ISRAEL/PALESTINE
THE BLACK BOOK

Israel/Palestine
The Black Book

Edited by
Reporters Without Borders

Pluto Press
London • Sterling, Virginia
in association with
Reporters Without Borders

First published in French by Editions La Découverte, Paris, as *Israel, Palestine – Le Livre Noir*, by Reporters sans frontières in association with Amnesty International, B'Tselem, Fédération internationale des ligues des droits de l'homme, Human Rights Watch, Palestinian Centre for Human Rights, the Palestinian Human Rights Monitoring Group and the Public Committee Against Torture in Israel.

First English-language edition published 2003 by Pluto Press
345 Archway Road, London N6 5AA
and 22883 Quicksilver Drive, Sterling, VA 20166-2012, USA

www.plutobooks.com

British Library Cataloguing in Publication Data
A catalogue record for this book is available from the British Library

Library of Congress Cataloging-in-Publication Data

Israel-Palestine
Israel/palestine: the black book / edited by Reporters Without Borders - 1st English-language ed.
    p. cm.
ISBN 0–7453–2142–9 – ISBN 0–7453–2141–0 Pbk.)
1. Arab-Israeli conflict--1993– 2. Human rights--Israel. 3. Jews--Crimes against--Israel. 4. Palestinian Arabs--/Crimes against--West Bank.
5. Palestinian Arabs--Crimes against--Gaza Strip.
I. Reporters sans frontières (Association) II. Title.
DS119.76.18725,2003
323.4`9`095694--dc21
                                2003006658

Designed and produced for Pluto Press by
Curran Publishing Services, Norwich

Printed and bound in the European Union by
Antony Rowe Ltd., Chippenham and Eastbourne, England

The statements and opinions in each report are the sole responsibility of the organisation that produced it.

Contents

[vii]

Preface

'Human rights transcend nationalism, religion and borders,' says Palestinian psychiatrist and human rights activist Eyad Sarraj. 'They're just the same under the Israeli occupation or the Palestinian Authority. Violations must be exposed because the best way to put things right is to speak up loud and clear.'

Sarraj sums up the sincere beliefs and the aim of the eight organisations that have produced this book - to describe the situation as accurately as possible and denounce the abuses on both sides.

Everyone knows about the conflict in the Middle East. You read about it in the newspapers, hear it on the radio and see it on television. The Israeli–Palestinian war is ever-present, stirring up emotions and setting off debates. Sometimes it wears you down. The scenes of violence, destruction and dead bodies sicken and overwhelm us. Too much hatred, too much argument, all buried under a mountain of accusations and disputes. It can turn us off and make us lose interest in the causes of the conflict.

We hope this book, by trying to establish the responsibility of all involved, will help the reader through the flood of news about the subject. News that each side tries to control. For the media has itself become part of the conflict, to judge by the propaganda and war of words between the two sides, waged with varying degrees of skill and success.

Israelis and Palestinians often try to manipulate the media to impose their view of the war and win international sympathy. To preserve a good image, the warring parties often stop journalists moving around or taking pictures freely. The price is frequent violence, with countless journalists roughed up, threatened, arrested, injured, wounded or even killed.

The originality of this book is that the hitherto hard-to-find reports of eight human rights organisations (Israeli, Palestinian and other) can now be read together. To avoid any accusation of bias, these respected organisations have been guided by two rules: to include only reports of abuses committed by their 'own side' and to give equal prominence to all rights violations, whoever was responsible for them.

A grim overall picture of human rights in the Middle East since the late 1990s emerges from this book. In the Palestinian lands occupied by Israel, discrimination is total, permanent and fierce, as in all colonial situations. The various retreats of the Israeli army since 1994 have not put an end to violation of Palestinian political, economic and social rights.

After 35 years of military rule, the Palestinians are now ruled by their own Authority, which has built up a record of flouting basic rights and committing many abuses. Palestinian organisations, used to pointing a finger at the Israelis, have had to denounce similar crimes committed by their own leaders. Palestinians who have been tortured in Israeli prisons have themselves become torturers.

Hopes of peace hid this for a time, as they hid the continuing creation of Israeli settlements, contrary to what has been promised, along with the demolition of Palestinian homes and seizure of farmland that go with it.

Since the start of the second Intifada, and especially the reoccupation of the main Palestinian towns and cities in the spring of 2002, human rights violations have become more widespread than ever. The Israeli police and army are now even using against the minority of Arabs who are Israeli citizens the same methods they used to crush the uprising in the occupied territories. And countless suicide attacks violate the most basic of human rights, the right to live.

Terrorism does not justify torture. Colonial oppression does not justify terrorism. In a situation where individuals are so little respected, human rights violations mount up and become entrenched, producing more and more victims, feeding hatred and the desire for revenge.

The only aim of this book is to tell the world this truth and remind it that only respect for the rights of those living in the Middle East can bring the peace and security they long for.

Reporters Without Borders, October 2002

Introduction

Jocelyn Grange

This book presents various investigations and reports by human rights organisations – Israeli, Palestinian or other – which have undisputed integrity and authority. But the partisan emotion that always erupts at the slightest criticism of either side has obliged us to adopt special rules. So the only reports by Israeli and the Palestinian organisations cited here are those that have criticised the behaviour of their own side.

Space prevents us from reprinting some of the reports in their entirety. Sections omitted have been left out with the agreement of the authors concerned and without altering the spirit of the report or the range of situations it criticises.

We have chosen to focus on the second Intifada, not just because the present conflict is more complicated and more intense than the first. The second Intifada is the result of a situation that has greatly worsened since the collapse of the 1993 Oslo negotiations, but is also the result of the multitude of human rights violations over the past half-century. So it is important to look at how things got to this point to better understand why and how the pattern of human rights violations arose.

Creation of a Jewish state in Palestine

The West Bank and the Gaza Strip have been occupied by Israel since the Six Day War in June 1967. That war released tensions that had been building for 20 years between the Jewish state and its Arab neighbours who had opposed sharing the Palestine Mandate territory recommended by the United Nations after the Second World War.

At the beginning of the twentieth century the Zionist movement, founded by a group of European Jews, had called on Jews everywhere to go and settle in Palestine and build a Jewish homeland where they would be safe from the persecution they had routinely suffered in Europe since the Middle Ages. But the Zionist ideal was not implemented in 'a land without people', as its early theoreticians had put it, but in a land inhabited almost entirely by Arabs.

Lord Balfour, who gave his name to the November 1917 declaration saying that Britain, as the then-occupier of Palestine, 'views with favour the establishment in Palestine of a national home for the Jewish people', admitted a few years later that his country had not taken account of the wishes of an existing community, but was deliberately seeking to recreate a new and permanent majority community there.

The Arab population of Palestine objected to both the British occupiers and the immigrant Jews, and did not see why they should have to pay the price of barbarism in Europe – barbarism that peaked with the horrors of the Nazis and sealed the fate of Palestine.

In November 1947 the international community, traumatised by the discovery of the Nazi gas chambers, approved at the United Nations the partition of Palestine into two states. This set off a war by an Arab coalition against Israel. After the peace accords with the defeated Arabs in 1950, Palestine was divided into three, with Israel controlling two-thirds of the land, Egypt administering the Gaza Strip and Jordan annexing the West Bank. The last two areas, in which the Palestine Liberation Organisation (PLO) wants to set up a Palestinian state, have been occupied by Israel since 1967.

Settlement of the West Bank and the Gaza Strip

Until it lost power at general elections in 1977, the Israeli left had created the first 24 Israeli settlements on the West Bank, under the 1971 'Allon Plan'. This provided for annexation of a corridor 5 to 10 kilometres wide along the 'green line' (the border between Israel and the West Bank) and another the same width in the Jordan Valley. The plan also said that 'settlements and permanent military bases' should be created there. The Israeli left saw these measures as a matter of basic security. Before the 1967 war, Israel feared Arab armies in the West Bank would attack Israel's coastal plain, which is only 15–30 kilometres wide. Occupation of the West Bank pushed the Arab–Israeli front line 50 kilometres to the east.

From 1977 on, the settlement policy was systematically implemented by Menahem Begin, who had managed to unite the secular and religious wings of Israeli right-wing nationalism to get himself elected prime minister. But to Begin and his ministers, such as Itzhak Shamir and Ariel Sharon, the settlement of the occupied territories was mainly an ideological affair. They wanted to reestablish the Greater Israel of Biblical times that stretched from the Mediterranean to the River Jordan.

In the space of a few months, nearly 3,600 hectares of land were designated for building new settlements. In 1980, the first international reports said more than a third of Palestinian lands had been seized by Israel. In 1982, a plan aimed to increase the number of settlements to 165 and the number of Jews living on the West Bank and the Gaza Strip to 1.3 million by 2010. The plan had a clear goal of annexation and spoke of 'integrating the occupied territories into Israel'. Both right and left-wing Israeli politicians then agreed to speed up the settlement process so as to absorb a million Jews who had arrived from Russia in the early 1990s.

Annexation of East Jerusalem

In 1947 the United Nations wanted to make Jerusalem a separate entity administered by the United Nations (UN), but this was never done because the city was divided in two after the 1948 war. The eastern part was annexed by Jordan and the western part became the Israeli capital. In June 1967 Israel occupied East Jerusalem, and a month later declared it would remain part of Israel. In 1980, the Israeli parliament proclaimed Jerusalem the 'one, eternal and indivisible' capital of Israel. The decision was condemned overwhelmingly by the UN member states.

Since 1967 about 160,000 Israelis have settled in East Jerusalem as part of a policy to make it demographically impossible to re-establish Palestinian sovereignty over that part of the city. In 30 years, more than 40 per cent of Palestinian land has been seized and its inhabitants expelled. New housing has been built for Israeli settlers to live in. The Israeli human rights group B'Tselem says 94 per cent of the housing put up in Jerusalem between November 1967 and February 1995 has been for Israeli Jews.

The Geneva Conventions

The UN Security Council has many times called on Israel to withdraw from the Occupied Territories, dismantle the settlements there and stop building new ones. The UN has also recognised, since 30 November 1970, the right of Palestinians to set up their own state there. Until that happens, the West Bank and the Gaza Strip are territories that come under the 1949 Fourth Geneva Convention on protecting civilians in wartime, which applies to occupied areas. This position is backed by the International Committee of the Red Cross (ICRC) and many resolutions of the UN Security Council.

The Israeli government claims the Convention does not legally apply to the West Bank and the Gaza Strip, but says it will nevertheless follow its humanitarian requirements, without saying clearly what it thinks they are.

The Fourth Convention spells out rules an occupying power must respect in its treatment of the local population, who are termed 'protected persons'. These rules forbid the occupying power, for example, to deliberately kill, mistreat or expel them. It also bars the occupants from installing their own civilians as settlers there.

The first Intifada

From December 1987, the Jewish state faced a daily rebellion by young Palestinians in the Occupied Territories — an Intifada (a rebellion using stones). In the previous 20 years of occupation, Israel had dealt with several episodes of unrest, and the Israeli army (Tsahal) was often called on to break up demonstrations. But unlike these protests, the Intifada lasted and turned into a war of attrition. The effect of the uprising and Israel's brutal repression of it caused a huge stir both internationally and in Israel itself. Knocked off its balance and clearly caught unawares, the Israeli army had great trouble controlling the uprising. By 1992, more than 2,000 people had been killed and about 40,000 wounded and injured. Use of torture by Israel became routine.

In 1994, a UN report denounced 'a routine and organised system of torture that recruited doctors to give it legitimacy'. Doctors were called in before each interrogation to certify that a prisoner was fit enough to undergo torture. Some Israel lawyers protested, but people who appeared before military courts had minimal rights. Such practices continued despite the Israeli High Court (supreme court) condemning certain kinds of 'moderate physical pressures'. But the Intifada gradually made the Israeli occupation untenable, and the international situation (the ending of the cold war and the outbreak of the Gulf War) forced Israel to negotiate.

The Madrid Conference and the Oslo Accords

A conference in Madrid in October 1993, sponsored by the USA
and Russia, brought together Israel, Syria, Lebanon, Egypt and
Jordan. The Israeli government, led by Itzhak Shamir, took part on
condition the PLO was not invited. The only Palestinians present
were from the West Bank and the Gaza Strip, and were part of a
Jordanian-Palestinian delegation. The Israelis and the Palestinians
tried to reach agreement on a five-year period of interim self-
government in the West Bank and Gaza, but the talks broke down
because the Palestinians insisted on recognition of their right to
sovereignty.

In 1992 the political situation changed, with the electoral victory
in Israel of a left-wing coalition led by Yitzhak Rabin, leader of the
Labour Party. Secret negotiations began, in London and then in
Oslo, between Israel and PLO envoys. Tentative agreement was
reached at the end of August 1993.

On 13 September, Yasser Arafat and Rabin signed a 'declaration
of principles' that signalled the start of the timetable set by the
Oslo Accords. Each side recognised the other's 'mutual legitimate
and political rights' and began a negotiation process based on
creation of an 'Palestinian Interim Self-Government Authority' in
the West Bank and the Gaza Strip for five years, leading to a
permanent agreement in accordance with UN Security Council
Resolution 242, which calls on Israel to withdraw its forces from
the lands it seized in 1967, and on neighbouring Arab countries to
respect Israel's borders.

To allow Palestinian self-government, Israel said it would pull
its troops out of all the Occupied Territories, except for the settlements, a few security zones (borders and military bases) and East
Jerusalem. Israel was to withdraw from more than 80 per cent of
the West Bank and the Gaza Strip. This would start in December
1993 and be completed by the end of 1994. Negotiations for a
permanent agreement were to start in the third year of the five-
year interim period and be completed by May 1999. They would
involve Jerusalem, the settlements, the borders and refugees. The
moment the Accords were signed, the Israeli right launched a furi-
ous media campaign against the government, which reached its
peak with the assassination of Prime Minister Rabin by a Jewish
fanatic in November 1995. On the Palestinian side, the Accords
were attacked by fundamentalist parties and several components
of the PLO.

The spirit of Oslo betrayed

The first phase of Israeli withdrawal came after a six-month delay (the Gaza–Jericho agreement of 4 May 1994), and the interim agreement on redeployment of the Israeli army in the West Bank was not signed until 28 September 1995. Extremists on both sides helped to slow down negotiations. In February 1994, an Israeli settler killed 19 Palestinians in the Tomb of the Patriarchs in Hebron, and in the spring of 1996, the fundamentalist Palestinian resistance movement Hamas began an unprecedented wave of attacks against Israel.

Tension grew and the Oslo Accords were renegotiated. Instead of wholesale withdrawal from the Occupied Territories, Israel proposed fragmenting the West Bank into three areas (the September 1995 agreement). This would include a fully autonomous area (Zone A) in Palestinian towns and cities, an area of shared power in Palestinian villages (Zone B), and an area where the occupation would continue (Zone C). Zone A covered only 6 per cent of the Occupied Territories and Zone B little more than 20 per cent. Israel would keep 70 per cent of the land and 80 per cent of the water. Palestinian self-rule was reduced to 100 or so tiny enclaves scattered throughout the West Bank. All the main roads would stay under Israeli control, which would allow Israel to seal off areas and prevent Palestinians moving around freely.

Israel's withdrawal from half of the city of Hebron in December 1996 and a part of the West Bank in 1999 (the Sharm al-Sheikh agreement) did not change things at all. Meanwhile, Israeli settlement of Palestinian lands was stepped up despite promises in the Oslo Accords, which had stipulated that neither side was to do anything to alter the status of the West Bank and the Gaza Strip while negotiations for a definitive agreement were still going on. Between 1993 and 1996 the number of settlers doubled to 300,000, and more and more roads were built. These roads linked the settlements to the Israeli national road network and prevented any Palestinian territorial continuity, something that was essential for creation of a Palestinian state.

Authoritarianism in the Palestinian self-governing areas

In the few territories it controlled, the Palestinian Authority worked to set up a state structure, with a president and a parliament elected on 20 January 1996 in the presence of international observers. The vote was a landslide for Yasser Arafat and his supporters. Their legitimacy and that of the Oslo Accords they supported was strengthened. But their huge victory prevented emergence of a legal opposition that would have enabled a truly parliamentary system to develop. Arafat ruled alone and ignored the parliament, even though legally it was the main institution of self-government.

The Palestinian Authority quickly came under fierce criticism. Cronyism, corruption and the personal enrichment of some of its leaders were frequent charges. Human rights violations were another complaint. The Palestinian police began systematically cracking down on opponents of the Oslo Accords, who were arbitrarily jailed and sometimes tortured. Fundamentalists were not the only targets of this repression, which Israel often called for. Nobody who criticised Arafat's policies too openly escaped the harassment of the Palestinian Authority.

The Camp David failure and the second Intifada

With the arrival in power of Binyamin Netanyahu's coalition government with the small religious parties in May 1996, the already chaotic negotiations ground to a halt again. When Labour Party leader Ehud Barak became prime minister three years later, optimism returned. During his election campaign, Barak had said Palestinians had a right to their own state. In June 2000 Barak and Arafat were summoned to Camp David, in the USA, by President Bill Clinton to sign a definitive agreement.

But the summit meeting failed. The Israeli prime minister wanted to annex 80 per cent of the settlements to Israel proper. This was about a tenth of the Occupied Territories. The Palestinians considered they had already made a historic compromise in 1993 by agreeing to give up 78 per cent of their historic homeland. The gap between the two sides on the refugee question seemed just as unbridgeable.

The Camp David failure laid the foundation for the second Palestinian Intifada. Tension was at its height when Israeli politician Ariel Sharon went to the Temple Mount escorted by Israeli police on 28 September 2000. The gesture was seen as a provocation by the Palestinians. The first clashes broke out in Jerusalem and spread swiftly throughout the Occupied Territories. A second Intifada, an Intifada for Jerusalem, was under way, but this time it was no longer just between Israeli troops and stone-throwing youths. Fatah's paramilitary Tanzim fighters and a section of the Palestinian Authority police took part in the fighting.

In January 2001, the two sides made a last attempt to negotiate, at Taba in Egypt. Discussion focused on the return of 96 per cent of the occupied territory to the Palestinians and shared sovereignty over Jerusalem. But the talks failed over the issue of refugees, and the violence worsened with the election of Sharon as prime minister in February 2001. Palestinians and Israelis then plunged into an endless cycle of violence which culminated in Operation Defensive Shield, launched by the Israeli army on 29 March 2002 in the Palestinian Occupied Territories.

The operation was triggered by a wave of suicide bombings inside Israel, notably one at Netanya on 27 March, the most deadly attack since the start of the second Intifada. In April 2002, all Palestinian towns and cities were the target of extensive Israeli military operations involving armoured ground forces, infantry and the air force.

PART I

ISRAEL

1 Killings committed by Israelis[1]

Amnesty International

The first killings of Palestinians during the Intifada were of those involved in demonstrations or bystanders. Many of the demonstrations were violent. Demonstrators threw stones at Israeli forces, sometimes using slingshots, and in Gaza and the West Bank, in some demonstrations they threw Molotov cocktails. The Israeli police, border police, special forces and the Israeli army responded using potentially lethal rubber-coated metal bullets and live ammunition. During some riots in the Gaza Strip and the West Bank, firearms were used by Palestinians, and after the first days there were gunfights between Israeli security forces and Palestinians armed with guns. However, in the first month approximately 80 per cent of the victims, according to Amnesty International, were killed in demonstrations in circumstances when the lives of members of the security services were not in danger.

The pattern of killings changed. Palestinian small arms shooting at Israeli Defence Force (IDF) posts and settlements led to an increasingly massive riposte from the IDF, resulting in an increased number of Palestinians being killed during the shelling of residential areas. From November 2000 the IDF increasingly pursued an openly avowed policy of extrajudicially executing individuals apparently suspected of planning attacks against Israelis. From January 2001 the IDF went increasingly on the offensive, invading Palestinian areas (including areas under full Palestinian control), shelling and demolishing houses, and razing orchards and crops.

---

1   Excerpt from *Israel/Occupied Territories/Palestinian Authority: Broken Lives – A Year of Intifida*, AI Index; MDE 15/083/2001, November 2001

The killing of Muhammad Jamal al-Dura

On 30 September 2000, the second day of the Intifada, Jamal al-Dura and his twelve-year-old son Muhammad were returning from a shopping trip to their home in al-Bureij refugee camp through Netzarim Junction. Although there were clashes between Palestinian stone-throwers and the IDF, there was no other route home. As the shooting intensified, they sheltered behind a barrel. The situation was described in a sworn affidavit taken by the Palestinian Centre for Human Rights from Talal Abu Rahma, a camera operator for the television channel France 2:

> Suddenly I heard a cry of a child. Then, I focused my camera on the child Muhammad Jamal al-Dura who was shot in his right leg. His father tried to calm, protect and cover his son with his hands and body. Sometimes the father Jamal was raising his hands asking for help. I spent approximately 27 minutes photographing the incident which lasted for 45 minutes. After the father and the child were evacuated by an ambulance to the hospital, I stayed 30 to 40 minutes. I could not leave the area because all of those who were in the area, including me, were being shot at and endangered. Shooting started first from different sources, Israeli and Palestinian. It lasted for not more than five minutes. Then it was quite clear to me that shooting was towards the child Muhammad and his father from the opposite direction to them. Intensive and intermittent shooting was directed at the two, and the two outposts of the Palestinian National Security Forces. The Palestinian outposts were not a source of shooting, as shooting from inside these outposts had stopped after the first five minutes, and the child and his father were not injured then. Injuring and killing took place during the following 45 minutes.

Muhammad died and his father was severely injured. The first ambulance driver at the scene, Bassem al-Bilbaysi, was killed by Israeli fire at the crossroads as he tried to rescue the father and son.

The IDF first stated that Muhammad al-Dura was killed by Palestinian fire. However, on 3 October 2000 the IDF chief of staff said that the IDF had conducted an investigation 'and as far as we understand, the shots were apparently fired by Israeli soldiers from the outpost at Netzarim'. On 10 October Amnesty International delegates, including a former senior police officer, Dr Stephen Males, a specialist in sensitive public order policing, visited the site. By that time the IDF had demolished the buildings by which Muhammad al-Dura and his father had sheltered, so the forensic evidence was lost. Photographs taken by journalists before the destruction showed a pattern of bullet holes in the wall just around the place where the two were sheltering. This suggested that Jamal and Muhammad al-Dura were targeted by the Israeli post opposite where they were cowering. On 11 October the IDF spokesperson in Jerusalem showed Amnesty International delegates maps which purported to show that Muhammad al-Dura had been killed in crossfire.

Demonstrations

In a demonstration or riot involving the use of stones, or even slingshots or Molotov cocktails, a well-trained police force should be able to contain and defuse the demonstrators without loss of life. The international standards for law enforcement officers are quite clear: they should respect and preserve life and minimise injury and damage. Israeli security forces have persistently breached international standards; they have also breached their own rules of engagement.

> In the performance of their duty, law enforcement officials shall respect and protect human dignity and maintain and uphold the human rights of all persons.
> (Article 2 of the UN Code of Conduct for Law Enforcement Officials (Code of Conduct). These rights include the right to life.)

> Law enforcement officials may use force only when strictly necessary and to the extent required for the performance of their duty.
> (Article 3 of the Code of Conduct. The commentary on this article clarifies that the use of firearms is considered as an extreme measure and states specifically that 'Every effort should be made to exclude the use of firearms, especially against children.')

> Law enforcement officials shall not use firearms against persons except in self-defence or in defence of others against

the imminent threat of death or serious injury ... and only
when less extreme means are insufficient to achieve these
objectives ... intentional lethal use of firearms may only be
made when strictly unavoidable in order to protect life.
(Principle 9 of the UN Basic Principles on the Use of Force
and Firearms by Law Enforcement Officials (Basic
Principles))

The demonstrations and riots in the early days of the Intifada were
studied by Amnesty International delegates, including a policing
expert. Confrontations took place at 'symbolic areas' – where land
had been confiscated, near checkpoints and on the way to Israeli
settlements. The Amnesty International delegation found that the
Israeli security forces, in policing the violent demonstrations, had
tended to use military methods rather than policing methods
involving the protection of human lives. The security forces had
moved swiftly from using non-lethal to lethal methods of control.
They had breached their own rules of engagement that allow the use
of firearms only when lives are in imminent danger, and then only
targeted to the source of fire, and had used potentially lethal force
randomly over a wide area. The weapons used – rubber-coated
metal bullets and live ammunition – were not suitable for policing
demonstrations. On many occasions Palestinian ambulances and
first aid workers were hindered from giving aid.

According to Amnesty International's findings, those demonstrations where the police or army did not arrive, did not seek
confrontations with the demonstrators, or used alternative, non-
lethal methods of controlling demonstrators were defused without
loss of life. For example, demonstrations in Nazareth and Umm
al-Fahm on 3 October 2001 to mark the first anniversary of the
killing of 13 Palestinian demonstrators in Israel became violent as
demonstrators threw stones at a police station in Nazareth over
a four-hour period. Police did not respond with fire and the
demonstrations were defused without loss of life. (...)

The children

A large proportion of those injured and killed by Israeli security
forces were children, usually present and often among those
throwing stones during demonstrations. Sometimes children
demonstrated on leaving school; sometimes they were called out
of school to demonstrate. Many children were apparently killed by

poorly targeted lethal fire; others, as the case studies indicate, appear to have been deliberately targeted. In many of the locations where children were killed there was no imminent danger to life or reasonable expectation of future danger.

Israeli government spokespersons and media have stated that the reason so many children have been killed has been the use by Palestinians of 'child soldiers'. However, the fact that children are participating in riots and confrontations with the army does not mean that they are child soldiers. A law enforcement force trained in riot control, and equipped and prepared as required by international standards, should not need to use firearms against stone throwers. Children throwing stones are not military objectives for lethal attack by the Israeli forces. The killing and wounding of children has revealed a reckless disregard for life by Israeli soldiers.

The Palestinian Authority (PA) as well as armed groups such as Fatah have reportedly taught children to parade or strip rifles in camps. Hamas training sessions using children have been filmed. There are some members of the Palestinian security forces aged under 18 who are armed. It is probable that during the year-long Intifada there have been children under 18 who have had possession of a gun or grenade and shot at Israelis or participated in gunfights, but it is uncommon. In general children do not carry guns. In every case investigated by Amnesty International, the killing of a child appeared to have been an unlawful killing.

Sami Abu Jazzar

Sami Fathi Abu Jazzar was declared brain dead after being wounded in the head on 10 October 2000 when Israeli soldiers shot at a crowd of some 400 people, mostly young elementary schoolchildren, who were throwing stones at an Israeli military post near Salah al-Din gate in Rafah in the Gaza Strip. Six others were injured. The children had been encouraged by older youths to leave their schools and demonstrate. Amnesty International delegates concluded that the lives of Israeli soldiers, whose position was heavily fortified and located far from the stone throwers behind two wire fences, were not in danger and there was no justification for the use of lethal force. Sami Abu Jazzar died the following day, on the eve of his twelfth birthday. (...)

The Israeli government's failure to learn from errors in crowd control, to investigate killings, and to hold anyone to account for unlawful killings has meant that children and adults have continued to be killed when lives have not been in danger. The Palestinian security forces have also failed in their duty to protect and respect the lives of children.

Gun carriers and demonstrations

According to official Israeli spokespersons, Palestinian gun carriers hide behind children. There are up to 43,000 armed members of at least eleven separate security services created by the PA. Many members of other political groups outside the armed forces, such as Fatah, also own guns.

As not all demonstrations have been observed by independent witnesses, and gun carriers have indeed been in some crowds of demonstrators, it cannot be said that Palestinian gun carriers have never sheltered behind children or other demonstrators. Investigations by Amnesty International have failed to find any specific instance where Palestinian gun carriers have used a demonstration as protective shield and shot at Israelis from among or behind the demonstrators. Such conduct would totally breach international humanitarian law.

The Israeli human rights organisation B'Tselem, which observed every demonstration that took place at Ayosh Junction in Ramallah for ten days – from 25 to 27 October 2000 and from 29 October to 4 November 2000 – found that gun carriers did not fire from among the demonstrators. Gun carriers who were among the demonstrators were removed by members of the Palestinian security forces. Its report stated:

> In half of the demonstrations that B'Tselem witnessed, there was gunfire from the Palestinian side. However, the Palestinians who fired were located a distance away from the stone throwers and were hidden inside buildings in the area. This separation was intentional, and B'Tselem saw PA personnel moving among the stone throwers and moving away people with firearms and people in uniform. In all the cases, Palestinian gunfire began after the demonstration had lasted at least an hour and after the soldiers had already fired 'rubber' bullets and live ammunition. In fact, after Palestinians fired, the soldiers stopped firing and did not

respond, except in one instance, on 27 October, when soldiers shot at Palestinians who opened fire. In viewing the occurrence from the observation points, it was noted that the soldiers' response was not affected by the size of the demonstration. The response to a demonstration of hundreds of Palestinians was identical to one in which 50 Palestinians participated. Two Palestinians were killed at the Ayosh Junction during the period that B'Tselem observed the demonstrations: Ghassan Yusuf Ahmed Salem 'Awiseh, 27, was killed on 27 October; Tha'ar Ibrahim Shalesh a-Zayed, 17, a resident of Jilazun refugee camp, was killed on 31 October. Both were shot when they did not constitute a life-threatening danger to the soldiers and were killed before the Palestinian side had opened fire.

Checkpoints

Many people have been killed or wounded at checkpoints when they have clearly posed no danger to the IDF. The circumstances include people crossing a checkpoint who reach for a handkerchief and those in a car manoeuvering for a better position in the queue. Usually the IDF initially claim that gunfire or grenades have been fired from where the person has been killed. Only when the cases are investigated (by human rights organisations or journalists, and on rare occasions by the IDF) does it become clear that negligent, reckless or nervous soldiers have killed unlawfully.

'No go' areas

In some places the IDF appear to have targeted people in the streets in an attempt to create a 'no go' area on the edge of a Palestinian town, usually near an Israeli settlement or border. In many cases Palestinians have fired at IDF soldiers or settlers, but the reprisal shelling of Palestinian areas is out of all proportion to Palestinian fire, which has usually involved small arms or grenades. The IDF response appears to be part of a tactic to empty areas of Palestinian towns by forcing the residents to evacuate.

In January 2001 Amnesty International delegates visited Rafah. They were warned by Palestinian residents not to approach the border because of the danger of casual shootings of civilians by Israeli soldiers. As a result, Amnesty International delegates remained 200 metres behind the areas examined during the

Fatima Jamal Abu Jish

Fatima Abu Jish, aged 20, was killed on 7 January 2001 as she was returning to her village of Beit Dajan from the hospital in Nablus where she worked as a receptionist. The IDF had set up roadblocks across the roads to the village, which villagers circumvented by following tracks through the fields. Such tracks were easily visible from the roadblocks, and soldiers at the checkpoints blocked the roads to the village as harassment rather than as a serious attempt to halt entry to Beit Dajan. As a result of the numerous checkpoints and blockades an 8 kilometre journey often took an hour.

The car in which Fatima Abu Jish was travelling with her sister and her brother-in-law reached the checkpoint at 5.15 p.m. and took the track. Theirs was the fourth car in a slow-moving tailback of some 20 cars. Suddenly a shot rang out. Fatima's sister looked back and saw Fatima slumped with blood trickling out of her mouth. The IDF first stated that soldiers had been firing in response to shots. It then admitted that no shots had been fired at the checkpoint and agreed to investigate the killing. Three days later, apparently as a result of their investigation, the IDF stated that a soldier had fired at the wheels of Fatima Abu Jish's car and disciplinary procedures would be taken against him. No reason was given why one car in a convoy should have been targeted.

previous visit on 10 October 2000. At that time, they had visited houses near the border that had been hit by bullets (they were now evacuated and empty) and investigated the killing of Sami Abu Jazzar. Previously, delegates had complained to the PA that Palestinian police should have held back stone-throwing children from approaching the border. In January 2001 all townspeople feared approaching the border to a distance of even 200 metres. Two months later, in another apparent attempt to maintain a 'no go' area, the IDF fired a stun grenade at Amnesty International delegates led by Pierre Sané, the then Secretary General, accompanied by several television crews and journalists and surrounded by some 30 children. No explanation was given by the IDF for firing a stun grenade at a group clearly made up of civilians who were posing no threat whatsoever to the soldiers.

Some of those killed or wounded near the border with Israel, whose cases Amnesty International delegates investigated, were bystanders or children playing games. The reckless shooting by Israeli soldiers of any people in certain areas has been highlighted by the number of shootings around UN staff and journalists. For example, Peter Hansen, Head of the UN Relief and Works Agency (UNRWA) was threatened by Israeli soldiers with guns on 30 August 2001 when he tried to enter Rafah to inspect houses that had been shelled and destroyed. On 16 September the Israeli army shot in the direction of delegates from Amnesty International and Human Rights Watch as they were examining the sites of recently destroyed houses 100 metres from the border with Egypt. There was no fire from Palestinian areas at the time.

More than 40 journalists, at least 30 of them Palestinian, had been injured by July 2001 while reporting during the Intifada. Reporters Without Borders (RSF) condemned the lack of serious investigations. When the Israeli Ministry of Justice closed the investigation into the shooting in May in Ramallah of TFI journalist Bernard Aguirre, RSF wrote:

> Three different television crews filmed the scene. Their films clearly show an Israeli border guard getting out of his vehicle, calmly taking aim and, with his cigarette between his lips, opening fire on the man, at a distance of 100 metres. The journalist, who had just finished an interview and still had his microphone in his hand, was hit in the chest. Fortunately the bullet-proof jacket he was wearing saved him.

Attacks on residential areas

In January 2001 Amnesty International delegates including a military expert went to a number of residential areas, Palestinian and Jewish, that had been targeted by gunfire. In all areas houses had been damaged and the lives of residents endangered. Delegates visited Palestinian areas, including Ramallah, Beit Sahur, Beit Jala, Hebron, Nablus, Tulkarem, Rafah and Khan Yunis, and the Jewish settlements of Psagot and Gilo. During a previous visit in November 2000, Amnesty International delegates had visited Beit Jala, al-Bireh and Jericho.

In Gilo and Psagot delegates saw a number of bullet holes in walls and windows. Houses were barricaded by sandbags, and in Gilo, a long concrete barrier gave extra protection to houses on the edge of town. The weapons used against these residential areas by armed Palestinians appeared to be AK47 rifles, but there was also evidence of the use of small arms such as .22 calibre weapons. In Gilo, about 400 metres away from the firing points on the edge of Beit Jala, the kinetic energy of the bullets appeared to have been largely spent by the time they reached houses. The settlement of Psagot is on a hill overlooking the Palestinian town of al-Bireh; delegates were shown places and houses where guns had been positioned which had fired at Psagot around 200 metres away. All the areas from which fire had come were in or near residential areas. Bullets had hit several houses, piercing windows in at least four houses, and a synagogue. In one house a bullet had gone through the kitchen window, narrowly missing a woman.

It was clear to Amnesty International delegates that IDF troops had responded to Palestinian attacks with disproportionate use of force. It did not seem to matter to the IDF whether the Palestinian attack involved a lone or several armed Palestinians. In some cases the IDF response lasted for several hours, well after the Palestinian attack had ceased. IDF weapons commonly used in these responses were the M16 rifle; the general purpose machine gun (GPMG); the .50 calibre Browning machine gun; and sniper rifles (the Galil and the M21). The damage to homes in the 'front line' was therefore extensive. Houses on the edge of Beit Jala next to Gilo showed damage over an extensive perimeter of about 1.5 kilometres, and there was widespread damage to almost every house in border areas in Beit Sahur, Khan Yunis and Rafah, with some dwellings rendered uninhabitable. Many other homes could not be occupied at night because of the threat of future shelling. (Most attacks occurred at night.)

During some exchanges of fire, weapons of large calibre were deployed against armed Palestinians shooting at settlements or Israeli military emplacements. The IDF admitted using 105 mm and 120 mm tank rounds against buildings that were frequently used as bases by armed Palestinians. The IDF also use the Apache attack helicopter which is supplied by the USA and armed with hellfire missiles and 30 mm cannon.

It appeared to Amnesty International delegates that on a number of occasions weapons had been used indiscriminately in such a way as to cause loss of life and injuries to Palestinian civilians. Grenade launchers, which seem to have caused the deaths of two children in Rafah and Hebron, recklessly endanger civilians when used against a residential area. Two types of grenade launchers have been used against Palestinian residential areas: the

M203 grenade launcher and the Mark 19, 40 mm, automatic grenade launcher. Unlike the M203, which fires single rounds, the Mark 19 has a 2,200 metre range and fires 48 high explosive and air-burst rounds in less than a minute. Each grenade has a lethal burst range of 15 metres. In addition, 40 mm high explosive shells have been used against Palestinian residential areas.

Extrajudicial executions

Israel has for years pursued a policy of assassinating its political opponents. Because extrajudicial executions are universally condemned, most governments who practise assassinations surround such actions in secrecy and deny carrying out the killings they may have ordered. Although the Israeli government prefers to talk about 'targeted killings' and 'preventive actions' (or 'pinpointed preventive actions') rather than 'extrajudicial executions', members of the Israeli government have confirmed that such killings are a deliberate government policy carried out under government orders. (...)

The extrajudicial killings carried out by Israel constitute 'wilful killings' which constitute a 'grave breach' of the Fourth Geneva Convention (Article 147) to which Israel is a High Contracting Party. The comprehensive list of war crimes set out in article 8 of the Rome Statute of the International Criminal Court includes grave breaches of the Geneva Conventions.

During the present Intifada the policy of extrajudicial execution was initiated with the killing of Hussein 'Abayat, a Fatah activist, on 9 November 2000. With the disregard for human life that was to mark such assassinations, two women bystanders were killed at the same time. Since then, until the end of August 2001, at least 30 people appear to have been 'targeted' for death and more than 20 others who happened to be near them have also been killed.

The present operations of extrajudicial executions are ordered – according to the Legal Adviser to the IDF, Colonel Reisner – at the highest level of the army and the government, and are carried out openly by whatever means seem most appropriate to the circumstances. The IDF claim that those who are killed are military objectives in a state of armed conflict. But the Israeli security forces who carry out the extrajudicial executions offer no proof of guilt, no right of defence. The identity of the person who authorises the killing is as secret as the information that allegedly 'justifies' such an extreme and unlawful action.

[21]

In some of the cases Amnesty International investigated, the targets were killed in circumstances where they might easily have been arrested. For example, Mustafa Yassin, aged 28, accused by the Israeli authorities of being an activist in Islamic Jihad, had spent nine hours in the custody of the IDF the day before 20 soldiers surrounded his house in Anin, in Area C, an Israeli-controlled area of the West Bank, and killed him on 23 July 2001. (...)

Killings committed by settlers

Palestinians frequently face attacks, including killings, by Israeli Jews living in the Occupied Territories. At the time of the 1967 war the only Jews in the West Bank were the Samaritan community in Nablus (numbering about 250). There are now well over 300,000 Jewish settlers living in new colonies (commonly referred to as 'settlements') throughout the West Bank, including East Jerusalem. Most Israeli settlements are in previously 'rural' locations, inserted between Palestinian villages, often on hilltops. Jews make up 98.4 per cent of the population of the settlements, most but not all of whom are Israeli citizens. While the rate of Israeli construction in East Jerusalem is now tailing off (owing to limited space), population increase and construction are continuing rapidly in the rest of the West Bank. Settlement expansion accelerated after the peace talks, particularly since the Oslo II interim agreement of 1995. Settlers are subject to Israeli criminal law in Israeli courts, whereas Israeli military orders and Jordanian criminal law are applied to Palestinians. Settlers pay Israeli taxes and receive Israeli benefits and services.

Bypass roads have been built for settlers to ensure their separation from the Palestinians and their freedom from the harassments of military occupation such as road closures. Outside East Jerusalem, Palestinians are prohibited from entry to settlements unless they have a permit, and settlers aged between 18 and 60 serve in a military 'guard service'; all are armed and have powers to arrest Palestinians.

Settlers have consistently been allowed to attack Palestinians with impunity. In most instances the violence of settlers against Palestinians is carried out by attacking (breaking glass, burning or occupying) houses or shops; frequently it is directed at people. In most cases such attacks appear to be random, directed indiscriminately at any Palestinian or Palestinian property nearby.

On many occasions settler violence during the present Intifada has come as a response to Palestinian attacks on a settler. If the IDF are present they normally fail to intervene; sometimes soldiers may attempt to intervene but they are not stationed in sufficient force to protect the Palestinian population. If the attack is in response to a Palestinian attack, soldiers may express approval. The IDF do not have the right to arrest settlers. (...)

Under the Fourth Geneva Convention all Palestinians are protected persons, and the Israeli authorities have certain obligations towards them, which should include protection from attacks. Article 27 states:

> Protected persons are entitled, in all circumstances, to respect for their persons, their honour, their family rights, their religious convictions and practices, and their manners and customs. They shall at all times be humanely treated, and shall be protected especially against all acts of violence or threats thereof and against insults and public curiosity.

Article 2(1) of the International Covenant on Civil and Political Rights requires states to undertake 'to ensure to all individuals within its territory and subject to its jurisdiction the rights recognised in the present Covenant'. Since the beginning of the Intifada at least ten Palestinians have been killed by settlers. In none of these cases has any settler been brought to justice. (...)

Collective punishment

> No protected person may be punished for an offence he or she has not personally committed. Collective penalties and likewise all measures of intimidation or of terrorism are prohibited (...). Reprisals against protected persons and their property are prohibited.
>
> (Article 33 of the Fourth Geneva Convention)

The Israeli authorities have consistently used closures, curfews and demolition of homes as a form of collective punishment against Palestinians.

Closures

The closure of occupied Palestinian territories began with the Gulf War in 1991.[2] In the name of 'security' the Israeli government barred Palestinians from the West Bank and Gaza from entering Israel without passes; such passes were only given to some Palestinians. Israel's control over the fluctuating number of passes was a means of pressure on the Palestinian population of the Occupied Territories.

The Gaza Strip was closed; vehicles of outsiders (apart from diplomatic or UN cars) were not allowed to enter. Gradually a fully-fledged border was erected. Sometimes, for instance on Jewish holidays or after bomb attacks, it is closed entirely and no one may enter or leave. Sometimes only foreigners or certain categories of foreigner are allowed to enter. The Gaza Strip is 45 kilometres long and never more than 12 kilometres wide. More than 20 per cent of this area is occupied by Israeli settlements, with a population of about 5,000 settlers, less than 0.5 per cent of the total population of the Gaza Strip. This area is barred to Palestinians. More than a million Palestinians, including 824,672 refugees, nearly 80 per cent of the total population, live in the remaining area.

The West Bank has often been partially cut off from Israel. This was more a means of harassment than a real attempt to prevent those alleged to be 'terrorists' from entering Israel (see below). Palestinian cars from the Occupied Territories have different number plates from those from within Israel, and from 1994 cars registered by Palestinians in the Occupied Territories have not been allowed to enter Israel. Except for a few Palestinian VIPs, Palestinians travelling from the Occupied Territories into Jerusalem have to travel by Israeli-registered taxis or buses. Few Palestinians have passes allowing them to enter Jerusalem.

Israeli closures of the West Bank during the first Intifada (from 1987 until 1993) and after the Oslo Accords have meant that those outside the Jerusalem municipalities have not been granted permits to live in Jerusalem, and are frequently prohibited even from entering the city. Palestinians from Jerusalem have the right to a Jerusalem identity card (ID) and drive Israeli-registered cars.

Closures have been of many kinds since the present Intifada began. Members of the IDF or the border police stand by the side of the road with traffic-slowing devices or a barrier. They may check every passport or ID card, or they may only stop and turn

2   However, restrictions on freedom of movement have been frequently used on Palestinians throughout the Israeli occupation; for instance, during the 1980s whole towns and villages were placed under collective travel restriction orders (in effect a prohibition from travelling abroad) sometimes for more than a year.

back certain cars, trucks or taxis. Barriers not staffed by soldiers come in different forms: a large pile of earth that blocks the road; a trench dug across the road; heavy concrete blocks; and even steel gates.

The Gaza Strip

The Gaza Strip has effectively been closed to the outside world for ten years. Any Gazan who wishes to leave the Gaza Strip has to apply for permission from the Israeli authorities. Those Palestinians from Gaza who have authorisation nevertheless have to return the same night; for some this means having to leave daily at 3 a.m. and return after 6 p.m. Most inhabitants of Gaza have never been outside this narrow strip of land. The frontier is a high wire fence. Normally the IDF say that those who are shot at the fence were trying to plant a bomb. Without proper investigations of each killing the truth of these assertions cannot be tested.

At Erez crossing into Israel, travellers – except for VIPs, the UN and diplomats – have to leave their cars behind. Israeli citizens need special permission from the Israeli civil authorities to enter Gaza and will usually be accompanied, at the insistence of the Israeli authorities, by Palestinian police.

Because the occupied areas of Gaza and the West Bank are divided from each other, one part of the peace negotiations was the construction of a bypass road to link the West Bank and Gaza. That bypass road was at last inaugurated in 2000. However, Gazans still needed a security pass before they were allowed to cross (and many were said to have used the opportunity to enter Israel). This bypass road was closed immediately after the Intifada began and has remained closed ever since.

Ever since the beginning of the Intifada an almost complete closure has been imposed on the Gaza Strip. For almost the whole period, Gazans have been unable to work in Israel. In addition, the Gaza Strip has at times been closed in at least two places, effectively dividing the strip into three and sometimes four parts with a checkpoint between each. The closures within the Gaza Strip are in the areas where the main north–south road is crossed by roads going to the settlements. Normally, whenever a settler car passes all Palestinian traffic is stopped, causing large traffic jams. However, for long periods during the Intifada the north–south road was only opened between 9 a.m. and 11 a.m. and between 3 p.m. and 5 p.m. This caused long traffic tailbacks; many residents had to wait in queues for two or more hours. It became almost impossible to travel to work or to study. On other occasions the north–south road was completely blocked in two or three places. Among other problems, such blocking left the middle area, including al-Bureij refugee camp and Deir al-Balah, without any hospital to serve the population.

The 'yellow areas' in the Gaza Strip are areas equivalent to Area B in the West Bank; they are areas near Israeli settlements where Israel exercises full security control but the PA exercises civil jurisdiction. During the period up until the Intifada many restrictions were placed on the daily life of Palestinians in these areas by the Israeli authorities; for instance, there were strict building regulations almost entirely limiting the possibility of building in these areas.

After the outbreak of the Intifada the Israeli authorities increased dramatically the restrictions they placed on those areas. In some areas, houses considered too close to settlements were destroyed. In most of these areas no one but the residents was allowed to enter or exit without Israeli authorisation.

The West Bank

Closures have also been used on the West Bank in the past, and have become increasingly harsh. During the years before the Intifada they would be imposed more or less heavily depending on Israel's assessment of the security situation or according to the government policy of the time; they tended to be imposed immediately after bomb attacks. Their purpose appeared to be to harass rather than to prevent all movement. Sometimes the blockage was absolute. At other times it was possible to persuade the security forces to let people through. Often the manned blockade could be avoided by taking a side road. This was perfectly obvious to the soldiers manning the blockade, since cars frequently came out only 50 metres down the road. The fact that the soldiers did nothing to stop such diversions added to the impression that closures are primarily a means of harassment rather than an effective response to a real security concern.

One feature of the Intifada has been the total closure of villages and even major towns. In answer to a petition against closures submitted by the Israeli Physicians for Human Rights on 18 December 2000, the IDF stated that they leave a single road to allow access to every village in case of medical emergency. In itself this causes delay and difficulty, since the road that is 'open' (or guarded by the IDF rather than closed with earth or concrete blocks) may change and not be known. In practice there is not always even one road open to a village. The Palestinian–Israeli organisation Ta'ayush, for instance, was unable to find a single road open for a convoy of trucks and cars bringing food and medical supplies to the villages of Burqin and Kufr al-Dik on 23 June 2001. One road, passing near a settlement, was closed to all Palestinians; others were blocked by trenches dug through the tarmac or by piles of earth. The convoy was eventually allowed by the army to dig a precarious pathway over the earth barrier, but the trucks carrying supplies were unable to cross. On 13 July 2001, after Palestinian attacks on Qiryat Arba settlers, the only route to Hebron that was open was one exposed to firing from the IDF and settlers and apparently booby trapped.

On 6 August 2001, following the killing of Tehiya Bloomberg, aged 40, from Ginot Shomron settlement, the Israeli army sealed off completely the West Bank towns of Nablus, Tulkarem, Jericho, Ramallah and Qalqiliya, and partially closed the towns of Hebron, Bethlehem and Jenin. On 12 September Nablus was again closed; no petrol was delivered and by 18 September there was no petrol in the town.

The closures accentuate the separation between different parts of the PA which, since the Oslo Accord, has never been allowed to operate as an entity. Direct routes are no longer permitted to Palestinian travellers and everyone has to make circuitous detours. The direct Ramallah–Bethlehem route is now frequently closed, and Palestinian travellers have to travel by the dangerous and precipitous Wadi Nar route, several kilometres longer. The straight easy road, taking about half an hour, from Nablus to Tulkarem now takes five hours. At times it is impossible to travel from Nablus to Jenin; several routes are used by those who needed to make the journey. Many villages have been closed for much of the past year. Farmers may not be able to reach their fields if they are close to settlements. Those who worked in Israel cannot go to work; those who work in neighbouring towns and villages face a more difficult, longer route, often subject to harassment, sometimes to ill-treatment, and even at risk of death. (...)

2 Excessive force used by Israeli Defence Forces[3]

B'Tselem[4]

This report investigates an incident that occurred in Beit Jala on the morning of 6 May 2001. It began when Fatah members fired at the Israeli checkpoint on the Bethlehem bypass road (Route 60, also referred to as the Tunnels Road). In reply, Israeli Defence Force (IDF) soldiers fired at Beit Jala with light weapons fire and tank shelling, and for the first time in this part of the West Bank, invaded Area A, which is completely under Palestinian Authority (PA) control. During the incident, five Palestinian civilians not involved in the hostilities were injured, including a five-year-old boy and a twelve-year-old girl. Among the armed Palestinians involved, one Fatah member was killed, and six members of the PA security apparatus were wounded. One IDF soldier was lightly wounded. This report will reconstruct, to the extent possible, the chronology of the incident, and analyse the degree to which Israel and the Palestinian Authority acted in accordance with the rules of international humanitarian law and international customary law.(...)

Chronology of events and eyewitness accounts

On Sunday, 6 May 2001, around 7.00 a.m., six armed members of Fatah positioned themselves on the hill between the Palestinian National Security checkpoint at the southern entrance to Beit Jala and the Talita-Qumi school. They opened fire on soldiers stationed at the IDF checkpoint on the Tunnels Road and at the IDF observation tower several metres away, which faces the school (...). According to information obtained by B'Tselem, a 14-year-old boy

---

3 Israeli Centre for Human Rights in the Occupied Territories.
4 Excerpt from *Excessive Force. Human Rights Violations during IDF Actions in Area A, Beit Jala, in May 2001*, May 2001.

was among the Palestinians who fired at the checkpoint. It should be noted that on that morning, there was no firing from Beit Jala at the homes of Israeli civilians in Gilo.

Tanks positioned near the IDF checkpoint fired a number of shells at the source of fire, and then two companies – one of paratroopers and the other of border police – invaded Area A and proceeded toward the school (*Haaretz*, 7 May 2001). One shell hit very close to a Fatah member, Muhammad 'Abiat, 45, and the fragments struck him in the head and killed him instantly. The IDF soldiers first took control of the house behind the school and then proceeded south toward the Fatah members, who had in the meanwhile retreated and entrenched behind the house near where the firing took place. When the IDF entered Area A, dozens of members of the PA's security services joined the Fatah members, and a gun battle ensued.

During the invasion, the tanks initiated heavy shelling at one of the hills in the Iskan neighbourhood, referred to by residents as Taleh Kubar, and at some houses in the neighbourhood. This firing ensued even though the battle was taking place 300 metres to the east, near the Duha neighbourhood. A member of Palestinian National Security described the events to B'Tselem (testimony given on 16 May 2001):

> Around 8.15 in the morning, we noticed two Israeli soldiers coming toward us on foot. There were several soldiers behind them. When we saw them, we retreated. We positioned ourselves around 50 metres from our checkpoint, in the direction of the Duha neighbourhood. We entrenched behind a pile of dirt and stones and began to fire at the Israeli forces. In the beginning, we were three policemen from National Security, but after we reported the entry of Israelis, Force 17 and Preventive Security forces joined us. All of us, including the Tanzim, who were involved from the start of the incident, fired at the Israeli forces who had invaded Area A, trying to prevent their advance. Then the tanks began to shell the area to the left of our checkpoint: Taleh Kubar and the area of the houses at the edge of the Iskan neighbourhood. The Tanzim have recently been using Taleh Kubar as a point from which to fire at the Israeli army post, but that usually takes place when it gets dark, because in daylight hours the soldiers at the post can identify them. In any event, there was no firing from Taleh Kubar that morning.

Most, but not all of the residents of al-Iskan, which overlooks the Israeli checkpoint, have abandoned their homes in recent months because of the frequent exchanges of fire between Fatah and the IDF soldiers at the checkpoint. The tank shelling of Taleh Kubar and al-Iskan on 6 May caused significant damage to five houses that were still occupied. In his testimony to B'Tselem, Akram 'Atallah, owner of one of these houses, stated:

> I have three children, aged four, nine, and twelve. All our money and savings were invested in building our new house, which we moved into exactly one day before it was shelled. At 7.30 a.m., I heard the sound of gunfire. I looked out the window and saw Israeli soldiers who had crossed the Palestinian checkpoint and entered Area A. I saw them exchange fire with the Palestinian fighters. I took my children and wife from the top floor to the ground floor and we hid behind a brick oven. The gunfire lasted about 15 minutes. Then we heard a loud explosion and saw that it was a tank shell. The shell struck around 3 metres from the house. I was afraid there would be more shelling, so I decided that we should move and stay under the stairs. From 8.00 to 9.30 we remained under the staircase. There was constant firing, and we decided to count the shells. The children counted 14 shells that hit nearby. My four-year-old son had to go to the bathroom, but I was afraid to take him upstairs, so he went in his pants. After three shells struck the facade of the house, we were afraid that the whole house would crumble, so we took advantage of a short lull in the firing to rush out of the house to go to my brother's house, which was next to ours. My brother and I concluded that we had to leave the house quickly and go to the nearby wadi [dry river bed], which was safer. When we got there, we found others who had also brought their wives and children to the wadi. I continued to observe what was going on from the wadi, because I wanted to know what was happening to my house. Around 11.00, a shell struck the roof tiles of the house, and the roof and the top floor went up in flames.... It is true that there is often firing from nearby open areas, but I can assure you that there wasn't any firing from my house, partly because there are many houses between us and the Israeli observation post.

The IDF also fired tank shells at the outermost residential area of the Duha neighbourhood. Neighbourhood residents did not abandon their homes, and it is still densely populated. Rawan 'Aziz Zawareh, aged twelve, an A-Duha resident, suffered facial wounds from shell fragments. Her mother, Fatma 'Ali Hamed Zawareh, described how her daughter was wounded:

> Around 7.15 a.m., three of my children left the house for school, which lies on the main road leading to Bethlehem. The three who went were Rawan, who is twelve, Tareq, who is nine, and Mahfuz, who is eight. I have two other children: Rana, who is four, and 18-month-old Raniyeh. About 7.30, I heard the sound of gunfire, and 15 minutes later shells began to fall near the houses. Around 10.30, when I was hiding with my two small children in an interior room of the house, I saw through the window my three eldest children arriving home from school and hiding behind a wall on a field about 20 metres from the house. They were crying and frightened. The shelling was still going on and they couldn't reach the house. I decided to go and get them and I managed to get to them. I took Tareq with my right hand and Mahfuz with my left hand, and Rawan walked in front of me. Suddenly we heard the shriek of a shell. It exploded on the dirt road, about 100 metres from us, and Rawan cried out. I saw that she had been wounded above the right eye. Blood was flowing from the wound. I picked her up and shouted for help. Tareq and Mahfuz cried and screamed. A few minutes later, National Security personnel arrived and took Rawan to the ambulance that was on the main road, at the entrance to the neighbourhood. It took her to the government hospital in Beit Jala. The physicians in the emergency room stopped the bleeding.(...) Now she is taking medication to stop the internal bleeding in her right eye.

IDF tank fire was also aimed at As-Sader, another neighbourhood of Beit Jala. At times, Palestinians fire from certain neighbourhood locations at the Tunnels Road and the Israeli District Coordination Office located at the edge of the Har Gilo settlement. Testimony from As-Sader residents indicates that there had not been any firing at Israeli targets that day. Most residents continued to live in their homes during the Intifada. One of the shells seriously injured five-and-a-half-year-old Nikola Bassam Hana Abu Ghanem when he was standing near his house. His father, Bassam Hana Abu Ghanem, described the incident:

> Our house lies on the hillside leading to the bypass road. It is around 1,000 metres to the road and there are many houses in that area. There has been lots of gunfire in the neighbour-hood in recent months. Numerous houses were damaged by bullets, but not our house. I often saw armed Palestinians firing from the hill above us, 200 metres from the house, toward the road. But on the day of the incident, they didn't show up and there wasn't any firing from the nearby hill. The sound of gunfire woke us at 7.30 a.m. The shots came from the bypass road and from al-Iskan. We weren't startled because we thought that we were far away and safe.(...) After my son Nikola awoke, he went to the road near our home to play with kids in the neighbourhood. Many kids had assem-bled there because a cement mixer and pump were being operated to lay a neighbour's roof. Around 8.20, my wife left the house to bring Nikola home for breakfast. They were 5 to 7 metres from the house when I suddenly heard a terrific explosion and my wife's screams. I ran outside and saw Nikola stretched out on the ground. His left arm was lying next to him, with only a piece of skin joining it to his shoul-der. The children nearby were crying and screaming. I took Nikola to the government hospital in Beit Jala. He was treated and then transferred by ambulance to al-Moqassad hospital, in Jerusalem. The physicians said that there was little chance that they would be able to save the arm.

During the battle between the invading IDF soldiers and the Pales-tinian security forces, the IDF soldiers fired at two ambulances of the Civil Defence Centre. The ambulances, properly marked by the Red Crescent, came to evacuate the wounded. The first ambulance reached the battle scene around 9.30. IDF soldiers fired at it during the course of the exchange of fire. It is unclear if the IDF fired at the ambulance deliberately.

The medic, Yehiye Nasser Hassan Tabiha, who suffered head wounds from the gunfire, stated to B'Tselem, on 8 May 2001:

> We stopped the ambulance on a dirt road some 50 metres from the National Security checkpoint. Suddenly, the Israeli soldiers who had advanced from the army post fired at us

from 50 metres away. We were in the ambulance. One bullet pierced the front windshield from the driver's side. The driver, Ahmad Hijazi, jumped out of the ambulance, and medic Ahmad al-Masir did the same. I got out and saw a person alongside me who had been wounded in the neck from [shell] fragments. I held him, sat him down on a stretcher in the ambulance and sat next to him, on the medic's seat. I tried to stop the bleeding from his neck. While I was treating him, a bullet pierced the right side of the ambulance and grazed my head, causing it to bleed. If I had been sitting normally with my head up, the bullet would have struck me flush in the head, Heaven forbid.

Another ambulance reached the scene around 10.30. The testimony of the driver, Rani Bishara a-Sha'ar, given on 8 May 2001, indicates that IDF soldiers fired at the ambulance, apparently deliberately:

I received a call to go to al-Iskan to evacuate a person who had been killed and to see if there were additional wounded. The dispatcher informed me that it was coordinated with the Israelis that they would not shoot at the ambulance during the evacuation. When I approached the National Security checkpoint, I came across an Israeli army jeep. I was ascending and the jeep was descending. The jeep stopped near me and I came to a quick stop. Two border policemen got out and aimed their weapons at us. I quickly engaged the hand brake and jumped out, as did Ahmad Abu-Zar, who was sitting next to me. Right at that moment, heavy firing at the ambulance commenced. Bullets broke the windows and many struck the body of the ambulance. My position at that moment prevented me from seeing the shots as they emerged from the rifles that those border policemen aimed at us a second before. Despite this, from the sound and from our location, I can't conceive that anyone other than those soldiers fired at us. At the time, I did not feel that my leg had been injured when I jumped out of the ambulance. Later, at the hospital, the physicians told me that I had broken it.

Around 2 p.m., seven hours after the incident began, the IDF soldiers abandoned the last houses that they had seized in Area A of Beit Jala and returned to their position on the Tunnels Road.

[33]

Criticism

During the incident described above, Israel and the Palestinian Authority violated several major provisions of international humanitarian and customary law intended to limit, to the extent possible, injury to civilians during hostilities. Israel violated the principle of proportionality, the principle requiring hostile parties to discriminate between combatants and civilians, and the prohibition on attacking ambulances. The Palestinian Authority violated its duty to prevent firing from within or near a civilian-populated area and to prevent children from participating in hostilities.

The principle of proportionality

This principle states that it is prohibited to initiate attacks, even when directed against a legitimate objective, if the injury and damage they are liable to cause is excessive in relation to the concrete and direct military advantage anticipated from the attack. The complexity of this principle, arising from the difficulty in determining what is 'excessive injury and damage' in relation to the 'military advantage anticipated', makes it difficult to clearly determine in some situations whether the attack is proportionate. In many cases, of course, it is difficult to expect soldiers or junior officers to weigh these considerations at the critical moment in time. The responsibility falls primarily on the upper military echelon when it plans or approves military actions, and when it gives general orders to those under its command regarding permitted responses in different situations.

Did the decision to invade Area A in Beit Jala, under the circumstances that existed on 6 May 2001 and in the manner employed, meet the test of proportionality? The immediate significance of the order to enter Area A was to place IDF soldiers in life-threatening danger much greater than if they had acted as on previous occasions and returned fire from a protected position. It was to be anticipated that not only would Fatah personnel fire at the invading soldiers, but that, at the least, members of Palestinian National Security, who staff the nearby checkpoint, would also open fire. The danger faced by the IDF soldiers led, as could be expected, to the use of additional means in the attempt to protect the attacking soldiers exposed to Palestinian fire. This protection included, for example, tank shelling.

Because the entire incident took place in a built-up, residential area (part of it densely populated), the decision to enter Area A exposed the civilians living in the Iskan and Duha neighbourhoods to extremely grave danger.

Was the military advantage anticipated great enough to justify endangering the lives of many civilians? The danger faced by the IDF soldiers at the checkpoint that day was no greater than it had been numerous times during the recent period. According to the testimony of one member of Palestinian National Security, Fatah has fired at the Israeli checkpoint an average of three times a week since the beginning of the al-Aqsa Intifada. The very night before the incident discussed in this report, Fatah members fired at the checkpoint from Taleh Kubar and, following a three-minute exchange of fire, the incident ended without injury. Thanks to the concrete walls that Israel erected, only one IDF soldier has been wounded at this checkpoint since the beginning of the al-Aqsa Intifada.

The invasion was never intended to prevent the firing because, according to Minister of Defence Binyamin Ben-Eliezer, Israel did not plan to conquer parts of Beit Jala and occupy them permanently. (*Haaretz*, 7 May 2001). Indeed, less than 48 hours after the soldiers retreated from Area A, firing resumed from al-Iskan at the Israeli checkpoint and at the tower facing the neighbourhood.

B'Tselem, a human rights organisation, does not have the tools required to examine all the military considerations taken into account in deciding on this action. However, it is absolutely clear that the relevant authorities did not take into account the principle of proportionality. This failure is apparent from the results: on the one hand, five civilians were injured and the lives of hundreds of civilians were endangered, and, on the other hand, the firing at the checkpoint recommenced a short time after the action.

Prohibition of indiscriminate attacks

The duty to distinguish combatants and other legitimate objectives from civilians who are not participating in the hostilities is basic and appears throughout international humanitarian law. An attack does not meet this requirement if, *inter alia*, it is not directed at a specific military objective or if it employs weapons that are not sufficiently precise to distinguish combatants and military objects from civilians and civilian objects.[5] In case of doubt whether a

5 First Additional Protocol to the Geneva Conventions, of 1977, article 51 (4).

civilian structure is normally dedicated to civilian purposes, it must be presumed that the use is solely civilian.

In its response to B'Tselem's query, the IDF spokesperson stated that, during the incident, 'IDF forces returned precise fire to the points from which the fire originated.'[6] B'Tselem's findings indicate a different reality, and raise the grave suspicion that the IDF violated the principle prohibiting indiscriminate attacks. The IDF breach occurred in two primary ways.

The first way relates to the use of tanks in the situation that existed on 6 May 2001 in Beit Jala. It is important to note that the legality of means of combat (except for those expressly forbidden) depends on the circumstances in which they are employed, particularly the damage that they are liable to cause to civilians. Tank shelling is extremely accurate when fired from up to 3,000 metres at a tank-sized object, and more so at homes. However, it is very difficult to precisely identify a source of light arms fire at a distance of more than 1,500 metres. The problem of identification is aggravated because the opposing combatants often move. In these conditions, and taking into account the pressure on the soldier responsible for protecting the other soldiers, the likelihood that the soldier will err in identifying the source of fire is great. The 'price' in civilian lives of a mistake may be extremely high when the shell is 105 or 120 mm (regardless of the kind of shell) in comparison with a mistake by light-arms fire (5.56, 7.62, and 9 mm).

A reserve officer in the armoured corps who recently served in a sector in the West Bank was involved in tank shelling of a populated area. His testimony, given on 20 May 2001, illustrates the problem:

> During the action, I was with the battalion commander on the hill overlooking the firing. The commander was getting reports all the time from three tanks that were at the site, ostensibly identifying the sources and position of the opposing fire, and requested permission to return fire. In every case, the commander checked the accuracy of the reports, and in many cases found that the identification was in error, and he ordered the soldiers not to fire. Many lives were saved thanks to the commander.

In light of the testimonies, primarily that of Akram 'Atallah and Bassam Abu Ghanem, which explicitly mention that there had

6 Letter of 29 May 2001 from Major Efrat Segev, head of the Public Relations Division, Office of the IDF Spokesperson.

been no shooting from or adjacent to their homes, it is apparent that at least some of the shells were fired at homes incorrectly identified as sources of fire. As mentioned, mistakes in identifying light weapons gunfire from a built-up area from such distances are common and expected. Therefore, the tank shelling in this case is indiscriminate because it is insufficiently precise to distinguish the legitimate objective from civilians and civilian objects.

The prohibition against indiscriminate attacks was also violated in another way. The tour of sites shelled in Beit Jala made by B'Tselem researchers reveals that the tanks fired dozens of shells at Taleh Kubar, which is in the Iskan neighbourhood, and at one of the hills in the Sader neighbourhood. The shelling occurred even though, according to an eyewitness, no firing had taken place that day from either of these locations.

This finding is consistent with the report in *Haaretz* on the briefing by Lt.-Gen. Shaul Mofaz, Israeli chief of staff, to officers of the Gaza division, in which he stated: 'The procedure states that for all mortar fire that lands in Israeli towns and villages, tank shells are to be fired according to predetermined targets. According to the procedure, these targets are the structures identified as sources of fire.'[7]

Additional testimony by the armoured corps officer quoted previously paints a similar picture:

> At the beginning of service, the battalion commander briefed us and told us from which sites the Palestinians generally fire at us. He said that if we are fired at, it is reasonable to assume that it comes from those sites. Though he did not state it expressly, it is very likely that many soldiers understood that, in every case, we are to return fire at the sites delineated by the battalion commander.

It appears, therefore, that during the incident, inherent in the IDF shelling of points in the heart of the civilian population is that the targets were predetermined points from which armed Palestinians had fired in the past. The IDF gunfire in this situation was indiscriminate because it was not directed at a specific legitimate objective, and was based on an unproven presupposition that was not established during the events, and in retrospect proved erroneous.

7　The IDF spokesperson did not deny the comments and stated that the IDF spokesperson 'does not relate to comments made in closed military forums'. Amnon Barzilai, 'Mofaz: excessive force in firing that led to death of the infant Iman Haju', *Haaretz*, 10 May 2001.

Immunity of medical teams and ambulances

The medical teams that treated and evacuated the wounded, and the ambulances that were involved, are entitled to special protection under international humanitarian law. Not only is it forbidden to intentionally harm them, there is a duty to assist the medical teams, as much as the circumstances allow, in carrying out their tasks.[8]

During the invasion of Beit Jala, the IDF fired at two ambulances of the Civil Defence Centre, which were properly marked by the Red Crescent, that arrived at the scene. In one of the cases, it is impossible to verify with certainty that weapons were fired intentionally at the ambulance or whether the ambulance was caught in the cross-fire. The testimonies relating to the second case indicate that the border policemen's shooting at the ambulance was deliberate, a flagrant violation of international humanitarian law.

Attacks from within a civilian population

The general principle prohibiting attacks that fail to discriminate between combatants and civilians, described above, is derived from the prohibition on initiating attacks from within or nearby the homes of civilians. The objective of the principle is to prevent injury to civilians from the other side's anticipated response. Humanitarian law also explicitly forbids the use of the civilian population as a means to obtain immunity from enemy attacks.[9]

Fatah members who fired on the day of the incident at IDF soldiers on the Tunnels Road were located on the hill in the Iskan neighbourhood, which is located only dozens of metres from civilian homes. Although the shots were not fired by persons formally affiliated with the PA, the PA is obligated to do what it can to prevent firing that exposes the nearby civilians to the risk of IDF return fire. The PA's responsibility is particularly clear in this case because the Fatah members were only some 100 metres from a Palestinian National Security checkpoint when they opened fire. Furthermore, a member of Palestinian National Security admitted in his testimony to B'Tselem (see his testimony above) that the security service is aware that firing from areas near the checkpoint at which he is stationed is routine.

8 Fourth Geneva Convention of 1949, articles 20 and 21, and the First Additional Protocol of the Geneva Conventions, of 1977, articles 12, 15, and 21.
9 First Additional Protocol to the Geneva Conventions, of 1977, article 51(7).

By refraining from taking measures to end the firing from and near civilian homes, the PA violated its duty to protect civilians who are not taking part in the hostilities. However, according to humanitarian law, such a violation does not in any way allow the IDF to relate to the area from which the firing is executed as one entity comprising a legitimate military objective.

Ban on involving children in fighting

International humanitarian law prohibits the combatant parties from recruiting children under 15 years old into their combat forces, and requires the parties to take the necessary measures to ensure such children do not take part in the hostilities.[10] It should be noted that human rights organisations throughout the world, among them B'Tselem, maintain that minors under the age of 18 should be prohibited from participating in hostilities.

Information obtained by B'Tselem indicates that the armed Fatah members who fired at IDF soldiers at the checkpoint included a 14-year-old child. The PA's failure to prevent his participation in the shooting and remove him from the hazardous area constitutes a flagrant violation of international humanitarian law. (…)

10 Ibid., article 77(2), and article 38 of the Convention on the Rights of the Child.

3 House demolitions and destruction of agricultural land[11]

B'Tselem[12]

On 10 January 2002, the Israeli Defence Force (IDF) demolished 60 houses, and partially demolished four more, in the Rafah refugee camp, near the Egyptian border. The action left more than 600 Palestinians homeless. The media in Israel and throughout the world published pictures of the residents and their demolished homes, and for several days, the demolition was at the heart of the Israeli public debate.

The debate focused primarily on how many houses the IDF demolished and whether the houses were occupied at the time. The IDF steadfastly maintained that only 22 houses had been demolished and that they had been abandoned for many months. The residents, human rights organisations and humanitarian organisations contended that the number of houses demolished was much higher, and that at least some residents were living in the houses when the IDF began its demolition. The public debate rarely addressed the question of whether the house demolitions were justified.

The reporting on the house demolition action in Rafah gave the impression that it was a one-time act that was executed in response to the killing of four soldiers the day before. However, since the beginning of the al-Aqsa Intifada, Israel has demolished hundreds of houses, uprooted thousands of trees, and destroyed thousands of acres of land in the Gaza Strip. In almost all the cases of demolition, the houses were occupied and the residents fled

11 Excerpt from *Policy of Destruction: House Demolitions and Destruction of Agricultural Land in the Gaza Strip*, February 2002.
12 Israeli Centre for Human Rights in the Occupied Territories.

when the bulldozers appeared at their doorsteps. The IDF implemented this policy primarily in the Gaza Strip, near the Israeli
settlements, bypass roads, and army posts.

Israel does not deny these acts, but claims that they are legal
under international humanitarian law. Officials justify the policy
on the grounds of 'pressing military necessity' as a result of the
fact that Palestinians conceal themselves in houses and orchards,
from which they commit attacks. The officials contend that,
because it is difficult for the IDF to protect Israeli civilians and
soldiers from such attacks, it is necessary to perform 'clearing
actions' on the land to prevent future attacks.

Israel calls this policy 'clearing', a name that conceals the
destructive and long-term consequences for the Palestinian residents in the Gaza Strip. Thousands of people have been made
homeless and thousands have lost their sole source of income for
many years to come. Israel caused this damage to people although
it did not contend that they themselves were involved in attacks,
or attempted attacks, against Israeli civilians or security forces.

This report examines Israel's policy of house demolitions, uprooting of trees, and destruction of agricultural land in the Gaza Strip.
The report does not discuss the similar, although less extensive,
actions carried out by the IDF in the West Bank. The first part of the
report describes the IDF policy. The second part criticises the policy,
based on the relevant provisions of international humanitarian law.

The policy

Since the beginning of the al-Aqsa Intifada, Israel has employed a
policy of house demolition, uprooting of trees, and destruction of
agricultural areas in the Gaza Strip. The policy is implemented in
areas near the Israeli settlements, on both sides of the bypass roads
along which the settlers travel, and near army positions, primarily
along the Egyptian border. The IDF spokesperson, asked by
B'Tselem to comment on this policy, responded as follows:

> The roads in Judea and Samaria and in Gaza constitute one of
> the main friction centres where intensive combat events have
> taken place in the last few months. The IDF is, of course,
> required to deal with these combat events and to provide
> protection to these who use the said roads, both soldiers and
> civilians. The vegetation and the fences on the sides of the
> roads often serve as hiding place to commit terror attacks,

and make it difficult for the IDF soldiers to protect Israelis who drive these roads from bombs and shootings. The security means that the IDF uses in order to provide a solution for this security need is, among others, exposing the areas on the sides of the roads, including flattening of the area, removing trees and destroying fences.

Several residents of the Gaza Strip whose property was destroyed and the Palestinian Centre for Human Rights, in Gaza, petitioned the High Court of Justice against the actions. Two of the petitions dealt with the army's demolitions near the Netzarim settlement, alongside the road joining the Netzarim junction and the settlement. The third petition dealt with the uprooting of orchards and destruction of greenhouses near the Kfar Darom settlement. The state's responses to these petitions were similar to the IDF spokesperson's response cited above:

> Among the major focal points of intensive combat in the Gaza Strip were the roads leading to the Israeli settlements (the Karni–Netzarim road and the Kisufim–Gush Qatif road). In this combat, the IDF had to protect the users of these roads, soldiers and civilians alike, from the acts of terror on these roads, both from attacks by people hiding on the sides of the roads, and those concealed in the groves and trees, and also from roadside explosive charges. (...) In these incidents, the vegetation on the side of the roads often hid the terrorists and made it very difficult for the army units to protect the road against the laying of explosives and against firing at people driving along the road. (...) Following the said incident, the IDF decided to initiate various operations to protect the road, among them IDF patrols, observation posts and the like. In addition, as part of these acts, it was decided to clear away areas to increase the visibility of the soldiers in the observation posts, and to prevent terrorists from infiltrating close to the road to lay explosives or open fire, and the like.[13]

These comments indicate that this policy is part of Israel's defence strategy in the Gaza Strip. The chief of staff had good reason when

---

13 Response of the state in HCJ 9252/00, Zalah Shuqri Ahmad al-Saqa *et al. v.* State of Israel. Identical arguments were also raised in the state's response in HCJ 9515/00, 'Ali Faiz al Wahidi *et al. v.* State of Israel and in HCJ 3848/01, Mahmud Muhammad 'Abd 'al-'Aziz Bashir *v.* State of Israel.

he stated that, 'the D-9 [bulldozer] is a strategic weapon here' (*Haaretz*, 28 December 2000) Part of this strategy is the creation of 'security strips' around places where Israeli civilians or security forces are situated. Various Israeli officials explicitly admitted that this protection against Palestinian attacks is the purpose underlying the demolition of dozens of houses in the Rafah refugee camp, near the Egyptian border. Following the extensive demolition of houses in January 2002, the former OC Southern Command, Yom Tov Samiah, contended that:

> These houses should have been demolished and evacuated a long time ago. Because the Rafah border is not a natural border, it cannot be defended. (...) Three hundred metres of the Strip along the two sides of the border must be evacuated. (...) Three hundred metres, no matter how many houses, period.

Regarding the same action, Prime Minister Ariel Sharon stated:

> In Rafah, the system is to smuggle through tunnels, and these tunnels are deep – from 12 to 18 metres. Israel has to take all the necessary steps to stop the smuggling of weapons.(...) No doubt the narrow corridor that we have there does not allow us to stop it.[14]

The report will next present data that demonstrate the consequences of Israel's policy in the Gaza Strip. The data will be followed by a description of the way Israel implements its policy. At the end of this section, the report will present several testimonies of residents whose property was damaged by IDF forces.

The facts

It is impossible to determine precisely the scope of Israel's destruction in the Gaza Strip. In some of the areas the IDF destroyed, primarily near the settlements, entry is prohibited. Therefore B'Tselem researchers were unable to examine the consequences of

14 The comments were made in response to a journalist's question on the demolition of houses in Rafah. See the Foreign Ministry's website (www.mfa.gov.il): 'PM Sharon on the IDF action in Rafah: effort to stop smuggling of weapons by the Palestinians', 13 January 2002.

the IDF actions, and even the residents themselves are unable to estimate the scope of the damage they suffered. In a letter of 14 February 2001, the IDF spokesperson informed B'Tselem that 'The IDF does not have a precise estimate of the number of trees or the size of the area that was cleared'. Another letter that B'Tselem sent to the IDF spokesperson requesting such data has not been answered despite repeated follow-up requests.

However, some assessment of the consequences of the policy exists. According to the UN Relief and Works Agency (UNRWA), since the beginning of the Intifada the IDF has demolished 655 houses in the refugee camps in the Gaza Strip, in which 5,124 people lived. In addition, the IDF partially demolished 17 houses, in which 155 people lived. The International Committee of the Red Cross (ICRC) published similar figures: from the beginning of the Intifada to December 2001, the organisation assisted more than 5,200 residents whose houses had been demolished. In comparison, Defence Minister Binyamin Ben-Eliezer stated that, 'The total number of Palestinian structures that were demolished in the Gaza Strip stands at about 300. This figure includes structures used for residential purposes, farming, and walls. In addition, some 175 greenhouses were destroyed.'

Regarding the number of trees and fields that were destroyed, Ben-Eliezer contended that, 'In total, some 5,500 *dunam* [4 *dunam* = 1 acre] of orchards of all kinds on the Palestinian side were uprooted and 4,500 *dunam* of planted fields and uncultivated land were destroyed.' The figures reported by the Palestinian Centre for Human Rights, in Gaza, were much higher: from the beginning of the Intifada to the end of July 2001, some 13,500 *dunam* of agricultural land, constituting some 7 per cent of the agricultural land in the Gaza Strip, were destroyed.

B'Tselem conducted detailed research on some of the areas in which the army's demolition actions took place. The research provided the following information.

Rafah – Egyptian border

The Egyptian border area is densely populated, and Rafah's refugee camps lie along the border, which contains Israeli army posts. The IDF demolished houses and destroyed agricultural land along a 16.5 kilometre strip near the border. The destruction in the populated areas was less than that on the agricultural land. In some locations, the destruction covered a 350–500 metre-wide strip. In other places, the destruction covered a 100–150 metre-wide strip. In certain locations, the destruction was less, comprising a 40–50 metre-wide strip.

Netzarim

Around the border of the settlement, the IDF destroyed a 500–700 metre-wide strip of land. Agricultural land north of the settlement, in the centre of which a mosque is located, was not destroyed, but the army prohibited access to the mosque. Along 700 metres of the road leading from the settlement to the sea, the IDF destroyed a 400-metre strip on both sides of the road. The IDF also built a 1.5 kilometre road for the settlers that goes directly to Karni. On both sides of this road, the army uprooted trees and destroyed crops along a strip of 250–300 metres.

Morag

An army post is located 2 kilometres east of the settlement. From both sides of the road that joins this post with the Morag junction, the army built dirt terraces, placed concrete blocks and demolished land along a strip of 200 metres. On a 200-metre-wide strip of the land located between the settlement and the Salah al-Din road, the army uprooted trees and destroyed crops. It also destroyed more than 600 *dunam* of land stretching from the settlement to the main roads surrounding it.

Kfar Darom

The army destroyed 200 *dunam* of agricultural land surrounding the settlement. In addition, it destroyed a 200–300 metre stretch of land on both sides of the roads leading to the settlement. In some locations, the strip extended to about 400 metres.

Implementation

The decision-making process relating to demolition of houses and destruction of agricultural land is not clear. In his letter to M. K. Ran Cohen, Defence Minister Ben-Eliezer contended that the division commander makes the decision to demolish houses, and that regarding uprooting of trees, the brigade commander also has the power to make the decision, according to the planned scope.

However, the head of the Civil Administration, Brig.-Gen. Dov Zadka, stated that commanders' demolition requests reach his desk:

> It isn't as if everyone gets up, chops, demolishes and breaks. The request comes to me. I check whether it is justified, pass it on to the legal advisor, and only then do we recommend to the major general that he approve such an action.

The demolitions generally take place in the middle of the night without any warning being given to the residents. In areas in which there are exchanges of fire between Palestinians and IDF soldiers, some of the residents, primarily women and children, previously abandoned the houses for safer locations. However in most cases several of the residents remained in their homes, primarily to protect their property. The dozens of Palestinian testimonies given to B'Tselem indicate that in many instances, these residents had to flee from their homes after they were awakened by the noise of tanks and bulldozers that were already at their doorstep. Some of their property was buried under the ruins.

On 10 July 2001, IDF forces demolished houses in the Rafah refugee camp. Eighteen were completely destroyed and one was partially demolished. The army also demolished six shops. The action left 272 people homeless. The IDF spokesperson contended that the demolitions were carried out 'following the increase in terrorist attacks in recent days' and because of 'the immediate security need to protect soldiers moving along the road'.

In this case, as in the house demolition carried out in January 2002, the IDF spokesperson contended that the houses were abandoned. However, testimonies given to B'Tselem indicate that some of the houses were occupied. Mithqal Abu Taha, 37, married and the father of two children, described on 10 July 2001 the IDF action:

> Yesterday, there was no Palestinian gunfire at the Salah al-Din gate. My married brothers and their families and my family and I spent the night at home, and it was quiet when we went to sleep. Around 12.40 a.m., I woke up to the sound of gunfire and shelling and the noise of bulldozers and tanks that we hear on a daily basis. We did not expect them to demolish houses in our area. Neither the Palestinian nor the Israeli side gave us any warning to vacate our houses.

We thought that the bulldozers were on their way to some other place. We are used to leaving the houses when the gunfire and shelling intensifies. We would flee to safer areas in the camp and stay there until the situation calms down. Suddenly, one of the children screamed, 'Get out, the Jews are demolishing the houses', and began to throw stones at the neighbours' doors to wake them up. He was sobbing and shouting. I was startled and went outside to see what had happened. I saw elderly people and women and men carrying their children, leaving their homes and going toward the northern part of the camp. I saw our neighbour Anwar Kalub, whose house is about 2 metres from the border, removing his children and his flock. Then I understood that they [the IDF] were demolishing the houses in our area. I rushed to wake up my three brothers and their wives and children, and we went outside without taking anything with us. About a half an hour later, one of my sisters-in-law yelled that she couldn't find her son, Hussein Abu Taha, 13. She began to scream, 'My son is in the house.' We couldn't get to the house because the gunfire was so intense. After a while, we saw him running toward us. I asked where he had been, and he said, 'I was sleeping and when I awoke I saw that they were demolishing my uncle's house. I saw the tin roof fall.' When the child fled from the house, a fragment struck him in the neck.

On 15 November 2001, IDF forces demolished 28 houses in the Khan Yunis area, near the Tofah junction. At least 125 people lived in the houses. The IDF spokesperson stated on 15 November 2001 that the action followed firing at the Neve Dekalim settlement and at IDF posts in the area, and was intended 'to eliminate the threat of gunfire'.

Osama Abu Amuneh, 40, married with seven children, who lived in one of the houses, told B'Tselem how the army demolished the houses:

On Wednesday (14 November 2001), at 11.00 p.m., we woke up to the sound of shelling. The shelling also woke the children. We were frightened because we didn't know what had happened. The children and my wife screamed and cried every time a shell was fired. We didn't know what to do. After half an hour of non-stop shelling, some

young men from the neighbourhood came and told me to
leave the house. They said the Israeli army had entered the
area and was demolishing houses without checking if
people were inside. We didn't get any warning [from the
Israelis] to leave the house. I couldn't leave because we
have many children, and the shooting outside was still
intense. At 11.45 p.m., the sound of shelling increased, and
we heard tanks coming from the Tofah checkpoint. The
tanks were moving westward and were about 70 metres
from my house. We heard two more enormous explosions.
The same young men came back and took the children
from the house without getting my consent. The children
were crying and screaming, and my boys asked me to go
with them, but I refused. We also evacuated everyone from
the house. I was the only one who remained. I stayed to
protect it and to see what happened. Ten minutes later, the
tanks approached the house. I also heard the sound of bulldozers. I was on the southern side of the house, the side
that does not face the main road. I heard the bulldozers
destroying the house. I didn't dare approach or peek
outside, because the tanks were firing long bursts of
gunfire in all directions and were shelling the area. When
I saw that thick dust was filling the house and that the
electricity had been cut off, I went outside through the
southern gate so that the Israeli soldiers wouldn't see me.

The army also did not give warning of its intention to destroy
fields and uproot orchards. Such warning would, at least, have
enabled the Palestinians to remove the irrigation pipes and other
objects from the fields. After returning from duty in Gaza, Captain
Rami Kaplan, deputy battalion commander in the reserves,
described the situation well (*Haaretz*, 27 April 2001):

We usually surprise them, entering the area aggressively
with engineering implements and tanks for protection. The
Palestinians leave the depressing tin huts carrying baskets,
run to the trees at the far end of the grove, and somehow
manage to pick some last oranges.

In some cases, the uprooting caused long-term damage, and in
some instances even irreversible damage. In late April 2001, IDF
forces destroyed agricultural land near the Kisufim junction. It

destroyed 15 *dunam* of crops and uprooted about 120 olive trees. Khaled Taher, a landowner, described how the army uprooted trees:

> The bulldozer uprooted a tree and then drove over it and crushed it. After it uprooted and crushed all the trees in the field, the bulldozer dug a big hole, put the trees in, and covered it with dirt. Then it flattened the land and moved on to the adjacent field.

Following the Palestinian attack on Aley Sinai, in October 2001, which killed Assaf Yitzhaki and the soldier Lior Herpaz, the IDF conducted extensive actions of destruction in the northern Gaza Strip area of Beit Lahiyeh. According to the IDF spokesperson's statement on 3 October 2001, the operation 'was intended to remove the Palestinian terror threat from the area's communities'.

Abdullah Abu Hileyl, 26, married with three children and a resident of Beit Lahiyeh, described the IDF action:

> Yesterday [4 October 2001], at 4.00 p.m., I was picking guavas when I saw three bulldozers accompanied by a tank and an armoured vehicle coming from the direction of the Dugit settlement. They stopped about 300 metres from my house. I immediately stopped what I was doing and went into my house. Within less than an hour, I heard the sound of moving bulldozers. I went outside and saw that the bull-dozers had entered the guava orchard and were uprooting the trees. I stayed in the house, which is in the area under Israel's control, until 7.00 p.m., when the bulldozers finished uprooting all the guava trees and flattening the ground. Then they moved eastward, passing by my house. Later, the bulldozers and the accompanying tank returned and entered another plot, where I grow eggplant. They destroyed the crops and cleared out the area, which was 6.5 *dunam*. Then the bulldozers turned eastward to land belong-ing to 'Atallah a-Tarzi, and uprooted two rows of citrus trees that were about 300 metres long. At 9.00 p.m. or so, the bulldozers returned to the army encampment. At 9.00 a.m., the bulldozers returned to 'Atallah a-Tarzi's grove and uprooted the remaining citrus trees. The Israelis destroyed a total of 21 *dunam* of his land, leaving him only 6 *dunam* of greenhouses for growing flowers, and a well. Then the

bulldozers went into a 27 *dunam* citrus grove field belonging to his brother 'Abdullah. They uprooted all the trees, and left the well. They went to a 30 *dunam* field of Yasser Zindah and began to uproot the vineyards there. In the afternoon, I went to pray while the bulldozers continued to destroy the crops.

In some cases, IDF soldiers did not allow residents to enter the sites where their property had been destroyed, and fired at residents to keep them away from the area. On 11 May 2001, in Deir-al-Balah, the army demolished the house of Saleh Abu Huli, 44, married with six children.

After the army completed the demolition, Huli tried to go to the site of his destroyed house to save some of his possessions. He described to B'Tselem what happened then:

> Later on, we went to the houses that had been destroyed. We saw that they had been totally demolished along with everything that had been inside. Some of the people lost money, gold jewellery and identity cards. When we got close to the houses, soldiers opened heavy fire at us even though journalists were present. We hid among the ruins, and the drivers who passed on the road stopped and hid behind their cars for about 15 minutes.

On 23 June 2001, the IDF destroyed houses and crops in the Barhameh neighbourhood in the Rafah refugee camp. 'Atta Barhum told B'Tselem on 23 June 2001 that 'Several times, we tried to remove the rubble to find money that was lost there and to take our possessions, but the tanks always came. Sometimes they were on this side of the border, and sometimes on the other.'

Similarly, after the demolition that took place in Rafah in July 2001, the soldiers did not let the residents of the houses approach the area. Khaled 'Abd al-'Ael, 37, married with seven children, described on 10 July 2001 the situation:

> The events ended at 4.30 a.m. Immediately afterwards, our neighbours and I went to the houses. We saw that the area had been totally demolished. Around 6.30 a.m., while we were in the area of the demolished houses, the soldiers at the Salah al-Din army post fired at us. We fled into the camp's narrow alleyways. (...)

Criticism

Israel's policy, described above, flagrantly violates international humanitarian law. The demolition of houses and the destruction of agricultural land cause extensive damage to the civilian population, which will bear the consequences for many years to come. Injury of this kind to the civilian population cannot be justified on the grounds of 'pressing military necessity', as Israeli officials contend.

Israel's actions constitute collective punishment because these Palestinians were not involved in the combat against Israel, even according to Israeli officials. Also, Israel did not give the residents any warning before damaging their property, and thus denied them the opportunity to state their claims before the relevant officials and entities. Despite these violations of international humanitarian law, Israel refuses to compensate the Palestinians whose property it damaged in these actions.

The ICRC, the delegation from the UN Human Rights Commission, and the Mitchell Committee, which examined Israeli policy during the current Intifada, harshly criticised Israel's extensive destruction in the Gaza Strip. They all determined that the policy violates international humanitarian law and called on Israel to cease implementation of the policy immediately. (...)

4 Israeli violations of freedom of the press[15]

Reporters Without Borders

Since September 2000, 45 cases of journalists injured by bullets have been recorded by Reporters Without Borders. In December 2001 the Israeli Defence Ministry publicised the conclusions of its inquiries. In most cases these superficial and partial conclusions deny all responsibility of Tsahal (the Israeli army). Palestinian journalists, the majority of those injured, have experienced more and more problems in moving about between the different territories.

The 15 months of violence between the Israeli army and Palestinians have had heavy casualties: over 1,000 people killed (about 800 on the Palestinian side and 200 on the Israeli side). The end of the year was marked by escalating violence with suicide attacks by the Hamas and the Islamic Jihad and retaliation by Tsahal in Palestinian towns. In this context journalists work in difficult conditions. Since the start of the second Intifada on 29 September 2000, 45 cases of journalists injured by bullets have been recorded by Reporters Without Borders (RSF). Some were seriously wounded. In most cases RSF imputed responsibility to the Israeli army and asked it to expedite its enquiries. In mid-December 2001, 15 months after the first clashes, the Israeli Defence Ministry made the results of its enquiries public. Only nine cases of journalists were mentioned in the document, which exonerated Tsahal in all cases but one.

Palestinian journalists, the majority of those injured, have also experienced more and more problems when moving about between the different territories. At the end of the year the Israeli authorities considered not renewing the press cards of Palestinian correspondents of the foreign press. At the same time, Tel Aviv publicised its project to create an Arabic television channel to

15 Excerpt from *Annual Report 2002*, May 2002.

counter the 'propaganda' of Arabic and especially Palestinian media. During the year a section of the Israeli press, usually known for its professionalism and independence, sometimes acted as a mouthpiece for the army and adopted the same vocabulary as that used by Tsahal.

Eight journalists wounded in shooting

On 9 February 2001 a photographer for the agency Gamma, Laurent van der Stockt, and a colleague with Reuters were covering demonstrations by Palestinian youths in Ramallah. The photographer was standing at about 50 metres from Israeli soldiers when a real bullet hit him in the knee. The demonstration had started after Friday prayers. The Palestinian youths had gone towards an Israeli roadblock near a Jewish settlement and thrown stones at the soldiers, who retaliated with rubber bullets and tear gas. The photographer was taken to a hospital in Jerusalem and then repatriated to France. He was bedridden for three months and suffers from serious after-effects. On the same day and in the same place Rebhi Ahmad Mohammed al-Kobari, Palestinian camera operator with the Palestinian television channel al-Sharq in Ramallah, was injured in the left knee by shrapnel after the Israeli army opened fire on demonstrators. The journalist was carrying his video camera and wearing a cap clearly marked 'TV'.

Ahmed Zaki, Palestinian correspondent for Oman Satellite Television, was hit in the knee by an unidentified projectile while covering clashes on 23 March at the entrance to Ramallah.

Zakaria Abu Harbeid, journalist with the local news agency Ramatan, was injured on 14 April at Khan Yunis, in Gaza, while taking photos of Israeli soldiers shooting at Palestinians. The journalist was hit in the hand and had to be hospitalised for several days.

On 20 April Laila Odeh, Jerusalem correspondent for the United Arab Emirates channel Abou Dhabi TV, was interviewing people in the Rafah area whose homes had been destroyed by Israeli raids in Gaza a few days earlier. As the journalist and her crew were about to leave, Israeli soldiers shot in their direction. Laila Odeh was hit in the thigh by a real bullet and immediately taken to Rafah hospital before being transferred to al-Shifa hospital in Gaza. According to her, the soldiers deliberately aimed at her. In the report put out on 18 December by the Israeli army, an 'action enquiry' could be decided on, if necessary.

Bertrand Aguirre, correspondent for the French channel TF1, was injured on 15 May while covering clashes in Ramallah between the Israeli army and Palestinian demonstrators. A bullet hit the journalist's bullet-proof jacket, causing bruising. The journalist was taken to Ramallah hospital for an examination. The journalist told Reporters Without Borders:

> I can't say whether the border guard aimed directly at me as a journalist, or even if he aimed at me personally. What is clear, however, is that he opened fire at a short distance, with real bullets, firing at body height, when his own safety was not threatened in any way whatsoever.

In September he was informed that the enquiry had been closed. To justify this decision, Eran Shangar, director of the police internal affairs bureau, explained, 'After examining the file, I decided not to prosecute the policeman for lack of evidence.' Yet three different television teams simultaneously filmed the scene. The films clearly show an Israeli border guard get out of his vehicle, calmly take aim, and with his cigarette between his lips, open fire with real bullets at human height, at a distance of about 100 metres.

On 15 June a Japanese freelance journalist was hit in the hand by shrapnel after Israeli soldiers had fired shots during clashes at the entrance to Ramallah.

Lu'ay Abu-Haikal was hit by a rubber-covered metal bullet on 6 July while covering clashes between Israeli troops and Palestinian demonstrators in Hebron. He was treated at Hebron hospital.

Six journalists arrested

Israeli soldiers arrested four journalists from the Palestinian public-sector channel Palestinian Broadcasting Corporation (PBC) – Ruba al-Najar, journalist, Jaghoub Jaghoub, camera operator, Bilal Aburish, production assistant, and Samir Abid Rabbo, sound engineer – on 24 April 2001 while they were doing a report in Nablus on the West Bank. An army officer accused them of filming Israeli military positions and vehicles. After taking the journalists to the Karne Shermon colony, soldiers blindfolded them and their driver, Hussein al-Gharnaoui, then interrogated them. They also searched them and viewed their videotapes. After eight hours of detention Ruba al-Najar, Jaghoub Jaghoub, Bilal Aburish and

Samir Abid Rabbo were released. Their driver was kept in detention on the pretext that he was involved in 'hostile activities'.
During clashes on Temple Mount on 29 July, Ahmed Husseini
Siam, who works for CBS, was arrested by police who also confiscated a videotape. Freelance journalist Maurizio Giuliano was
arrested on 30 October at an Israeli roadblock when crossing
Allenby Bridge between Jordan and the Occupied Territories. He
was manhandled by a police officer. He was then also detained for
a few hours on the Jordanian side.

Fourteen journalists physically attacked

On 10 May 2001 Hossam Abou Alan, photographer for Agence
France-Presse, Mazen Dana, camera operator with Reuters, and
Nael Shiyoukhi, sound engineer for Reuters, were covering the
Jewish carnival in Hebron when they were set on by Jewish
settlers.

During clashes on Temple Mount on 29 July, nine journalists –
Nasser Atta (ABC News), Rachid Safadi (al-Jazira), Atta Awassat
(*Yediot Aharonot*), Fatem Awalan (Nile TV), Gevara Bouderi (al-
Jazira), Mahfuz Abu Turk (freelance, working mainly for Reuters),
Muna Qawasmi (al-Ayyam), Amar Awad (Reuters) and Nasser
Abdel Jawad (camera operator) – found themselves face to face with
several hundred policemen after the demonstrators had fled or
taken refuge in the mosque. The police, who had been about to
charge, attacked the journalists and beat them with truncheons. Atta
Awassat was hit with the butt of a rifle.

Tarek Abdel Jaber, journalist, and Abdel Nasser Abdoun,
camera operator, both with Egyptian state television, were
attacked on 13 August by an Israeli soldier at the Qalandia roadblock between Jerusalem and Ramallah. The soldier hit Abdoun in
the face and the groin, so that he fell to the ground. According to
the two journalists, other Israeli soldiers present did nothing to
stop this assault. Abdel Nasser Abdoun was taken to Makaset
hospital in Jerusalem where he spent three hours. The Israeli
soldier was sentenced to 21 days in jail and prohibited from being
in a position of command.

Pressure and obstruction

Tsahal soldiers shot warning shots in the direction of three Reuters
journalists, Christine Hauser, Ahmed Bahadou and Suhaib Salem,

on 8 March 2001 in Gaza. The journalists, who wanted to film and take photos of an Israeli military installation in Netzarim, and were clearly identifiable by their equipment, had to throw themselves to the ground. The soldiers asked them to leave. One of them went over to the journalists to tell them that they were not allowed there. The Israeli army spokesperson, Olivier Rafowicz, later commented that 'because of the very tense situation in Gaza, civilians are not allowed to go near Israeli defence force posts'. 'The army simply shot warning shots. The Reuters crew had not informed the army of its presence in the area', he added.

In early May the head of the army education department, General Eliezer Stern, ordered the suspension of the Israeli army weekly *BeMahaneh*. According to an army spokesperson, 'articles in the newspaper (dated 4 May 2001) did not correspond to army standards'. An article published in that issue described a homosexual reserve colonel.

On 1 August a group of Palestinian journalists was blocked for several hours at a roadblock at the entrance to Nablus. The next day an ANN (Arab News Network) crew was held up for two hours at the same roadblock. Mohamad al-Sayed, journalist, Ahmed al-Asi, camera operator and their driver were insulted after Mohamad al-Sayed (an Arab Israeli) refused to interpret for the Israeli soldiers.

The armoured car of Elizabeth Dalziel of Associated Press was hit by bullets during shooting on 5 October between Israeli soldiers and Palestinians in Hebron. After the first bullet hit the windscreen of the vehicle clearly marked 'TV' and 'Press', the journalist tried to flee. At least five other bullets then hit the car, one of which burst a tyre. The photograph said she did not see who opened fire but it seemed that the shots came from Israeli positions. This took place in the Abou Sneineh district, one of the two parts of Hebron into which the Israeli army made an incursion that day, killing five Palestinians. The Israeli army announced on 6 October that it was investigating the origin of the shots. In early 2002 the results of the enquiry had still not been disclosed.

In the autumn Ziad Abou Ziad, Palestinian member of the legislative assembly and managing editor of the magazine *Palestine–Israel Journal* (edited jointly by Israelis and Palestinians), was banned from entering Jerusalem where the head office of his newspaper is situated. 'Some people fear dialogue between our two peoples more than anything else', explained the journalist.

A television crew from the Lebanese channel al-Manar, owned by the Shiite Hizbullah movement, was shot at on 18 November by Israeli soldiers close to the border town of Kfarchouba. According to Hizbullah, one Asian and several European journalists were present and were also shot at. The Israeli soldiers shot at the journalists' feet.

On 13 December the Israeli army destroyed a Palestinian broadcasting installation in Ramallah by blowing up the main antenna. Palestinian radio and television had already stopped broadcasting the previous evening due to bombings. These official media were then forced to use private-sector broadcasting antennae.

On 18 December the Israeli Government Press Office (GPO) announced its plan not to renew the press cards of Palestinian journalists working for foreign media. Instead, they are to be given a 'special assistant' orange card valid only for the Territories, which does not allow automatic access to Israel. The Israeli authorities justified this measure by claiming that Palestinian journalists 'spread propaganda and do not meet journalistic standards for balanced coverage'. According to the GPO, between 500 and 600 Palestinian journalists currently have a press card.

5 The heavy price of Israeli incursions[16]

Amnesty International

> The Palestinians must be hit and it must be very painful. We must cause them losses, victims, so that they feel the heavy price.
>
> (Ariel Sharon, Israeli Prime Minister, speaking to the press on 5 March 2002)

Since 27 February 2002 the Israeli Defence Force (IDF) has launched two waves of incursions into the Palestinian areas occupied by Israel in 1967, using tanks, armoured personnel carriers (APCs) and Apache helicopters. In the six weeks up to 11 April 2002 more than 600 Palestinians may have been killed and more than 3,000 injured.

The declared aim of the incursions into the Occupied Territories, which were continuing as this report was written, was, according to a briefing on 1 March 2002 by the Commander of the West Bank division Brig.-Gen. Yitzhak Gershon, 'To clarify that there isn't and will not be a safe place for the terrorists and their senders. Our intention is to destroy the terror infrastructure in the refugee camps, if they are found.' He added that 'It is important to clarify that this activity is not intended against the population which is not involved in terrorism. We have made all efforts to prevent causing harm to civilians.'

However, the IDF acted as though the main aim was to punish all Palestinians. Actions were taken by the IDF which had no clear or obvious military necessity; many of these, such as unlawful killings, destruction of property and arbitrary detention, torture and ill-treatment, violated international human rights and humanitarian

16 Excerpt from *Israel and the Occupied Territories. The Heavy Price of Israeli Incursion*, AI Index: MDE 15/04/2002, April 2002.

law. The IDF instituted a strict curfew and killed and wounded armed Palestinians. But it also killed and targeted medical personnel and journalists, and fired randomly at houses and people in the streets. Mass arbitrary arrests were carried out in a manner designed to degrade those detained.

Amnesty International delegates who visited the area between 13 and 21 March saw a trail of destruction: homes, shops and infrastructure demolished or damaged; apartments trashed and looted; cars crushed and lamp posts, walls and shopfronts smashed. The IDF had deliberately cut electricity and telephone cables and water pipes, leaving whole areas without power and water for up to nine days. David Holley, an independent military expert, one of Amnesty International's delegates, said:

> The military operations we have investigated appear to be carried out not for military purposes but instead to harass, humiliate, intimidate and harm the Palestinian population. Either the Israeli army is extremely ill-disciplined or it has been ordered to carry out acts which violate the laws of war.

The first incursions were ended by a gradual and partial Israeli pullback after the arrival of US envoy Anthony Zinni on 14 March. However, the destruction and gross violations of human rights inflicted by the IDF between 27 February and 20 March (when the IDF finally pulled out of areas round Bethlehem) reached unprecedented levels during the second wave of incursions, 'Operation Defensive Shield', which started on 29 March 2002 with an attack on President Yasser Arafat's headquarters in Ramallah. The IDF spread through Ramallah, then entered Bethlehem, Tulkarem and Qalqiliya from 1 April, followed by Jenin and Nablus from the nights of 3 and 4 April. Towns were declared closed military areas, with strict curfews imposed on those within the towns. The IDF showed a widespread disregard for life, law and property. People from outside the invaded areas, including journalists, UN agencies, other humanitarian workers and even diplomats, were prevented from gaining access to offer aid or report on what was going on.

With six main cities and many villages effectively under siege, blocked off from the outside world, and with movement within the towns prohibited, a humanitarian disaster loomed as supplies of food and water ran out for many Palestinians. Ambulances, including those of the International Committee of the Red Cross

(ICRC), were not allowed to move, or suffered lengthy and life-threatening delays. Medical personnel or those who tried to help the injured were fired on, and the wounded bled to death on the street. With movement banned, those who died could not be properly buried; they remained in houses or morgues, or were hastily buried in parking lots or gardens. In the ten days until 7 April, according to IDF figures, 200 Palestinians were killed and 1,500 wounded; on 12 April the IDF admitted that the real figures of those killed were in hundreds in Jenin alone. As the IDF tried to keep journalists and outsiders away from areas where they were carrying out operations, many of the reports of large-scale human rights violations by the IDF, including extrajudicial executions, expulsions, and massive house destruction by the IDF, could not be verified. At first the families of Palestinians arrested had no idea where they were, or even whether they were alive or dead. On 11 April 2002 official IDF figures stated that since 29 March, more than 4,000 Palestinians had been arrested and more than 350 were in administrative detention. A military order, issued on 5 April, banned visits to detainees by lawyers for the first 18 days of their detention.

During the month before 27 February, twelve Israeli civilians were killed by Palestinian armed groups. Since the beginning of the Intifada, the targeting of Israeli civilians by Palestinian armed groups and individuals, through suicide bombs and drive-by shootings, has been a grim feature. With the first incursions a sharp escalation of suicide bombings by Palestinian armed groups took place, deliberately targeting Israeli civilians. Between 2 March and 1 April at least 40 civilians were killed in such attacks. The attacks included the killing of ten Israelis, including six children, standing outside a synagogue in Beit Yisrael; the 9 March killing of ten Israelis in a café in West Jerusalem; and the killing of 26 Israelis celebrating Passover at the Park Hotel in Netanya. Amnesty International has unreservedly condemned such deliberate killings of civilians by armed groups as violations of the right to life. This report focuses on the human rights abuses that accompanied IDF incursions into the Occupied Territories after 27 February. Other abuses, including those perpetrated against Israeli civilians by armed Palestinian groups, have been and will be addressed in separate statements and reports. No crime, however appalling, can excuse the wanton disregard of international human rights and humanitarian law carried out daily in the Occupied Territories during the post 27 February incursions by the IDF under the orders of the Israeli government headed by Prime Minister Ariel Sharon. (...)

Violations of the right to life

> Every human being has the inherent right to life. This right shall be protected by law. No one shall be arbitrarily deprived of his life.
>
> (ICCPR, article 6(1))

Without proper investigations, which are not taking place, it is impossible to say how many of those killed by the IDF were armed Palestinians who were actively engaged in targeting Israeli forces. However, the use of force by the IDF appears to have been disproportionate and often reckless. There are also reports of extrajudicial executions.

The IDF incursions into Palestinian refugee camps and towns have encountered resistance by Palestinian armed groups. Amnesty International delegates witnessed the exchanges of fire between the two sides on two occasions during their recent visit. (...)

On 17 March Amnesty International delegates in Deheisheh camp and Bethlehem witnessed heavy exchanges of fire by both members of the IDF and armed Palestinian groups. Delegates saw some 200 armed Palestinians in civilian dress as they passed through the streets of Deheisheh and Bethlehem. Palestinian bystanders, including children, in the town appeared to be at risk of being targeted by the IDF or shot by either side in cross-fire.

During Amnesty International's research in other areas, its delegates were told that Palestinians who had weapons and who were not members of armed groups had shot at the IDF forces.

During Israel's incursion into Jabaliya on 11–12 March the IDF unlawfully killed bystanders by shooting randomly. Any Palestinian seen by the IDF on the top of a building appeared to be targeted by the IDF. In addition, there were many cases in all areas where Palestinians who apparently misunderstood instructions by the IDF – standing still, or coming forward or retreating when ordered to do something different – were shot. One IDF conscript told Amnesty International in February, 'Any person that is considered a threat can be killed. "Threat" is a very fluid notion – as big as the ocean.'

Eight Palestinians watched the incursion on the roof of their house in Tel al-Za'tar quarter in north Jabaliya when it started around 10.30 p.m. As IDF Apache helicopters flew overhead the eight hastened to leave, but 'Abd al-Rahman Muhammad 'Izz al-Din, aged 55, the last person to flee, was shot in the back, apparently by IDF snipers on a neighbouring roof, just as he reached the door to the roof to go downstairs. His son Walid 'Abd al-Rahman 'Izz al-Din, 35, turned to rescue him and was himself shot dead minutes later by a bullet that passed from his shoulder to his heart. Ambulances tried to reach the 'Izz al-Din house but were unable to do so. An ambulance operative from the Palestinian Red Crescent Society (PRCS) said, 'It took us more than an hour to enter the house. A tank was standing at every entrance to the house.'

In Salah al-Din Street a deaf and mute man, Samir Sadi Sababeh, aged 45, died when the IDF prepared to demolish a small metal workshop on the other side of the street from where he sheltered. Around 10.30 p.m. on 11 March the IDF summoned all residents of the flats beside the workshop to leave, allowing them no time to collect their possessions. The IDF called Samir Sababeh to join the residents being evicted from their houses. When he failed to come, they shot and killed him.

Huda al-Hawaja, aged 31, a mother of five children living in Aida refugee camp in Bethlehem, was killed on 8 March when IDF soldiers used explosives to open the door of her house in order to occupy it as a strategic post. The incident was recorded by a reporter of Israel's Channel 10 TV and shown on Channel Two. According to the Israeli newspaper *Haaretz*:

> During the briefing before entering the house, the soldiers are told to break down the door with a hammer, and if that didn't work, to use an explosive brick. That's what they do. The result: the mother of the family is mortally wounded and lies on the floor bleeding. The children stand behind her choking back tears. The father tries calling an ambulance but it is trapped between checkpoints. The soldiers continue moving through the house by cutting through the walls. (...)

Raffaele Ciriello, aged 42, an Italian freelance journalist, was killed in Ramallah at 9.30 a.m. on 13 March when he was shot by a machine gun mounted on an IDF tank about 150 metres away. The IDF reportedly did not allow ambulances to approach him, and he was carried to hospital by Palestinians. According to Amedeo Ricucci from the Italian TV station Rai Uno, there was no Palestinian fire at the time Raffaele Ciriello was shot.

In the latest incursions, there seems to have been an even greater readiness to kill. Some extrajudicial executions have taken place. Other killings appear to be cases of what the Israeli army describes as 'death kill verification' – the extrajudicial execution of those wounded. Amnesty International condemns such practices.

At midnight on 29 March the IDF attacked the Cairo-Amman Bank where members of Force 17, a PA security force, engaged them from the third floor. After the IDF had stormed the building, five bodies of members of Force 17 were found; each one had been wounded and shot at close range with a single shot to the head or throat. (...)

Healthcare workers targeted

> Each party to the conflict shall be obliged to apply, as a minimum, the following:
> (1) Persons taking no active part in the hostilities, including members of armed forces who have laid down their arms and those placed hors de combat by sickness, wounds, detention, or any other cause, shall in all circumstances be treated humanely. (…)
> (2) The wounded and sick shall be collected and cared for.
> (Common Article 3 of the Geneva Conventions)

Articles 20 and 21 of the Fourth Geneva Convention require respect and protection for medical personnel and convoys. Amnesty International condemns the fact that the Israeli authorities have consistently violated the right to life by failing to respect the principles of medical neutrality. During the first week of Operation Defensive Shield according to a statement given by Peter Hansen, the director of the UN Relief and Works Agency (UNRWA), on 5 April 2002, more than 350 ambulances had been denied access and 185 ambulances had been hit by gunfire. 'I would strongly suggest that when 185 ambulances have been hit, including 75 per cent of UNRWA's ambulances (...) this is not the result of stray bullets by mistake hitting an ambulance, this can only be by targeting ambulances', he said.

Since 27 February 2002 six medical personnel have been killed and many wounded by IDF fire. The head of the Palestinian Red Crescent in Tulkarem told Amnesty International delegates on 18 March 2002, 'I find it safer now to send patients needing dialysis or other medical treatment by taxi, rather than by ambulance.'

The Israeli invasions of March and April 2002 saw an unprecedented attack on medical personnel. The IDF's consistent fire on ambulances travelling to the injured halted ambulances for days at a time. The IDF has also fired on civilians, including women, who ventured out to carry the injured. After two medical assistants travelling with ambulances were killed within the space of a few hours on 7 March, the ICRC told ambulances not to move, and during the whole of 8 March, while clashes were continuing in Tulkarem refugee camp and the wounded were lying in streets and homes, not a single ambulance was able to leave the station.

The ICRC tried to coordinate the movement of ambulances by contacting the Civil Administration (the Israeli military government in the Occupied Territories) and obtaining IDF authorisation first. They were delayed, and even with this coordination they were frequently shot at. Nor was the ICRC emblem any protection. In a public statement, the ICRC on 5 April 2002 stated that it was 'obliged to limit its movement in the West Bank to a strict minimum'. It continued:

> Over the past two days, ICRC staff in Bethlehem have been threatened at gunpoint, warning shots have been fired at ICRC vehicles in Nablus and Ramallah, two ICRC vehicles were damaged by IDF tanks in Tulkarem and the ICRC premises in Tulkarem were broken into. This behaviour is totally unacceptable, for it jeopardises not only the life-saving work of emergency medical services, but also the ICRC's humanitarian mission.

Two doctors and four paramedics were killed by IDF fire between 4 and 12 March 2002. Amnesty International investigated the killings of Sa'id Shalayel, Kamal Salem and Ibrahim Jazmawi.

On 4 March 2002 Dr Khalil Suleiman, aged 58, was killed when the clearly marked PRCS ambulance he was travelling in was hit by gunfire from members of the IDF. Dr Suleiman was head of the PRCS Emergency Medical Service (EMS) in Jenin in the West Bank. Also injured were four Red Crescent paramedics and the driver who were travelling in the ambulance. An injured girl was being transported in the ambulance at the time.

On 7 March, the first day of the Israeli army's entry into Tulkarem, the use of ambulances was allowed only in coordination with the ICRC, accompanied by the ICRC ambulance. However, after

5 p.m. the ICRC ambulance had to leave. As it grew dark a clearly marked UNRWA ambulance on its way to collect three wounded people was attacked by a missile from an Apache helicopter. Kamel Salem, an UNRWA sanitation worker with medical training, sitting in the ambulance beside the driver, was killed. Another ambulance, with Ibrahim Muhammad Jazmawi as the medical assistant, had been at the scene, and his ambulance returned to the centre. Meanwhile more calls came to help the wounded, including three injured in a car accident. The PRCS tried to coordinate its movements with the IDF through the ICRC, and waited nearly an hour before it eventually got agreement to send out ambulances. Two PRCS ambulances left to collect the three injured people. However, two minutes from the hospital in a main shopping street of Tulkarem they saw a tank facing them. The ambulance of Ibrahim Jazmawi reversed about a metre. The tank fired on both ambulances, killing Ibrahim Jazmawi and damaging the second ambulance. The surviving ambulance staff escaped on foot. After half an hour a group of ambulance staff were able to return on foot to collect the body of Ibrahim Jazmawi. After that the ICRC told the ambulance staff not to move, and they remained inactive for the whole of 8 March, despite continuing clashes and casualties in the camps. (...)

Demolition and destruction

> Any destruction by the Occupying Power of real or personal property belonging individually or collectively to private persons, or to the State, or to other public authorities, or to social or cooperative organisations, is prohibited, except where such destruction is rendered absolutely necessary by military operations.
>
> (Article 53 of the Fourth Geneva Convention relative to the Protection of Civilian Persons in Time of War of 1949)

In every refugee camp they occupied, Israeli soldiers left a trail of destruction. Tanks rolled over parked cars, broke down walls and house fronts, and knocked down lamp posts and street signs. Sometimes they rolled for no apparent reason into the front of houses. Electricity, water and telephones were cut for as long as the Israeli army remained in occupation. Meanwhile wall-piercing bullets and sometimes tank rounds were shot for no apparent reason into shop fronts or houses.

From the beginning of the incursions, homes of 'wanted' men or those who had carried out attacks on Israelis were demolished. During the invasion of Jenin on 5 and 6 April 2002, at least 20 Palestinian homes in Jenin refugee camp were demolished, either to make the narrow roads wide enough for tanks, or because they contained armed Palestinians who refused to give themselves up.

Not only does the IDF action in destroying property when not absolutely necessary and trashing apartments breach article 53 of the Fourth Geneva Convention, it also breaches article 33 of that Convention, prohibiting collective punishment, pillaging and reprisals.

In Ramallah the house of Afif Ahmad, containing six people, was hammered by wall-piercing fire and missile rounds on 12 March from a tank, as six members of the family lay in fear on the floor for four hours. The IDF entered and occupied those houses and apartment blocks that appeared to be in strategically advantageous positions. Residents in the houses were confined to a single room or a single flat for as long as the IDF occupied the town – sometimes for as long as four or five days. The soldiers occupying flats systematically trashed them, opening drawers and wardrobes and scattering their contents, tearing clothes, damaging pictures, throwing televisions or computers down stairs. There were reports of looting from many areas; sometimes victims complained to the IDF who took no action. In one flat in Deheisheh camp belonging to Amal 'Abd al-Mun'im, the family Qur'an had its pages cut out and scattered over the floor, and a report by B'Tselem had been pierced over and over again, apparently by a knife or bayonet. She told Amnesty International:

> They came on Saturday 9 March, 25 soldiers with armoured cars. They put us all in one room – there were six of us, [my husband], my four children and myself. They stayed about five hours and we were confined to one room. Then they took my husband away. They stayed four days in the house. When we came back we found everything destroyed. My house is three storeys high and they destroyed everything. They stole two video cameras each one [worth] $300. They took all our money, the computer which cost about 8,000 shekels. They were using the toilets but they didn't clean anything. We found their excrement everywhere – they filled towels with shit and smeared it on the wall, in the kitchen and our dishes. They tore up the Qur'an and broke everything.

In many houses entered by the IDF the soldiers broke open holes in walls in order to reach neighbouring houses. This is a recognised military technique in town fighting, sometimes known as 'mouse-holing', to provide soldiers with escape routes. The Israeli soldiers called it 'walking through walls'. In the houses visited by Amnesty International, the making of holes from one house to the other always created chaos in the rooms on either side. Sometimes holes were made from one apartment to another when it was possible for soldiers to have entered from a verandah or window. In Balata refugee camp, according to Palestinians, about 30 holes were made to enable Israeli soldiers to pass through a row of houses up to the UNRWA school.

In al-Am'ari camp, Ramallah, 30 soldiers came without warning into the house of Halima al-Nabi around 7.30 p.m. on 12 March 2002. They went up to the top floor, trashed the apartment and broke a hole through the wall of her son's apartment next door, although there was a verandah and a door which could have given access. They spent about three hours there, then from the flat of her son Jamal al-Nabi they tried to break through to the house of another son, Nabil al-Nabi, but found the concrete wall too thick. So they used a window, descending into the bedroom where all of Nabil al-Nabi's eleven children slept together. They scattered clothes and cushions around, broke the glass of family photos, tore the Qur'an and threw the television downstairs. They stayed in the house for three days, until the morning of 15 March, while the family was shut into their grocer's shop downstairs with one mattress between the 13 family members. 'Some of the children were scared to death and we took two, aged five and six, to hospital', said Halima al-Nabi. (...)

Arbitrary arrests and inhuman treatment

(...)
Testimony of Jamal Issa, aged 37, from Tulkarem refugee camp:

> The IDF came to my house at 6 a.m. [on 8 March]. They gathered everyone, three families, in one room and we stayed there from 6 a.m. until 10 a.m. when we were moved to another house. They collected 20 people in the same house. Then we were taken to the school where we stayed for four or five hours, blindfolded and with our hands bound. They collected all our IDs and tried to sort us in

groups. After three hours they took us to the DCO [District Coordination Office]. We stayed the night at the DCO, about 60 of us, handcuffed and blindfolded, treated as terrorists and humiliated. The basic rights of prisoners were denied to us. We asked to go to the toilet and they refused. We spent a night of shouting and crying. After that some were transferred by buses to Kedumim and others to Huwara military camp. There wasn't a prison in Huwara; it was better than the other place, they removed the blindfolds and handcuffs. We spent six days without any interrogation and then they released us. We hoped that someone would tell us why we were taken. We had been scared the whole time because they had threatened to kill us, but in the event we were more frightened of the release than of detention as we were left at the military camp checkpoint, where we collected our IDs, and we had to find taxis and go past all the Nablus settlements. It took us four hours to get home. (...)

During Operation Defensive Shield, up to 11 April more than 4,000 Palestinians were arrested, mostly in house to house searches. In some places mass arrests took place after broadcast orders to all males between 15 and 45 to report. This reportedly took place in al-Bireh on 30 March; many men who reported at the Diaspora School were put on buses and taken to Ofer. They were reportedly blindfolded and handcuffed, and held in the open until their interrogation after three days. The interrogation was minimal: name, birth and personal details. After questioning they were taken to a tent and given blankets and wooden pallets to sleep on. Most were released at Qalandiya after seven days. Other detainees arrested in Ramallah reported being held in the open in half-finished houses or school yards; they were kept lying down, and handcuffed and hooded when they went to the toilet. Detainees said that they were sometimes beaten.

With strict curfews in place in most towns, families whose relatives had been arrested did not know whether they were alive or dead. Israeli human rights organisations who tried to trace detainees were inundated with appeals, but were unable to find information from the IDF, who said that they themselves had no idea of the names of those they had arrested. A military order, number 1500, was issued on 5 April 2002 allowing the army to hold detainees for 18 days without access to lawyers before being brought before a judge (who could renew the lack of access order).

As a result of reports that detainees had toes and fingers broken, four human rights organisations, B'Tselem, the Association for Civil Rights in Israel (ACRI), HaMoked and Physicians for Human Rights (PHR) petitioned the Israeli High Court of Justice (HCJ) that such treatment should cease; the HCJ rejected the petition. (...)

6 Operation Defensive Shield[17]

International Federation of Human Rights Leagues

The International Federation of Human Rights Leagues (FIDH) and Médecins du Monde (MDM) commissioned an investigation into the situation regarding human rights and international humanitarian law in the town of Nablus in the West Bank, as it has evolved since Operation Defensive Shield carried out by the Israeli army in Nablus between 3 and 22 April 2002. (...)

The mission found evidence in particular of numerous breaches of the Fourth Geneva Convention relative to the Protection of Civilian Persons in Time of War, a convention ratified by Israel: impeding access to medical care; cruel treatment inflicted on the wounded; violence to the life and health of protected persons (either deliberate or as a result of the indiscriminate and disproportionate use of force); outrages on the dignity of persons; humiliating or degrading treatment; use of human shields. The mission also found that the Israeli army carried out arbitrary mass arrests in Nablus. The conditions of detention and treatment of detained persons appeared to fall well short of the rules of international humanitarian law and the provisions of the Convention against Torture and other Cruel, Inhuman or Degrading Treatment or Punishment. In addition, the destruction of real and personal property and other acts perpetrated by the Israeli army constituted collective punishment, which is forbidden under international humanitarian law.

---

17 Excerpt from *Operation* Defensive Shield – *Nablus Joint Investigative Mission Médecins du Monde – FIDH West Bank – 28 April to 5 May 2002.* Most of the elements that involved the local work of Médecins du Monde are not dealt with in this book, since the organisation declined to be associated with it.

Chronology of events[18]

(...) Everyone was aware that Tsahal forces had been standing by for around a week at the gates of the town. Resistance to an Israeli attack had been organised. Although the Palestinians remain discreet about the number of men involved and the exact make-up of the group, the mission estimated that several hundred armed men retreated into the old town. Combatants or individuals wanted by the Israelis attempted to flee the town and went into hiding in the surrounding hills. Orders were apparently issued to members of the Palestinian public force to disperse throughout the town until the Tsahal forces withdrew, and not take part in any clashes. The mission met three members of the Palestinian naval forces who confirmed this strategy:

> We knew the Israeli army was going to enter Nablus and bomb the barracks where we were normally quartered. We were ordered to retreat with our weapons to a rented apartment very near the camp. We were given orders not to use our weapons against the Israelis.

The four main entrances into Nablus – there are also a dozen or so smaller entrances – were reinforced with sandbags, which the mission saw when visiting these defensive installations. Explosives – 'Palestinian cocktails' – were also stored near certain entrances to seek to deny access to the Israelis. On 3 April, at around 9 p.m., 200 tanks, armoured cars and other military vehicles, supported by air cover, entered the town. Entering simultaneously at three points, from the Jerusalem road (particularly those troops from the military camp at Huwara), from the Mount Jerezem road and from the Haifa road, the armoured vehicles soon began to lay down sustained fire, dead ahead and on their flanks, hitting homes and garbage bins on their advance through the suburbs (a technique known as 'hosing down', used to protect themselves against potential booby traps). The worst destruction took place in the first few days.

The number of Tsahal troops deployed in Nablus is difficult to evaluate, probably around 1,500 at the least. A Tsahal spokesperson claimed that the Israeli troops engaged in Nablus consisted 'exclusively of uniformed soldiers, no settlers, and that, despite the high risks, Tsahal had not hesitated to bring in infantry'.

18 Reconstructed by cross-referencing interviews.

Although the Palestinian authorities had told the population to remain at home and officially 'no instruction to fight was given to the population', the three camps were encircled and were fired upon, as was the old town. The first victims date from this time.

At around 8.30 p.m. Hachim, the head of the Askar camp, received a phone call telling him that Israeli tanks were inside Nablus. At 10 p.m. the camp was plunged into darkness as the power supply was cut off. A 50-year-old man, Abdul Nabi Saleh, died of a heart attack. The water supply system and the power supply were swiftly put out of action, at least in certain neighbourhoods, as passing tanks broke pipes and snapped cables. On the first night, the power station was fired upon by tanks and aircraft. Certain armoured vehicles took up positions on higher ground in the hills for a better aim.

On 4 April, heavy-calibre weapons were used against the Balata camp. A house opposite the cemetery (Makdoushi Street, Balata), owned by one Mahmoud Titi (aged 29), came under particularly heavy fire on 4 April and was destroyed by shells from a tank stationed on the far side of the cemetery and from Apache helicopter gunships (Tsahal website on 8 May 2002). The mission noted traces of the impact of small-calibre bullets and also gaping holes in the house. Some of the shots were so powerful that they continued through the neighbouring house. Also on 4 April, unexploded ammunition began causing victims in the Balata camp. On 5 April, the Askar camp came under fire from heavy arms.

Reassured by the fact that the Israeli army had not entered the camp, refugees began emerging from their homes. At no point had the Israelis announced a curfew. A civilian by the name of Mohamad Gandour (aged 22) was hit by a bullet and died at 1 p.m. Late in the afternoon, a further bombardment hit the centre of the camp, killing four refugees: Kamal Mellaha (35, a shopkeeper), Youssef Abuzed (38, a taxi driver), Yasser Chawiz (24, unemployed) and Hani Chalabi (40, a tiler). None of the bodies was recovered in one piece. Seven people were wounded: Shahaban Gheth (29), Louai Madani (23), Mahmoud Madani (26), Ahmad Nassala (20), Muhamad Yaish (15), Emran al-Kirm (21) and Muhamad Jurf (20).

The Red Crescent was notified but was unable to send in emergency assistance until the afternoon of the following day, 6 April. Tanks positioned at one of the entrances to the camp denied all access. At around 6 p.m., using another access route, the emergency services were able to reach the seven wounded and remove them. On the way, they collected an eighth wounded person. Once out of the camp, the ambulances were intercepted outside a furniture factory known as 'Dajhani'. Soldiers checked identities and directed the wounded to the military camp at Huwara. Four of the eight wounded left the camp around 11 p.m. and were taken to the Itirad hospital in Nablus. Three were questioned by the mission while still at the Itirad hospital. They confirmed the account of events given above. The members of the mission also met the eighth victim evacuated by the ambulances.

On 6 April, troops took over the telecommunications commercial and technical centre opposite Nablus town hall. The town's communications with the outside world were cut off, as were internal communications in certain neighbourhoods, while Internet access and the Palestinian mobile telephone network Jawal were both paralysed.

On 7 April, sporadic firing continued and the Askar and Balata camps were shelled. The Israeli army was still encircling the camps.

From 8 to 10 April, there was fighting in the old town of Nablus. Pockets of resistance held out in certain blocks of housing. The International Committee of the Red Cross (ICRC) confirms the timing:

> Violent fighting broke out in the old town of Nablus on 8 April. Three ambulances were hit by bullets in the morning and two others had to return to base after warning shots were fired in their direction. Subsequently, all ambulance movements were suspended until the afternoon. Red Crescent teams then brought around 50 wounded from the old town to the hospital.
>
> (*ICRC News* 02/15)

The most violent fighting took place around El Yasmina, a crossroads of alleys protected from sniper or helicopter fire by its many arches, which offer considerable shelter.

On 9 April, a diplomat accompanying a humanitarian convoy and a group of journalists halted at the gates to the town by 'particularly aggressive soldiers and settlers' claimed to have witnessed 'constant missile fire from Apache-type helicopters' between 11 a.m. and 1 p.m.

On 10 April, Tsahal made loudspeaker appeals to the population to leave their houses in ten minutes because 'heavy bombing will follow'. The same day, the Israeli army entered the Aim

Betelma camp, supported by heavy artillery fire at 1.30 and 6 a.m. Five inhabitants of Aim Betelma were killed during the Israeli operations: Ihab Farmahi (29), Khalil Anis (26), Salam Jabour (32), all civilians having taken up arms and killed while fighting in the old town, and Amjad Catani (29, killed on 9 April as he 'was going to the well for water because there was none in the house', according to his entourage) and Mutassim Ayad, aged 15, killed outside his home. The camp head reported 13 wounded, including two who were still in hospital. These two had been wounded while fighting in the old town. Some 80 people were arrested. Sixty-five were later freed, and 15 were still in detention at the time of the mission's visit to the camp (four imprisoned in Mejido and eleven in Ofer). There was widespread destruction. Three houses were no longer habitable, 40 had been damaged, and 15 cars had been put out of action.

On 12 April came the first lifting of the curfew, between 2 p.m. and 6 p.m. (although according to other sources the curfew was first lifted only on 14 April).

On 14 April, the Israeli army entered the Askar camp under heavy artillery cover and the curfew was lifted from 2 p.m. to 6 p.m. At 8 p.m. the tanks began their incursion into the centre of the camp, supported by Apache helicopter gunships. According to the report of the camp head:

> There were tanks and helicopters everywhere. The power supply, restored on 12 April, was cut again. There were four wounded and an enormous amount of damage, in particular a lot of cars were destroyed (18 cars crushed or burned, nine houses destroyed, six houses rendered uninhabitable and 45 damaged.

Between 15 and 18 April a number of searches and arrests were made, in the Askar camp in particular (400 people were arrested, and some are still being held without trial).

On 18 April, Tsahal forces left the Askar camp and the curfew was lifted for the third time. On 21 April, the Israeli army withdrew from the Askar camp. On 22 April, Israeli forces withdrew from the whole of Nablus. Operation Defensive Shield therefore lasted 19 days in Nablus. Israeli hopes of arresting large numbers for questioning were disappointed, since only 14 wanted activists were arrested and only 2,500 weapons were seized, out of a total of some 150,000 estimated to be in Palestinian possession.

Palestinian sources report 85 dead, 289 wounded, hundreds taken in for questioning, buildings and infrastructure destroyed over the period. The governor of Nablus, Mahmoud Alul, maintains that 'Sharon's goal is to destroy as much as possible, to kill as many as possible to put pressure on the Palestinian people, to break us and to create more obstacles in the path of peace.'

The spokesperson for the Israel Defence Force (IDF), Lt.-Col. Adir Haruvi, interviewed by telephone, maintained for his part that:

> The objectives pursued by Tsahal in Nablus were identical to those pursued in other Palestinian towns: to put an end to the acts of terrorism that have made so many innocent victims among Israeli civilians. Entering the towns is the only effective way to put an end to the unjustified violence to which many groups, such as Hamas, the Jihad, the Tansims, Force 17, and so on, resort. Tsahal therefore sought to destroy the arms factories and arrest the terrorists (...). The weapons used were chosen to cause the fewest possible civilian casualties (...) civilian losses in no way correspond to Tsahal policy. Civilians would not have been affected as they were if the Palestinian combatants had not fought in the town centre.

In mid-May 2002, ditches were dug around these Palestinian towns and ringed with barbed wire fences through which to 'filter' people and goods. These fences have been installed for an indefinite period. Since the FIDH-MDM mission to Nablus, the town has suffered further incursions and is under permanent military control.

Obstruction of emergency aid workers

The mission heard many accounts of the action of the emergency services being impeded during this period. Members of the mission found that ambulances had been rendered unusable through complete destruction (wreck of an ambulance seen in the old town), and at least one (a UNRWA ambulance) was put out of action as a result of a projectile lodged in its radiator.

The ICRC confirms both the attacks and the obstacles to the movement of ambulances. For 8 April, it reports 'Three ambulances were hit by bullets in the morning and two other ambulances had to return to base after warning shots were fired in their direction. Subsequently, all ambulance movements were suspended until the afternoon' (*ICRC News* 02/15). (...)

Kamel, aged 47, an ambulance driver interviewed by the members of the mission in the Red Crescent office in Nablus, gives his account:

> On 6 April, around 4 p.m., I was supposed to collect a man with wounds to his legs at the far side of the Askar camp. We'd known about him for two days. The third day, after coordinating, we were allowed to go and collect him. There was also an ICRC car with me. When we reached the road block, I got out of the ambulance and took out the stretcher. The car with the wounded man in it was waiting on the other side of the road block. The man had been brought there by his family. We went up to the road block with the stretcher. The ICRC man had an ICRC flag with him. There were two tanks about 300 metres away. They both started firing. We all fell to the floor. The ICRC man waved his flag. Soldiers came out of the tanks and encircled us. They asked us to pull up our clothes, put up our hands. The discussions lasted about 30 minutes. The soldiers were in contact with the camp at Huwara. Then they took me and another man to go into the houses around. I had to stand right in front of a soldier and knock on the doors of the houses myself and ask the people inside to let us in. We did that at three houses. We went in, and there were families inside, but mainly women, in fact. Then we all had to put our hands on our heads. It must have taken 15 minutes for each house. Then we were able to collect the wounded man. That day, there was too much firing around the hospital, so we took him to the Red Crescent. We carried on treating him. The following day, after more coordination, we were able to take him to hospital. (...)

In addition to the fact that obstacles were placed in the way of the movement of ambulances, or that such movements were purely and simply forbidden, other obstacles to medical care also arose from the fact that medical staff – doctors and nurses – were unable to reach their place of work. (...)

The chances of getting medical help have been greatly reduced by the deliberate destruction of the Nablus telephone exchange.

The use of mobile phones was quickly curbed by destroying the electrical installations in the neighbourhoods where the Jawal satellite receiver dishes are. The use by Nablus residents of mobile phones that go through the Israeli network has also been greatly limited. The network continues to function (including in the Jewish settlements around Nablus), but the phones cannot be recharged whenever the army cuts off the electricity supply. The lack of water, electricity and food also causes problems at the hospitals.

Ill-treatment of the wounded and injured

Numerous accounts tell of cruel treatment inflicted on the wounded and sick, not only arising from the obstacles placed in the way of emergency medical assistance (see above), but also as a result of other acts reported in certain accounts. (...)

Mohamad spoke of 'kicks' being inflicted on wounded persons in a military camp. He too was wounded on 5 April in the Askar camp, at around 7.40 a.m.:

> I had gone out to get cigarettes for my father. I bought the cigarettes and was on my way back home, walking along the avenue, when I found myself flying through the air and then landing on the ground. I hadn't heard anything, and at that time there was no curfew. There were other people lying on the ground. A man carried me to the camp medical centre. They dressed my injuries and put me on a drip. The drip was soon finished, and nobody replaced it. There was no electricity. I stayed there until 5 p.m. the next day. There were two of us in the ambulance, both wounded. As we were leaving the camp we were stopped by a tank. We stayed there for maybe three hours. It was cold, the soldiers had left the back doors of the ambulance open. The ambulance driver asked if he could close the doors because I was cold. The soldier refused. There was a Red Cross car with us. The soldiers took us to the Huwara military camp. There were two ambulances, surrounded by army vehicles. When we arrived in the camp, they took me out of the ambulance on the stretcher and put me in a tent by myself. I was afraid. Then they brought in another wounded man. A soldier told me he was a doctor and was going to take care of me. He gave me oxygen with a mask over my nose, put me on a

[77]

drip and asked me if I was Russian [the victim has blue eyes and light brown hair]. He spoke in Arabic. They wrote a number in Hebrew in red felt tip on my arm. Then they brought in another wounded man. I tried to look at him. A soldier kicked him. The soldier who was with me stopped me looking by asking me to look at his finger held up in the air, which meant I was looking at the roof of the tent. I asked him what they were going to do with the others. They didn't answer. I heard them taking the wounded out of the tent I was in. Later I heard cries. Then they brought in two other wounded people, and put them on drips too. When my drip was finished, the soldiers said they were going to take me to Israel to treat me. I didn't want to go. I wanted to go to Nablus. They tried to convince me, saying I would get better treatment. I asked if I went, if the others were coming too. They said I would be going on my own in a helicopter. I didn't want to go. I heard a helicopter landing. They asked me if I was afraid. Yes, I was afraid. They promised they would bring me back afterwards to the Askar camp. I ended up agreeing as long as my father came with me. They told me that wasn't possible. The soldier then wrote something on my forehead.

At 1 a.m. they put me in a small military truck with another wounded person. There were three soldiers with us. I asked where we were going but they didn't answer. One gave his weapon to the other wounded person and told him to shoot. He didn't want to. Afterwards, they asked me. I didn't want to, either. We met up with an ambulance. They put us in the ambulance and I don't remember what happened after that. I heard that four of the wounded that night never came out of the camp. (...)

Endangering life and personal safety

(...) Deliberate incidents of endangering life and personal safety

It emerges from numerous accounts recorded by the mission that members of the Israeli armed forces deliberately killed, wounded or struck certain protected persons under the terms of the Fourth Geneva Convention.

On 10 April 2002, at around 6 a.m., all men aged between 15 and 45 were ordered by loudspeaker to gather at the water point in the

Aim Betelma camp. In the Ayad house, two people were concerned: Mutassim (aged 15) and his elder brother, the father being over 45. The elder brother was not there: his father had sent him to stay with neighbours for safety. The family house lay on the edge of the camp, and the shelling was very close. A bulldozer had in fact demolished a wall just next to the house where the children had used to play. Some 15 minutes after the loudspeaker announcement, while people were out in the road on the way to the muster point, Mutassim came out of the house. This would have been at around 6.15 a.m. The neighbour living opposite called out to him and told him he was too young, he should go back inside. A burst of machine gun bullets struck the boy as he was running back towards his father inside the house. The boy died in his father's arms. The body was taken to the camp medical centre. Two bullets were shown to the members of the mission. One of them was flattened. The third remained in the boy's body.

Suna, aged 32, and her father were also victims of tank fire:

> We were in the courtyard, my father and I. We saw the tanks, which were aiming in our direction. I felt something hit me in the back and I fell to the ground. I think I must have passed out for a few minutes. My father was 4 metres from me. He had been killed by a bullet in the chest. Neighbours dragged me away to shelter me from the firing. (...)

It also appears from certain accounts that persons providing technical services and civilian protection were targeted. One Palestinian official reports:

> During the incursion, the role of the town council was to try and guarantee the emergency services (water, electricity and health care). From the fifth day onwards, the power supply repair department was able to start getting back to work to a certain extent, but despite an agreement negotiated with the DCO, the staff in charge of these repairs were subjected to abuses: they were searched, forced to undress, were struck or even fired upon, which caused the death of some members of staff. (...)

It emerges from the various accounts cited above that Israeli soldiers in many cases deliberately killed, wounded or offered violence to protected persons. There were therefore breaches of both article 31, stipulating that no physical or moral coercion may be exercised against them, and article 32 which expressly forbids:

> any measure of such a character as to cause the physical suffering or extermination of protected persons in their hands. This prohibition applies not only to murder, torture, corporal punishments, mutilation and medical or scientific experiments not necessitated by the medical treatment of a protected person, but also to any other measures of brutality whether applied by civil or military agents.

These breaches are also more specifically breaches of Common Article 3 of the four Geneva Conventions, in particular of section 1 a) which prohibits, at any time and in any place whatsoever with regard to protected persons, 'violence to life and person'. (...)

Consequences of indiscriminate and disproportionate use of force

It emerges from numerous accounts that persons were wounded by an indiscriminate and disproportionate use of force. Raeda, a young woman of 26, reports the following events:

> On the evening of 3 April, I was at home with my two aunts. I live in the old town of Nablus, in the al-Yasmeen area. We were watching the news from Qatar on the television. Ours is an old house on three floors. We were on the second floor. There was a whistling noise, and I went out on the balcony. It collapsed with all the three floors. The tanks weren't in the old town yet. I was the last one out of the wreckage. I called out so people would find me. The ambulance came quickly. There were ten of us in the house in total. One of my brothers suffered burns, another had a broken leg, another had injuries to his eyes.

Her two aunts were killed, but she had not yet been told of this. 'She was in no state to receive too much bad news all at once', the Palestinian woman psychologist treating Raeda told us. The mother of two young children, this young Palestinian studying English was one of the first civilian victims of Operation Defensive Shield. Interviewed at the Rafidia hospital, she is suffering from a multiple fracture of the seventh cervical vertebra with compression of the spinal cord, injuries which have results in quadriplegia. (...)

Humiliating and degrading treatment

Many accounts report outrages upon personal dignity, humiliating and degrading treatment inflicted upon protected persons under the Fourth Geneva Convention.

Hassan relates what happened after being arrested with eight others:

> The soldiers had their colleagues take photos of them with us. The posed with our blindfolded heads in each hand. When we got out of the military truck in the Huwara camp, it was a tragedy. We were blindfolded and there were lots of soldiers, men and women, waiting for us; they hit us, they sang, danced and applauded all around us in Hebrew. This lasted for about an hour. They insulted my religion: they took off my blindfold, they spat on the Qur'an and then threw it on the ground.

Isham, Rashid and Mohammed recounted that during the journey from Nablus to the Huwara camp. 'the Israeli soldiers took "souvenir photos", especially with Rashid who is very big and very strong.(...) When we arrived at the Huwara camp, there were settlers there, children in particular. They looked at us like we were animals in a zoo.' Other accounts report similar scenes, like the one mentioning a 'photo session'. Many witnesses were interviewed who had been verbally insulted or who had been forced to insult Palestinian officials.

The members of the mission also found that the practice of the Israeli army forcing people to undress constituted an outrage on the honour and dignity of the Palestinians. (...)

The facts recounted in these accounts constitute breaches of article 27 of the Fourth Geneva Convention which stipulates that 'protected persons' – that is, those persons who, at a given moment and in any manner whatsoever, find themselves, in case of a conflict or occupation, in the hands of a party to the conflict or occupying power of which they are not nationals:

> are entitled, in all circumstances, to respect for their persons, their honour, their family rights, their religious convictions and practices, and their manners and custom. They shall at all times be humanely treated, and shall be protected especially against all acts of violence or threats thereof and against insults and public curiosity.

These breaches result also from breaches of numerous other provisions, such as articles 16, 28, 31 and 32, for example. (...)

Use of human shields

The mission heard several accounts of the use of civilians as human shields by the Israeli army. One such account was given by Hassan: he told how Israeli soldiers, not daring to approach him, sent a Palestinian civilian to search him:

> As I was lying on the ground and holding out my identity papers, someone came up to me. It was a professor from the University of Nablus that they had arrested. He apologised and told me he was obliged to check that I was not carrying any weapons.(...) The Israeli soldiers asked my brother and me to remain standing in front of the soldiers: that was to protect them against any shooting from the house. An officer asked us if there was anyone in the house. I said there was no one left in the house. He said I was lying and that if he found someone he would kill me. He told us he was going into the house with us going first, as a shield. As we walked up to the house, every 2 metres or so the officer made us stop, rested his elbow on my shoulder and fired at the house.

This recalls the account given by Kamal the ambulance driver:

> Then they took me and another man to go into the houses around. I had to stand right in front of a soldier and knock on the doors of the houses myself and ask the people inside to let us in. We did that at three houses.

It clearly emerges from these accounts that there were breaches of article 28 which prohibits the use of protected persons under the Fourth Geneva Convention (article 4) as human shields: 'The presence of a protected person may not be used to render certain points or areas immune from military operations.'

Conditions of detention and treatment of prisoners

During their incursion into Nablus, the Israeli armed forces arrested hundreds of people, some of whom were still in detention when the members of the mission visited Nablus. Many of these arrests were made following loudspeaker announcements ordering all men of a certain age to assemble at a designated point. Such an announcement was made in the Aim Betelma camp on 10 April, but also in other parts of Nablus. According to one of the witnesses questioned:

> In several parts of the old town and in the south of Nablus, on 14 or 15 April loudspeakers ordered all men aged 14 and over to come out onto the street and gather at the Jamal Abdel Nasser school. Identity cards were checked. Three groups were formed: civilians, combatants (including those arrested in the old town after surrendering) and Palestinian police officers. All the combatants, the police officers and a number of civilians were put into trucks and taken to the Ofer military camp.

It is clear from the accounts given that the arrests carried out by the Israeli armed forces present in Nablus were arbitrary mass arrests. With a handful of exceptions, the arrests were aimed not at designated individuals but against all Palestinian men of a particular age group. (...)

Among the witnesses interviewed by the mission, there were many who had been arrested and detained. Many accounts were gathered but the two which follow are particularly enlightening: one, Hassan's account, is illustrative of poor conditions of internment and cruel treatment inflicted on internees, and the second [not included in this extract] is that of Isham, Rashid and Mohamed.

Arrested on 3 April with eight others and detained for several days, Hassan, who was the victim of many of these breaches, recounts:

> All nine of us were taken in tanks (seven in one tank and two in another) to a private building being built in the University of Nablus district, and that had been requisitioned and converted into the HQ of the Israeli army following its incursion into the town (some 30 people living in the building had been 'parked' in two apartments). All nine of us had to kneel down in the staircase, blindfolded and with our hands tied behind our backs. We stayed like that for three days (4, 5 and 6 April). We were not allowed to talk to one another and we spoke to the Israeli soldiers in English.

In response to my request, after the first day, and since it was very cold, we were supplied with blankets. We were given a little water when we asked for it. The soldiers put two biscuits in my mouth and something sweet, but I couldn't tell what it was. I was given nothing else to eat during the three days. Every four hours or so, the guard was changed. This is how I kept track of time.

There were two sorts of soldiers: some were very aggressive and violent, and systematically struck us as they passed. Some of us, like my brother, kept the marks for a certain time. We couldn't get medical certificates to prove it: after we were freed, we spent some time in a village outside Nablus and now [almost a month after the events], you can't see anything. Other soldiers were very polite and very human, and even told the others to stop hitting us. It was these soldiers I tried to speak to whenever we had to ask for something. One of these soldiers even offered to share his rations with us, but we preferred to say no because we didn't know exactly what it was. (...)

On 5 April I asked to see a doctor because my arm was hurting [an infection in the nerve dating from prior to the events, but made more painful by the wearing of handcuffs]. A doctor came to see me. He said he couldn't do anything but he asked the soldiers to handcuff my hands in front of me and not at my back: they agreed to this. In the same way, on the few occasions we asked to use the toilet (not a real toilet, but a container), they let us do so. On one trip to the toilet, my brother's handcuffs were also shifted from his back to his front. Then he had to help all the others to urinate.

After three days, on 6 April, all nine of us were taken away, handcuffed and blindfolded, in a military truck in which they had first loaded the Israeli soldiers' dustbins (the blindfolds were taken off during the trip). In the truck there were two soldiers: an Israeli (probably Special Forces) and a Druze. They struck us during the trip. Most of the blows were designed not to leave traces and not to break any limbs; even so, they left bruising and caused bleeding in some cases, including my brother. The insults were never-ending. (...) I spoke in Arabic to the Druze who was very violent at the beginning. His behaviour changed over the course of the trip, which lasted over two hours (via the settlements). When we arrived in the Huwara camp at around 1 a.m. on, 7 April, he was completely different.

When we got out of the military truck in the Huwara camp, it was a tragedy. We were blindfolded and there were lots of soldiers, men and women, waiting for us; they hit us, they sang, danced and applauded all around us in Hebrew. This lasted for about an hour.(…) Then they searched us and took all our personal belongings (watches and so on), except for our clothes. Some of our things were returned to us when we were freed, but not others.

After we had been searched, around 2 a.m., they took us into a tent with about 150 people in it. In the tent, Israeli soldiers took advantage of the fact that I was blindfolded and handcuffed to push me from one side to another to make me lose my balance. I had to lie on the floor, on my back. Soldiers, men and women, came to 'play' with us: some of them made us open our mouths, and they spat into them and put earth in them. I was lying next to someone else. I asked him who he was in Arabic but an Israeli soldier intervened. He hit me in the forehead with his rifle butt to shut me up and struck the other person with his boots. I asked to be allowed to go to the toilet. A soldier took me out of the tent (it was raining), hit me and took me back into the tent without my being able to go to the toilet. Then the soldiers left. I managed to sleep for two or three hours, then I was woken up by being kicked. The soldiers threw us food and cheese. Since I didn't feel I should be treated like a dog, I refused to eat. We had to march on the spot for an hour, an hour and a half, then we went somewhere else in the open air.

Three hours later, that would be on 7 April at around 11 a.m., when up till then no one had asked us any questions, they started questioning us individually. To transfer us from one place to another, we had to hold onto the clothes of the man in front, rest our head on his back and move along like that. During the interrogation, they took off our handcuffs and blindfolds. Someone introduced himself to me as the officer in charge of the intelligence services (Shin Beth) for the north of the West Bank. He spoke Arabic. The interrogation lasted 20 or 30 minutes. The questions started off very general, then became personal. The officer knew everything about me, he wasn't looking for anything special, he didn't take any notes except for the telephone numbers for the house and for the mobile phones. He obviously knew the numbers and he even said, 'You haven't given me all the numbers, there's one missing.' And there was one missing. At no time did they inform me why I had been arrested. (...)

Once this first interrogation was over, I was taken into another room and questioned again by a soldier. After the two interrogations, the Israeli soldiers took a lunch break. I again had to march on the spot, then around 6 p.m. I was freed along with my brother and a third person. This person left, but my brother and I refused to leave the camp without a letter from the authorities stating that we had been freed. We kept on insisting. Finally they took a photo and wrote on it 'freed from Huwara camp'. We walked 300 or 400 metres to the village of Kufr Kalil, where we found the third person freed with us, and we stayed with friends for a week. The curfew was permanent and we were afraid of coming under fire from snipers. (...)

Destruction of property and housing

Members of the mission found evidence in the town of Nablus and in the three refugee camps (Askar, Balata and Aim Betelma) of numerous cases of destruction of real and personal property, both private and public, and in particular of infrastructure. Clearly visible were substantial damage to roadways, the systematic destruction of power and communications networks, destruction of residential buildings (including a several-storey building at the entrance to Nablus, reduced to rubble), official buildings (such as the governor's offices, or the prison), walls riddled with bullet holes in certain districts (particularly the main street in Askar), vehicles, including private cars, destroyed and so on. The mission visited the telephone exchange and found evidence of considerable destruction and damage: doors blown open with explosives, cables picked out and severed. According to the Palestinian technicians, 'the lines to Jenin, Qalqiliya and Tulkarem in particular were cut, while the Israeli mobile network serving the settlements continued to function'.

It was the old town that suffered the most damage. One resident told us of his visit to the old town when the curfew was first lifted:

I came out, and it looked like there had been an earthquake: the old town was in ruins. The Protestant church (west wall), the Orthodox church, the soap factories, many houses, the pavements, the shops, the electricity pylons, etc., all were destroyed.

On its visit to the Casbah, the mission noted the destruction of certain buildings (such as the soap factories, many shops and a number of houses), as well as considerable damage to shops (windows shattered, blinds smashed in or riddled with bullets) and to dwellings.

Assessments of the destruction have been made, in particular by the municipality of Nablus. In its communiqué no. 2 of 20 April 2002, the municipality listed the material damage caused to the Casbah, a centre of interest to UNESCO which has been concerned for several years to safeguard certain buildings such as the Khan al-Walat caravanserai. (...)

'Grave breaches' of international humanitarian law as defined by article 147

The MDM-FIDH mission found that the acts reported above and carried out by Israeli soldiers in the course of their incursion into Nablus correspond to the definition of grave breaches given in article 147 of the Fourth Geneva Convention:

> Grave breaches shall be those involving any of the following acts, if committed against persons or property protected by the present Convention: wilful killing, torture or inhuman treatment, including biological experiments, wilfully causing great suffering or serious injury to body or health, unlawful deportation or transfer or unlawful confinement of a protected person, compelling a protected person to serve in the forces of a hostile Power, or wilfully depriving a protected person of the rights of fair and regular trial prescribed in the present Convention, taking of hostages and extensive destruction and appropriation of property, not justified by military necessity and carried out unlawfully and wantonly.

Persons protected under the Convention, as defined by articles 4 and 5 of the Convention, were victims of acts constituting wilful killing, inhuman treatment, great suffering wilfully caused, or serious injury to body or health, unlawful confinement, deprivation of

the rights of fair and regular trial in accordance with the Convention, extensive destruction not justified by military necessity and
carried out unlawfully and wantonly.

In the light of the Rome Statute of the International Criminal
Court, FIDH and MDM consider that certain acts recorded by the
mission may be qualified as war crimes. Article 8 of the Rome
Statute states:

> For the purposes of this Statute, 'war crimes' means:
> a) grave breaches of the Geneva Conventions of 12 August
> 1949, namely, any of the following acts against persons or
> property protected under the provisions of the relevant
> Geneva Convention: wilful killing; (...) wilfully causing
> great suffering, or serious injury to body or health; (...)
> unlawful deportation or transfer or unlawful confinement.
> (b) other serious breaches of the laws and customs applica-
> ble in international armed conflict (...) intentionally direct-
> ing attacks against the civilian population as such (...);
> intentionally directing attacks against civilian objects, that
> is, objects which are not military objectives (...); etc.

Other breaches of international law

The law of armed conflicts is a specific body of law but does not
exclude other rules: it does not exclude the continuing validity of
the general rules of international law applicable in normal circumstances, such as the individual rights of the person.

The argument that these rights, in particular those enshrined in
the International Covenant on Civil and Political Rights (ICCPR),
do not apply in the West Bank and Gaza because these zones are
not subject to Israel's national sovereignty and jurisdiction is inadmissible, and has indeed been rejected by the relevant bodies of
the United Nations, which upheld the application of these obligations to all territories over which Israel exercises de facto control.
This position is all the more justified in that Israel considers that
the Israeli settlers established in the Occupied Territories enjoy the
rights enshrined in international agreements, and is willing to
answer for the application of these agreements in the settlements,
which are located in the very same areas of jurisdiction. Certainly,
fundamental laws may be suspended or derogations from them
may be made, but only within the strict limits laid down by the
instruments in which they are provided for. Furthermore, the

possibilities for suspension and derogation must be interpreted restrictively, and certain rights are so fundamental that no derogation may be made in their respect.

Many facts recounted in the accounts gathered by the mission and set forth above constitute simultaneous breaches of instruments governing the law on international armed conflicts and such fundamental instruments governing human rights as the Universal Declaration of Human Rights (UDHR) and the ICCPR. (...) Among the provisions breached is the right to life (articles 3 of the UDHR and 6 of the ICCPR). Breaches of the right to life are constituted by intentional attacks on civilians, indiscriminate and disproportionate attacks, and the obstacles placed by Tsahal in the way of the emergency medical services.

Other breaches of the right to life were constituted by the illegal execution of Palestinians suspected of collaboration with the Israeli authorities. The members of the mission would like to stress the issue of collaboration and the illegal executions of Palestinian civilians believed, rightly or wrongly, to be 'collaborators'. The highly sensitive information acquired by the mission on this subject is extremely limited. 'Four Palestinians accused of being collaborators were executed. Some were caught trying to dismantle explosives placed by the Palestinian resistance at the entrances to the old town', one Palestinian official admitted. Collaboration by Palestinians with Israel is 'the outcome of a long occupation and control exercised by the Israelis over the everyday life of the Palestinians', was the brief comment of the Governor of Nablus when interviewed by the mission. (...)

Under the terms of the ICCPR, there can be no derogation from the right to life or the prohibition on cruel and inhuman or degrading punishment or treatment. The State of Israel cannot therefore claim 'a public emergency which threatens the life of the nation' as a justification for any legal derogation.

Other fundamental rights were also violated, such as the right to liberty and safety, and the prohibition on arbitrary arrest and detention (articles 3 and 9 of the UDHR and 9 of the ICCPR). It emerged from many accounts submitted to the mission that hundreds of people from the town of Nablus were arbitrarily arrested. Contrary to the express provisions of article 9, section 2 of the ICCPR, the persons interviewed were not informed, at the time of their arrest, of the reasons for that arrest, and were not informed of the charges laid against them. In addition to being deprived of their liberty, these persons

[89]

were not able to petition a court to pronounce immediately on the legality of their detention, as provided for by article 9, section 4 of the ICCPR. Nor can the State of Israel take refuge behind an assertion of 'a public emergency which threatens the life of the nation' to claim any derogation from those rights. While it is true that these rights are not mentioned expressly as rights not subject to derogation in article 4, section 2 of the ICCRP, there can be no derogation from the right to liberty and to safety, and the prohibition on arbitrary arrest and detention, in view of their nature as imperative standards of international law. The same is true of article 10 of the ICCPR which provides that 'all persons deprived of their liberty shall be treated with humanity and with respect for the inherent dignity of the human person'.

The accounts gathered by the mission and reported above also showed 'manifest breaches of the Convention of 10 December 1984 against torture and other cruel, inhuman or degrading punishment or treatment' (article 16). Certain of the facts reported constitute inhuman or degrading punishment or treatment. Most obvious among them are the many days of curfew, the many obstacles to free movement placed in the way of the inhabitants of Nablus,[19] the many insults and humiliations to which they were subjected, the detentions which followed the arrests made by the Israeli forces during their 'incursion' into Nablus,[20] the conditions of detention to which the persons arrested were subjected, the demolition and destruction of dwellings, and so on. In its recommendations to the State of Israel, the United Nations Committee against Torture considered that the Israeli policy of house demolitions could, in certain circumstances, constitute cruel, inhuman or degrading punishment or treatment.

Under the terms of the ICCPR, there can be no derogation from the right to life or the prohibition on cruel and inhuman or degrading punishment or treatment. The State of Israel cannot therefore claim 'a public emergency which threatens the life of the nation' as a justification for any legal derogation. (...)

---

19 *Conclusions and recommendations to Israel by the Committee against Torture at its 495th and 498th meetings on 20 and 21 November 2001*, T/C/SR. 495 and 498,section 6, i).

20 On the issue that administrative detention constitutes treatment contrary to article 16 of the Convention, see among others the *Conclusions and Recommendations to Israel by the Committee against Torture at its 495th and 498th Meetings on 20 and 21 November 2001*, T/C/SR. 495 and 498, section 6, e).

Conclusions[21]

Invocation of the international responsibility of the State of Israel and obligation to make reparation

The State of Israel may be held internationally responsible as a result of the breaches of the law of armed conflicts committed by members of its armed forces. Such breaches of the law of armed conflicts may be imputed to the belligerent state when they originate with one of its agencies and the position of the agency 'responsible' in the military hierarchy is immaterial as regards the state's accountability for the action.

Under the terms of international law, the State of Israel is required to make reparations for the consequences of its actions. Israel could not hide behind breaches of international law committed by the Palestinians as a means of release from its international responsibility on the grounds of a material breach of a treaty as grounds for terminating or suspending the treaty – the *exceptio non adimpleti contractus* – as set out in article 60 of the Vienna Convention on the Law of Treaties. Section 5 of the same article expressly states that exception does not apply to 'provisions relating to the protection of the human person contained in treaties of a humanitarian character'. The argument advanced by Lt.-Col. Adir Haruvi, that 'all this would not have happened if there had been no terrorist attacks on Israeli citizens', is therefore inadmissible. The law of armed conflicts is also closely related to imperative standards of international law, from which no derogations are permitted. This also explains the fact that, apart from the provisions of the law of armed conflicts which themselves refer – explicitly or implicitly – to a state of necessity to justify the non-application or limited application of certain rules, the state of necessity can never constitute a circumstance negating the illegal nature of a breach of the law of armed conflicts.

Other aspects of the responsibility of the State of Israel: obligation to prevent and punish breaches

The obligation to 'respect and ensure respect for' the relevant texts, as is required particularly under Common Article 1 of the

---

21 Among the conclusions of the original report, are two parts, 'State responsibility' and 'The international responsibility of the State of Israel', that have not been reproduced here.

four Geneva Conventions, implies an obligation to prevent breaches of international humanitarian law. In this respect, the importance of Israel's duty to disseminate the provisions of that law – among the members of its armed forces but also, by extension, among its civilian population – cannot be underestimated. Armed conflict is a context which, per se, favours the loss of all references as regards the limits of what is permitted and what is forbidden. Minimum training in the laws of war is therefore indispensable. Other elements of a policy of effective prevention of breaches of the law of armed conflicts are also essential, such as psychological training to put young soldiers on their guard against their own reactions and impulses, or such as the fight against the cult of obedience or the culture of contempt for others.

It should be noted that the State of Israel may be held internationally responsible if it is proven that breaches were committed by Israeli civilian settlers. The Israeli state should in any event take the necessary measures to ensure that such persons are prevented from committing atrocities, which in particular implies disarming them, as the General Assembly has demanded on numerous occasions. According to Lt.-Col. Adir Haruvi, spokesperson for the IDF, 'only uniformed soldiers took part in the military operations, and no settlers'. It nonetheless emerges from several accounts recorded on the spot by the members of the MDM-FIDH mission that settlers were, in any event, present within the Huwara military camp. Members of the mission were also able to see for themselves that armed settlers were present at checkpoints. It was confirmed to members of the mission, by certain foreign diplomats among others, that armed settlers were sometimes carrying out inspections themselves at checkpoints – in particular the Huwara checkpoint at the entrance to Nablus – and showed themselves to be particularly aggressive.

'Respecting and ensuring respect for' the relevant texts also supposes repressing breaches thereof. If the breaches concerned are grave breaches, the State of Israel is required by international law to take criminal proceedings against the perpetrators, in accordance with the special requirement to repress grave breaches of the law of armed conflicts, an obligation incumbent on each Contracting Party. Other breaches of the law of armed conflicts, which do not constitute grave breaches, should also be subject to legal proceedings, at least in so far as they are rendered criminal by internal Israeli law or when they are likely to constitute other breaches of this law. As regards repression, the members of the mission noted the assertion of the spokesperson for the IDF, Lt.-Col. Adir Haruvi, that 'if members of Tsahal acted incorrectly and committed breaches of international law, they will be severely punished. Such behaviour is totally contrary to Israeli army policy. Over 100 cases are currently under examination.'

It is also necessary to allow the victims of breaches to obtain fair and adequate reparation. The State of Israel is also required to ensure the prevention and repression of breaches of fundamental rights, in particular cruel, inhuman or degrading punishment or treatment, and to enable the victims to obtain reparation.

Responsibility of third-party states

The fulfilment of our prescribed international obligations in accordance with the principle *pacta sunt servanda* as enshrined in article 26 of the Vienna Convention on the Law of Treaties implies two distinct obligations: respecting the relevant texts, and ensuring the respect of those texts. This supposes not only that states party to the treaties will ensure that their armed forces respect the law of armed conflicts, but also that the armed forces of their counterparts will also respect them. Thus, as in the cases covered in this report, when a third-party state to an armed conflict or its representatives find evidence of breaches of the law of armed conflicts, that state is obliged not only morally but also legally to respond, particularly by addressing claims to the state responsible. The performance of this 'obligation of response' to which states are bound should also take other forms. In this respect, it is important to underline the importance of implementing conditional clauses based on respect for human rights which figure in certain agreements with the State of Israel, in particular the association agreement between the European Union and Israel (article 2), which the European Parliament has recommended should be suspended (resolution of the European Parliament of 10/04/2002, P5 TAPROV (2002) 0173).

Individual criminal liability

The rules of international criminal law have established certain actions as international criminal offences for which their perpetrators, co-perpetrators and accomplices must answer individually. Among such offences are included war crimes, that is, certain grave breaches of the law of armed conflicts which states have decided to prosecute at international level, along with torture and cruel, inhuman or degrading punishment or treatment.

Any individual who has committed a war crime must be prosecuted and sentenced irrespective of his or her quality – either as a member of the Israeli armed forces and hence of an Israeli State agency or as a private individual, such as a settler, for example. The accounts heard by the MDM-FIDH mission did not make it possible to identify the individuals guilty of such breaches, among other reasons because 'in the old town, for example, there were no soldiers on foot in the streets. They all stayed in the tanks in order not to expose themselves'. (…) Lt.-Col. Adir Haruvi, spokesperson of the IDF, gave no answer as regards which Israeli troops were involved in the military operations in Nablus. Certain witnesses spoke of the presence of the Golani division. The cooperation of the Israeli authorities is necessary in order to identify and seek out those directly responsible for breaches. In so doing, the Israeli authorities would be complying with the international obligation incumbent on the State of Israel to repress breaches of the law on armed conflicts.

Difficulties in identifying the direct authors of breaches do not prevent the Israeli superior officers concerned, who are more easily identifiable, from being held individually responsible. Superior officers may be held responsible as indirect authors of breaches committed not only when they gave the order to commit certain war crimes, but also when they failed to take the measures necessary to prevent or repress such crimes.[22] While it is not possible to conclude from the findings of the mission to the West Bank carried out by MDM and the FIDH that orders were actually given to commits acts constituting war crimes, it is nevertheless important to stress the general nature of certain methods used by Tsahal and which constitute such acts. One such, among others, is the practice of using civilians to a certain extent as human shields. These practices were mentioned in a number of accounts gathered by the mission in Nablus, but also in many other accounts gathered elsewhere in the West Bank by other associations, in particular in Jenin by Human Rights Watch, to the extent that one can only wonder how far these may constitute 'recommended

---

22 See also articles 6 and 5 of the Statutes of the Nuremberg and Tokyo Military Tribunals, and also the Yamashita affairs, US Military Commission, 7 December 1945, LRWTC, 4, pp. 1 and following cited in David, E., no. 4.54, p. 559; List (Hostages Trial) Nuremberg American Military Tribunal, 19 February 1948, A.D. 1948, p. 652 and others.

methods' or methods taught to young Israeli soldiers. However it may be, the passivity of superior officers in the face of actions of which, in the circumstances, they could not reasonably claim to be unaware, is sufficient to make them criminally liable.

The authors of this report would like to point out that there is no statute of limitations on war crimes, nor is any amnesty possible.[23] Individuals prosecuted for war crimes should no longer be able to invoke the two classic cases of defence, which are, on the one hand, force of law or of duly constituted authority, and on the other, the state of necessity.

The actions reported in the witness accounts gathered and presented in this report are those of certain Israeli soldiers. The members of the MDM-FIDH mission would wish to stress that certain witnesses insisted on the fact that Israeli soldiers behaved very correctly towards them. (...)

---

23 The fact that there can be no amnesty for war crimes derives from the fact that there is no statute of limitations on such crimes — if it is accepted that there can be no such statute of limitations, then there can be no amnesty, since the consequences of an amnesty are wider-ranging than those of a statute of limitations (on this issue, see David, E., no. 4.212, p. 655), and from the need to combat impunity.

7 Operation Defensive Shield, Jenin[24]

Human Rights Watch

Israeli authorities have repeatedly stressed the military significance of the Israeli Defence Force (IDF) operation inside Jenin
refugee camp, stating that it was imperative to stop attacks against
Israeli civilians, both by halting the individuals involved and by
destroying the infrastructure they used. Israeli officials claim that
many of the suicide bombers who carried out attacks against
Israeli civilians came from the camp. A number of ranking Palestinian militants from the Islamic Jihad, Hamas, and al-Aqsa
Martyrs Brigade groups also lived in the refugee camp.

The battle inside Jenin refugee camp

Armed Palestinians had prepared for the attack by setting up
positions at the perimeter of and within the camp, and by laying
booby traps in many areas. Located on hills southwest of Jenin's
city centre, the camp's dense housing and narrow, twisting alleys
made for a very difficult environment in which to conduct close-
range urban combat. When Human Rights Watch investigators
visited the camp, residents spoke openly about the preparations
made by the militants, who have been estimated in media reports
as having numbered between 80 and 100. Children could be seen
walking around with unexploded Palestinian pipe bombs they
had dug out of the rubble. A de-mining worker told Human
Rights Watch that he had defused 40 Palestinian-made bombs in
a single day.

But the presence of armed Palestinian militants inside the camp,
and the preparations made by those armed Palestinian militants in
anticipation of the IDF incursion, do not detract from an essential

24 Excerpt from Human Rights Watch, *Jenin: IDF Military Operations*, May 2002.

fact: Jenin refugee camp was also home to more than 14,000 Palestinian civilians. The IDF had an obligation under international humanitarian law to take all feasible precautions to prevent a disproportionate impact of its military incursion on those civilians.

Most witnesses interviewed by Human Rights Watch described the first two days of the incursion as consisting of tank, helicopter and gunfire. IDF tanks and troops took up positions around the camp's perimeter during the night of 2 to 3 April. While accounts differ according to location, witnesses in the area of the camp immediately above the hospital reported seeing small numbers of IDF soldiers enter the camp on the morning and late afternoon of 3 April. Armed Palestinians took up positions at the camp entrance, and also reportedly at other edges of the camp. As the days passed, the armed Palestinians were increasingly forced back into the camp centre, fighting in small groups that became increasingly isolated.

To enable tanks and heavy armour to penetrate to the camp, the IDF sent in armoured bulldozers to widen the narrow alleys by shearing off the fronts of buildings, in places several metres deep. In the initial days, Palestinian fighters held off the IDF to the west of the camp, while to the east bulldozers penetrated the hilltop district of al-Damaj, overlooking the centre of the camp. The IDF infantry managed to enter the northern entrance to the camp, throwing smoke grenades to provide cover as they went from house to house. Although helicopters were present, at that stage they primarily provided air-to-ground support. IDF soldiers 'mouse-holed' from house to house, knocking large holes in the walls between houses to provide routes of safe passage from to the outer perimeters of the camp to the centre. In numerous cases, they used Palestinian civilians and detainees as human shields as they moved from house to house, and as Human Rights Watch has documented in previous incursions elsewhere in the West Bank and Gaza Strip, forced civilians to perform the most dangerous tasks of entering and checking buildings during house-to-house searches.

The third day of the incursion, in the early morning hours of 6 April, US-supplied helicopters started firing missiles into the camp, often striking civilian homes where no Palestinian fighters were present. The missile fire, which began in the early morning hours, caught many sleeping civilians by surprise. The chaos and destruction caused by the bombardment allowed the IDF to move closer to the centre of the camp. On 9 April, 13 Israeli soldiers died in a major ambush in the Hawashin district.

[97]

After the 9 April ambush, the IDF relied heavily on missile strikes from helicopters. It also extensively used armoured bulldozers, which allowed the IDF to penetrate districts where previously it had not been able to consolidate control. The change in military strategy arguably helped to defeat the armed Palestinians in the camp, but as described below, the new tactics had an unacceptable impact on the civilian population and infrastructure of the camp.

The IDF continued to use armoured bulldozers throughout the operation. On 10 April, armoured bulldozers were sent to widen an alley in Abu Nasr district, to the west of Hawashin. At this time, the bulldozers were still primarily being used to widen streets. On 12 April, civilians in the Matahin area of the camp, located above the main UN Relief and Works Agency (UNRWA) school, were likewise warned to leave their homes in advance of their being destroyed by bulldozers. Many heeded the call. Armoured bulldozers soon arrived to clear a broad path for the IDF's armoured vehicles, levelling many of the homes in their path.

Towards the end of the IDF operation, the fighting and destruction was mostly focused on the central Hawashin district of the camp. The majority of the fighting appears to have subsided by 10 April, but isolated pockets of Palestinian militants continued to hold out for some days. The bulldozers appear to have continued razing homes even after most of the fighting had ended. At the end, the bulldozers had done much more than creating paths for the IDF tanks and armoured cars in Hawashin district: the entire area, down to the last house, had been levelled.

Civilian deaths and illegal executions

During its investigation, Human Rights Watch found serious violations of international humanitarian law. The organisation documented 52 Palestinian deaths in the camp and its environs caused by the fighting. At least 22 of those confirmed dead were civilians, including children, the physically disabled, and elderly people. At least 27 of those confirmed dead were suspected to have been armed Palestinians belonging to movements such as Islamic Jihad, Hamas, and the al-Aqsa Martyrs Brigade. Some were members of the Palestinian Authority's (PA) National Security Force or other branches of the PA police and security forces. Human Rights Watch was unable to determine conclusively the status of the remaining three killed, among the cases documented.

Because of the large number of homes in the refugee camp that were demolished by the IDF, it is possible that the total number of casualties will climb somewhat, though not dramatically, as recovery efforts proceed. Corpses continued to be recovered on a daily basis in the camp as Human Rights Watch was carrying out its research in the camp, but residents in the camp had already identified those persons as killed before their bodies were recovered. Because the IDF has not made available the full list of names of those arrested during the operation, some families are unsure whether relatives have been arrested by the IDF or have been killed in the camp.

It does not appear that there are larger numbers of 'missing' persons from the camp. The residents of the camp gave consistent lists of the known or suspected dead in the camp, and those lists did not grow significantly while Human Rights Watch conducted research in the camp.

Some of the cases documented by Human Rights Watch amount to unlawful and deliberate killings. However, the organisation did not find evidence of systematic summary executions.

During its investigation, however, Human Rights Watch documented unlawful and deliberate killings, and the killing or wounding of protected individuals as a result of excessive or disproportionate use of force. Such cases are in violation of the international humanitarian law prohibitions against 'wilful killing' of non-combatants. The organisation also found instances of IDF soldiers deliberately impeding the work of medical personnel and preventing medical assistance to the wounded, with no apparent or obvious justification of military necessity. Such cases appear to be in violation of the prohibition against 'wilfully causing great suffering or serious injury to body or health'.

At least four persons were killed by the IDF because they were outside during curfews or walked in areas declared 'closed' by the Israeli army. Such use of lethal force to enforce curfews or 'closed' areas is a widespread practice by the IDF. The use of lethal force against civilians who do not abide by curfews or are found in 'closed' areas is unjustified, and a violation of the international humanitarian law provisions prohibiting the targeting of civilians. International humanitarian law requires that the IDF use less lethal means to enforce its curfews and 'closed' areas.

In addition, the dimensions of the destruction and the temporal sequence of the demolition of homes and property found by Human Rights Watch researchers suggest that these were carried out unlawfully and wantonly, and did not meet the strict requirements of military necessity and proportionality.

There is strong prima facie evidence that in some of the cases documented grave breaches of the Geneva Conventions, or war crimes, were committed. Such cases warrant specific criminal justice investigations with a view to identifying and prosecuting those responsible. (...)

Shooting of Hani Abu Rumaila, 3 April

Hani Abu Rumaila, aged 19, spent the night of 2 April at the house of his grandmother. When the IDF first reached the Jenin camp and gun battles erupted at about 4.00 a.m. on 3 April, he ran home to his parents' house and informed his father that tanks had arrived at the outskirts of the camp. Then he decided to return to the gate of the house and watch what the IDF soldiers were doing. His stepmother, Hala' Abu Rumaila, explained how Hani was killed at about 5.30 that morning:

> The Israelis had just arrived and Hani wanted to open the main gate to the house. He wanted to see what was going on outside. Then, [as he opened the gate], they [IDF] shot him in the leg. He started screaming. When he tried to stand up and run back home, they shot him in the abdomen and chest.

A nurse living nearby tried to come to Hani's rescue when she heard the screaming, but was herself killed by the IDF soldiers (see below). The family then called an ambulance, which removed Hani's body to the hospital. Because of the intense fighting, Hani's family could not make their way to the hospital for funeral arrangements, and Hani was buried in a temporary communal grave at the back of the hospital. Hani was unarmed at the time of the killing, and was not a member of any Palestinian militant group, according to his family. Normally when a Palestinian militant is killed, family take some pride in the fact that the dead relative was in an armed group opposing the occupation, and make no effort to deny the militant history of the deceased.

The Abu Rumaila family showed Human Rights Watch the nearby home that had been occupied by IDF soldiers during the Jenin offensive and from which they believed IDF soldiers had fired on Hani Abu Rumaila. That home is located about 100 metres down the street from the Abu Rumaila home, diagonally across the street, and had a clear line of sight to the gate of the Abu Rumaila home where Hani was shot. (...)

Shooting of Ahmad Hamduni, 3 April

Eighty-five-year-old Ahmad Hamduni was left virtually alone at his home when the fighting broke out in Jenin refugee camp, because his family had moved to an area south of Jenin two days before. When the fighting reached his area around 3.00 p.m. on 3 April, he moved to the home of another elderly neighbour, 72-year-old Raja Tawafshi. The two elderly men first had some 25 relatives staying with them, but at about 5.00 p.m. those relatives left the house, leaving the two elderly men alone.

After the men finished their evening prayers, Israeli soldiers suddenly attacked the home. Raja Tawafshi recalled how his neighbour was killed by the soldiers soon after they entered:

> After I had finished praying, they [the soldiers] shot one door of my gate off and it flew into the room. I stood up and they shot at me. I raised my hands. They shot a sound bomb [concussion grenade] inside and the soldiers came inside with their guns. I stood up with my hands up, and [Ahmad Hamduni] was behind me.
>
> Because he is an old man, [Ahmad Hamduni] hunches over. The soldiers were worried [about the hunch in his back] and shot him immediately. I told them, he is an old man, and I tried to touch him. Then the soldiers told me to go out of the room.

The soldiers proceeded to search the entire three-story home, pushing Tawafshi in front of them at gunpoint: 'The soldier put the gun to my back and they searched the house, pushing me in front of them.' While the soldiers were inspecting the top story with Tawafshi, an IDF missile hit the floor, narrowly missing the group. The soldiers then returned downstairs, placed Tawafshi's hands in plastic cuffs, and tied him to a chair next to the body of his neighbour, which they had covered with a carpet. Tawafshi explained how he was kept in the chair all night:

> They tied my hands and feet and put me in the seat. They tied me to the seat with plastic tape, wrapping it around my

chest and legs. They brought a blanket and put it over me. I was thirsty and asked for some water in Hebrew. They said no. Later, I needed to go to the toilet. They asked me to shut up. I was suffering, but nobody helped me. I was in the chair from 7.00 p.m. until 5.00 a.m. Then they came, cut me loose and took the blanket.

The soldiers then took Tawafshi out of the home at gunpoint and demanded that he check the homes of four neighbours before they finally allowed him to go home. (See below for a further discussion of the coerced use of civilians during the Jenin operation.) (...)

Bombing death of 'Afaf Disuqi, 5 April

At about 3.15 p.m. on Friday, 5 April, Israeli soldiers ordered Asmahan Abu Murad, aged 24, to come with them to knock on the home of the neighbouring Disuqi family. As she came outside, she saw a group of Israeli soldiers, including one who was holding a bomb with a lit fuse which he was attaching to the Disuqi home: 'I went outside and saw one soldier with a bomb; the string was already lit. They told me, "Quickly, put your fingers in your ears." All of the soldiers went away from the bomb, then one soldier threw the bomb and the others started shooting at the door.'

Aisha Disuqi, the 37-year-old sister of 52-year-old 'Afaf Disuqi, explained how the latter went to the door to check on the smoke and to open it for the soldiers, and was killed in the explosion that followed:

> We were inside in a room and saw some smoke. The soldiers were asking us to open the door. My sister 'Afaf went to the door to open it, and while she was opening it, the bomb exploded. When the bomb exploded, we were all screaming, calling for an ambulance. The soldiers were laughing. We saw the right side of her face was destroyed, and the left side of her shoulder and arm was also wounded. She was killed that first moment.

Asmahan Abu Murad, who was outside with the soldiers in front of the door, corroborated in a separate interview with Human Rights Watch that the soldiers were laughing after the killing of 'Afaf Disuqi: 'After the explosion, I heard her sisters scream for an ambulance. The soldiers were laughing. Then they told me to go back inside.' After the explosion, the soldiers did not enter the Disuqi home. They told Asmahan Abu Murad that she could go home, and the soldiers then left the scene. During the time of the incident, there was no active combat or firing in the neighbourhood. The remorseless murder of 'Afaf Disuqi, an unarmed civilian, constitutes a war crime.

'Afaf Disuqi's family took her body inside the home, and repeatedly tried to get an ambulance: 'We had a mobile but could only receive incoming calls. Every time someone called, we asked for an ambulance, but it was prohibited [for the ambulances to move].' The body remained at the home from Friday until the next Thursday, when the family was able to move the body to the hospital. (...)

The bulldozing death of Jamal Fayid, 6 April

Jamal Fayid, aged 37, lived with 17 other family members in the Jurrat al-Dahab area of the camp, next to the Hawashin district. Fayid, disabled from birth, could not speak, eat or move without assistance. For the first two days the family sheltered themselves from the fighting in a small room beside the kitchen. Other relatives had joined them there for safety.

Shooting around the house and from IDF helicopters intensified on the afternoon of the second day, 4 April. On 5 April, the house was hit by a missile and the second and third floors began to burn. Fayid's family tried to run onto the street from the main door, but were forced back when Faziya Muhammad, an elderly aunt, was shot in the shoulder just before she reached the door. They broke a side window and climbed out, but were unable to lift Fayid through the window. They ran down the stairs shouting at the soldiers to hold their fire. The family then ran towards an IDF position in a house diagonally opposite. An IDF medic briefly treated Muhammad's injury, and the family eventually made their way to Fayid's uncle's house a short distance away.

Early the next day, 6 April, Fayid's mother and sister returned home to check Fayid's well-being. He was unharmed. Fayid's sister told how she and her mother ran to IDF soldiers in the street to ask permission to retrieve him:

> We tried to beg the soldiers that there was a paralysed man in there. We even showed them his identity card. The ones on the street told us to go away. So we ran to [soldiers in] a

neighboring house and said the same. We begged and begged. So eventually they let five women into the house and try to carry him out.

Fayid's mother, aunt, sister, and two neighbours entered the house. Shortly afterwards they heard the sound of a bulldozer approaching:

> It came and began to destroy the house. We could hear people on the street shouting, 'Stop! There are women inside the house! Stop!' The soldiers even knew we were in there because they had said we could go into the house and get Jamal out.

Despite the shouting, the bulldozer continued. The women ran out as the house swayed and crumbled around them, crushing the paralysed Fayid in the rubble. The soldier in the bulldozer cursed at them, calling them bitches. The women ran into another house for safety. The IDF medic who had helped them the day before raged and swore at the bulldozer driver.

The women stayed in the area for three days, then returned again to the rubble when the incursion had ended. 'At night we slept somewhere else, and during the day we came here to find him. We looked all day yesterday, but we could not find him.' Fayid's body was recovered from the rubble on 21 April, 15 days after the house was demolished on top of him. It is difficult to see what military goal could have been furthered or what legitimate consideration of urgent military necessity could be put forward to justify the crushing to death of Jamal Fayid without giving his family the opportunity to remove him from his home. This case requires investigation as a possible war crime.

Use of Palestinian civilians as human shields

IDF soldiers in Jenin engaged in the practice of human shielding, forcing Palestinian civilians to serve as 'shields' to protect them from Palestinian militants. The practice of human shielding is specifically outlawed by international humanitarian law. (...)

Among the most serious 'human shielding' cases documented in Jenin by Human Rights Watch were the cases of four brothers, a father and his 14-year-old son, and two other men who were used to shield IDF soldiers from attack by Palestinian militants while the

IDF soldiers occupied a large house located directly across from the main UNRWA compound in the camp. In separate interviews with Human Rights Watch, the victims described how they were forced to stand on the balcony of the house to deter Palestinian fighters from firing in the direction of the IDF soldiers.

The Palestinian civilians also described how the IDF soldiers had forced them to stand in front of the soldiers when the soldiers fired at Palestinian fighters, while resting their rifles on the shoulders of the Palestinian civilians.

Imad Gharaib, aged 34, was one of the four brothers. On Saturday, 6 April, at about 6.00 a.m., a group of 30 to 40 IDF soldiers entered the Gharaib family home, and forced the Gharaib brothers to walk in front of them as they searched the home. One of the IDF soldiers abused Imad, beating him with his rifle and threatening to shoot him if he did not reveal where he had hidden his gun (Imad said he does not possess a gun):

> He asked me if I had any guns. I said, 'No, I am only here with my family.' He started beating me with the back of his gun, hitting me many times, insisting that I had a gun. (...) He [then] threatened to shoot me and put the gun to my face. Then he moved the gun a bit and shot the television.

After the soldiers had inspected the home they tied the men up, and half an hour later, walked them over to a large neighbouring house in which the IDF had set up a temporary base; the house was located directly across from the main UNRWA compound. The men were forced to stand outside, facing the Palestinian gunfire:

> They ordered us to walk in front of them. (...) There was some shooting at the [IDF] soldiers [by Palestinian militants higher up in the camp.] They started pushing us and brought us down to another house. There, they put us on the veranda where we could be seen [by the Palestinian fighters]. The soldiers were sitting inside the salon. We were facing the shooting. The soldiers did this to protect themselves. We could be clearly seen – if the fighters saw us they would not shoot.

Kamal Tawalbi, a 43-year-old father of 14 children, and his 14-year-old son were also taken to the same house and forced to stand facing the Palestinian gunfire. The IDF soldiers also placed them at the windows and forced them to stand in front of the soldiers as the soldiers shot at Palestinian fighters in the camp:

> They took me and my son. They put me in one corner and [my son] in the other corner [of the balcony]. The soldier put his gun on my shoulder. I was facing the soldier, we were face to face, with my back to the street. Then he started shooting. This situation lasted for three hours. My son was in the same position – he was facing the soldier, the soldier had his gun on his shoulder, and was shooting.

The soldiers also treated Kamal Tawalbi and the other men with cruelty. During his interview with Human Rights Watch, Kamal Tawalbi – who had been taken from his home by the IDF soldiers, while his home was burning from a helicopter strike – broke down in tears as he recounted how the IDF soldiers had tried to make him believe that his family had been killed while he was in custody:

> I heard the noise from my family. I was very worried. Then another missile hit the house. I started screaming, 'My children, my children!' [One of the soldiers] said, 'Shut up, because your family is dead, the house collapsed on them.' He was a Bedouin from Beersheva, his name was Yusi. I started crying after this. When Yusi saw I was crying, he kicked me in the leg. He stomped on my foot and hurt it badly.

Both men recalled how the soldiers had forced the men to lie face down on a floor covered with broken glass, and had tied their hands painfully tight behind their backs with plastic handcuffs. The men were then arrested and taken to a military camp for interrogation, and subsequently released at the village of Rumanah. (...) In an interview with the *New York Times*, a group of Israeli soldiers in Jenin admitted that they had used Palestinian civilians to shield themselves from attack by Palestinian fighters. 'Yes, because of the snipers [we used Palestinian civilians]', one of the soldiers stated. 'If the sniper sees his friend there, he won't shoot.' A soldier also told the *New York Times* that they had used Palestinian civilians to open the doors of homes out of fear of booby traps: 'We had a soldier who opened a door and was killed by a booby trap that went off in his face. We let them [Palestinian civilians] open the door. If he knows it is booby trapped, he won't open it.'[25] (...)

25 Serge Schemann and Joel Greenberg, 'Israelis say Arab dead in Jenin number in dozens, not hundreds', *New York Times*, 15 April 2002.

8 The Israeli army turns on the media, 29 March–15 June 2002

Reporters Without Borders

'It's the first time I've seen this in more than 20 years', said a foreign reporter working in Jerusalem. Since the start of the second Intifada, and especially since 29 March 2002 when the Israeli army began its incursions into Palestinian towns, countless journalists have been arrested, threatened, roughed up, prevented from moving around, deported, injured, or had their accreditation withdrawn or passports confiscated. Israel has ratified the International Covenant on Civil and Political Rights (ICCPR), whose article 19 guarantees 'freedom to seek, receive and impart information', but the Israeli army has in practice stopped journalists from freely reporting on their operations. The press freedom situation has never been so bad in all the history of Israel.

Closed military zones: 'Keep moving, there's nothing to see'

The Israeli army declared the city of Ramallah a 'closed military zone' on 30 March 2002. On 1 April, it was Bethlehem's turn. Between 2 and 3 April, the foreign media found the towns of Qalqiliya, Nablus, Tulkarem and Jenin more and more difficult to get into, and for several days no journalist was able to enter the Jenin camp while military operations were going on there. In early May, foreign minister Gideon Meir said the army's restrictions were to protect journalists, not prevent them working. Israel had every right to declare closed military zones, he said. Journalists managed to get into some towns anyway, but it soon became clear they were not welcome.

More than 60 of them came under gunfire. At least four shots were fired at Palestinian Associated Press photographer Nasser

Nasser on 4 April while he was taking pictured of armoured vehicles in Ramallah. The next day, journalists in a convoy of seven bulletproof vehicles with press markings were driving towards Palestinian leader Yasser Arafat's headquarters, where US mediator Anthony Zinni was visiting him, where Israeli soldiers fired warning shots and stun grenades at them. As the convoy turned round, the CNN vehicle was hit by a bullet which broke its rear window. The City Inn hotel in Ramallah was the regular target of shooting when many journalists were staying there in April.

Wounded and injured journalists: where are the investigations?

At least eight journalists have been wounded by gunfire since 29 March. They include Carlos Handal, a camera operator for the Egyptian station Nile TV, who was seriously wounded in the jaw. But shooting at journalists is nothing new. Since the beginning of the second Intifada in September 2000, Reporters Without Borders has counted 55 cases of journalists being wounded by gunfire, mostly Israeli, it said after on-the-spot investigation. Several journalists, mostly Palestinians, were seriously wounded, even though some were clearly identifiable as journalists and standing apart from the clashes when hit. With very few exceptions, no serious enquiry into the incidents has been made or punishment meted out to those responsible, even when this responsibility was clear, as in the case of the French TF1 TV reporter Bertrand Aguirre, wounded on 15 May 2001 in Ramallah.

In September 2001, Israeli legal officials decided to drop their enquiry into the incident. Eran Shangar, head of the police internal affairs department, said that after reviewing the case, he had decided, for want of sufficient evidence, not to prosecute the policeman responsible. Yet when Aguirre was shot, three television crews were filming the scene. An Israeli frontier guard was clearly seen getting out of his vehicle, preparing his gun and, cigarette in mouth, calmly opening fire from a distance of 100 metres. The journalist had just finished doing a piece to camera and was still holding an open microphone in his hand when he was hit in the chest. By chance, his bulletproof vest saved him. The investigators thus had all the proof they needed about who fired the shot.

Accreditation not renewed, or else withdrawn or refused

Several hundred Palestinian journalists were not able to get their journalist cards renewed in 2002. Awadh Awadh, who works for the French news agency Agence France-Presse (AFP), was refused renewal for supposed security reasons. In many cases, the Israeli authorities simply said the applications were 'being studied'. Talal Abu Rahman, the France 2 television camera operator who filmed the death of the young boy Mohammed in Gaza in October 2000, could not get his card renewed even though he had had one for more than ten years. Some journalists were more lucky and got cards valid for a several months (instead of the normal two years), while others were given new cards reserved for 'media assistants'. Such accreditation, even if it does not permit the holder to go freely between zones, at least makes passage easier through checkpoints. Without it, journalists risk arrest. The non-renewal of cards especially handicaps the big news agencies that use Palestinian stringers in Palestinian Authority territory. This March, Israeli press office spokesperson Danny Seaman warned that any Palestinian found without the necessary documentation (meaning a press card) inside Jerusalem Capital Studios (JCS), the building that houses all the main international media, risked arrest, and the media whose office he or she was found working in could be fined 70,000 shekels (about 15,000 Euros).

Jassim al-Azzawi, special correspondent of the Abou Dhabi TV satellite station, was deported on 7 April. A few days earlier, the Israeli government press office had withdrawn his accreditation along with that of Laila Odeh, of the same station. Both were accused of putting out 'anti-Israeli propaganda'. Why should they be treated well when they were mouthpieces of the enemy, asked Seaman? There was a limit to freedom of expression, even in a democratic country, he added after their deportation. Two days earlier, for the first time since Reporters Without Borders began working in Israel, the press office refused to give accreditation to representatives of the organisation. Seaman said this was because it had become a 'political' organisation, since it had added Israeli army chief of staff Shaul Moffaz to its worldwide list of predators of press freedom in November last year.

Six Palestinian journalists imprisoned

Many foreign journalists have complained to the Israeli army, and the local foreign press association has made many protest statements against these violations of press freedom. 'If this is how they treat me, then I can imagine what they're doing to the Palestinians', said Keith Miller of the US television network NBC. Palestinian journalists who for years have put up with intimidation by Israeli soldiers have been singled out for humiliation since 29 April. At least 20 have been arrested. On 2 April Atta Iweisat, a photographer working for the Israeli daily paper *Yediot Aharonot* and the Gamma photo agency, was arrested in Ramallah in the presence of foreign journalists. He was handcuffed and made to kneel on the ground for several hours in pouring rain.

Most of those arrested, including Aweisat, were freed on 15 June, but six are still imprisoned. They are Khalid Ali Zwawi, of the daily *El Istiqlal*, Maher el-Dessuki, of al-Quds Educational TV, Kamal Ali Jbeil, of the daily *Al-Quds*, Hussam Abu Alan, an AFP photographer, Yusri el-Jamal, a Reuters sound operator, and Ayman el-Kawasmi, head of a local radio station, El Horriya. They were placed in preventive detention for three months. El-Dessuki, Jbeil, Abu and el-Jamal are being held at the Ofer detention centre near Ramallah, where they sleep in tents with several hundred other prisoners. Alan needs special treatment for a head wound he received several years ago, but has not been able to get it. Some of the journalists held are suspected of 'helping a terrorist organisation'. AFP and Reuters protested to the Israeli authorities about this and demanded, in vain, to know what evidence there was against their journalists.

Palestinian media offices attacked

Between March and June 2002, the offices of the Palestinian media, whether government or privately-owned, were especially targeted by the Israeli army. On 30 March, Israeli soldiers entered the main building in Ramallah of the Palestinian radio and television network, Voice of Palestine. On 19 January, the Israeli army had dynamited the building and destroyed all its equipment. On 3 April, after arresting two journalists in the offices of al-Rooat, a local Bethlehem television station, soldiers destroyed equipment and seized videos. On 10 June Israeli soldiers ransacked the Reuters office in Ramallah and confiscated equipment.

The Israeli army criticised many Palestinian media for 'extremist' broadcasts. Since the beginning of the second Intifada, both government and privately-owned Palestinian media (which have broadcast official propaganda) have regularly aired programmes glorifying martyrs and inciting people to hatred and murder.

Foreign media also under Palestinian pressure

Both Palestinian and foreign journalists have also come under pressure from officials of the Palestinian Authority (PA). After the 11 September 2001 attacks in the USA and the joyful demonstrations they set off among Palestinians, the PA, fearing its international image would be harmed, tried to prevent Palestinian and foreign journalists from reporting such events.

On 11 September 2001, the Palestinian Security Service summoned a freelance camera operator working for Associated Press to warn him not to send the film he had taken of demonstrations in Nablus. Later, the PA's government secretary, Ahmed Abdel Rahman, said the PA could not 'guarantee the life' of the camera operator if the film was broadcast.

On 12 October 2000, many journalists who went to the scene of a lynching of two Israelis in Ramallah were physically attacked by Palestinian police and civilians, who seized their film and in some cases cameras too. French TF1 TV reporter Bertrand Aguirre was set upon by Palestinians after filming the scene.

To win the war of words and pictures, the Israeli minister in charge of public broadcasting and the prime minister's office regularly appeal to the Israeli media to be 'patriotic'. Journalists in the state-owned media have been told what words to use, to talk not of Israeli 'settlements' in the Palestinian territories but of 'localities' or 'villages'. Dead Palestinians are not to be called 'victims' but 'deaths'

Many readers of the left-wing daily *Haaretz* cancelled their subscriptions in protest again the way the paper covered Operation Rampart (the army incursions into the West Bank towns). *Haaretz*, known for its strong criticism of the army, has set itself apart from Israeli public opinion, which mostly backs Prime Minister Ariel Sharon's policies and the army's actions in April and May. The two biggest Israeli newspapers, *Maariv* and *Yediot Aharonot*, which aim to reflect Israeli majority opinion, rival each other to display their patriotism.

9 Torture in Israel[26]

Public Committee Against Torture in Israel

On 6 September 1999, concluding approximately a year and a half of deliberations, nine justices of the Supreme Court of Israel, sitting as High Court of Justice (HCJ), published their decision in the case of HCJ 5100/94 The Public Committee Against Torture in Israel *v.* The Government of Israel *et al.* (henceforth, the HCJ ruling). The ruling, issued after a struggle carried out over many years by the Public Committee Against Torture in Israel and other human rights organisations, determined that systematic torture inflicted by the General Security Service (GSS) for some twelve years, following the recommendations of the Landau Commission, did not fulfill the requirements of Israeli law.

The ruling led to a significant change in practice. Some of the torture methods permitted by the Landau Commission disappeared entirely, or almost entirely, among them violent shaking, covering the head with a sack, playing powerfully loud music, and tying to a small tilted chair.

Unfortunately, however, it cannot be stated that two years after the HCJ ruling there is no more torture and cruel inhuman or degrading treatment (henceforth: ill-treatment) in the GSS interrogation wings. (...)

This report analyses both the positive and negative aspects of the HCJ ruling, describes the present situation, and offers conclusions regarding the failure of the HCJ ruling to place a complete end to the plague of torture in Israel. (...) The second part of the report also describes the widespread phenomenon of violence and humiliation of Palestinian detainees by IDF soldiers and the Israeli police. Palestinians are often beaten and humiliated by the detaining authorities, then taken to GSS interrogation facilities where they are exposed to additional ill-treatment. (...)

---

26 Excerpt from *Torture and Ill-treatment in GSS Interrogations Following the Supreme Court Ruling (6 September 1999 –6 September 2001)*, September 2001.

The report is based on legal material, on data and information provided by Palestinian and Israeli human rights organisations, attorneys, and other persons and organisations, and on affidavits and testimony taken from victims of torture and ill-treatment by the GSS.

The High Court decision: positive and negative aspects

The current situation in GSS interrogation wings (...) was and continues to be influenced largely by the HCJ ruling. It is therefore important to examine the ruling and its implications, and particularly to understand to what extent the ruling, despite its impressive achievements, has enabled the continuation of torture and ill-treatment of Palestinian interrogees [This deviation from standard English corresponds to the Hebrew *nehqar*, and is used throughout to refer to detainees under GSS interrogation.] The following analysis does not focus on theoretical aspects of the ruling, but on those aspects which bear practical implications. (...)

Positive aspects

The HCJ ruling was, first and foremost, a step unprecedented in its courage. In accepting the petitions of the Public Committee Against Torture in Israel, the Association for Civil Rights in Israel, HaMoked: Centre for the Defence of the Individual, and individual lawyers, the Supreme Court positioned itself against not only the security system, but the entire political establishment – the Knesset, the government, the state attorney, and the state comptroller – all of which supported, with almost no reservations, the system of institutionalised torture that had been in place for twelve years: that is, since the government adopted the recommendations of the Landau Commission in 1987. The Supreme Court also positioned itself against a public that to a large extent supported this system of torture. Moreover, the Supreme Court did a near complete about-face, overturning a series of its own decisions that had upheld both the theoretical and practical aspects of Landau's formula for permitting torture.

The Supreme Court ruled that GSS interrogators have no more authority than ordinary police interrogators. They are authorised only to carry out a 'reasonable investigation' which is 'is one free of torture, free of cruel, inhuman treatment of the subject and free of any degrading handling whatsoever'. The Supreme Court thus put an end to practices of torture that were permitted in advance, recorded in detailed instructions, discussed and determined in the meetings of the Government Ministerial Committee, approved by Knesset committees, and protected by the State Attorney's Office.

In response to claims of the State Attorney's Office, implying that international law permits torture and ill-treatment in the form of 'moderate physical pressure' under certain conditions, the Supreme Court aptly defined the provisions of this law in its reference to international treaty law – to which Israel is a party – which prohibits the use of torture, 'cruel, inhuman treatment' and 'degrading treatment'. These prohibitions are 'absolute'. There are no exceptions to them and there is no room for balancing.

In practice, the Supreme Court outlawed one by one all of the methods of torture permitted by the Landau Commission, beginning with violent shaking, continuing with squatting and the 'shabeh' methods (covering the head with a sack, playing loud music and tying to a small, tilted chair), and ending with sleep deprivation (as a means of applying pressure) and painful shackling. The court ruled that these methods cause suffering (and when applied cumulatively – as in the 'shabeh' method – 'particular suffering and pain') to the interrogees and degrade their dignity, and are therefore illegal.

The Supreme Court ruled that the defence of necessity is individual and applies only retroactively, and is therefore not a source of authority for granting a priori permission to GSS interrogators to use physical pressure. In so doing, the court removed the legal foundation used by the Landau Commission for granting permission in advance for using means of torture.

Negative aspects

While the Supreme Court referred to, as stated, the provisions of international law, it refrained from considering the petitions in light of international standards set by such law; it also refrained from applying fully these very provisions to GSS interrogators. In addition, the court left loopholes that enable the GSS, under the cover of secrecy that protects it from external investigations, to use methods of torture and ill-treatment, and claim – even if such claims are for the most part false – that they constitute a 'reasonable interrogation' in accordance with the ruling.

Refraining from directly defining the Landau Commission's 'permissions' as torture

It is clear from the ruling that the Supreme Court does not accept the state's claim that GSS interrogation methods 'do not cause pain and suffering' and therefore do not constitute torture, or even ill-treatment, prohibited by international law. The Court ruled, as mentioned, that these methods offend interrogees' dignity and degrade them, as well as cause 'real pain and suffering' and even 'particular pain and suffering'.

The above notwithstanding, the Supreme Court avoided using the appropriate term for the Landau methods – torture. The conclusion that they constitute torture and ill-treatment is clear, but it is implicit – not explicit. This avoidance may have stemmed from the fact that the court itself had permitted, as mentioned, the use of these very means in the past, and that in its ruling it did not rule out permitting them retroactively in the future.

The direct result of this avoidance of an explicit statement has been that even in the year 2001, Israel continues to argue before the institutions of the UN that 'the methods which had been employed in investigations by Israel's security service (referred to as the "Landau Rules"), do not constitute torture or cruel, inhuman or degrading treatment and do not violate the provisions of the Convention [against torture]', and bases this claim on the argument that 'the Court, in its Judgment, did not reject the arguments of the State that such interrogation methods did not constitute torture or cruel, inhuman or degrading treatment and do not violate the Convention [against Torture]'.

Even if this is a dubious claim, given the above, and given that it ignores the fact that the Supreme Court did not reject the petitioners' claim that it is indeed torture we are talking about, it is clear that an explicit and not merely implied statement by the Court would have rendered it impossible to make such claims. Moreover, an explicit statement by the Court that these methods constitute torture would have attached to these methods the stigma that they deserve, and would have thus discouraged the State both from applying them and from justifying their use.

'The ticking bomb' and 'defence of necessity' – an opening for 'legal' torture

While the Supreme Court prohibited the government from authorising the GSS to torture or ill-treat detainees, it did not prohibit

GSS interrogators from torturing or ill-treating interrogees under all circumstances, as required by the provisions of international law binding upon Israel. The HCJ ruling states:

> We are prepared to assume that – although this matter is open to debate – (…) the 'necessity' defence is open to all, particularly an investigator, acting in an organisational capacity of the State in interrogations of that nature. Likewise, we are prepared to accept – although this matter is equally contentious – that the 'necessity' exception is likely to arise in instances of 'ticking time bombs', and that the immediate need ('necessary in an immediate manner' for the preservation of human life) refers to the imminent nature of the act rather than that of the danger. Hence, the imminence criteria is satisfied even if the bomb is set to explode in a few days, or perhaps even after a few weeks, provided the danger is certain to materialise and there is no alternative means of preventing its materialisation. Consequently we are prepared to presume, as was held by the Inquiry [Landau] Commission's Report, that if a GSS investigator – who applied physical means of interrogation for the purpose of saving human life – is criminally indicted, the 'necessity' defence is likely to be open to him in the appropriate circumstances. A long list of arguments, from both the fields of ethics and political science, may be raised for and against the use of the 'necessity' defence. This matter, however, has already been decided under Israeli law. Israel's Penal Law recognises the 'necessity' defence.

In other words, if a GSS interrogator were convinced that the case at hand qualified as a 'ticking bomb' situation, the law allows him or her to apply all of the 'physical means of interrogation' that the Supreme Court generally prohibited in its ruling – that is, to torture the interrogee. After the fact, this matter would be brought before the attorney general, who would then decide if, in fact, the case were indeed a 'ticking bomb' situation.[27] If so, the defence of

27 The State Attorney General, Dr Eliyakim Rubinstein, indeed composed and even published a document containing the principles according to which he would guide himself in such cases. See *State Attorney General, GSS Interrogations and the Necessity Defence – Framework for Attorney General's Deliberation (following the HCJ ruling)*, Jerusalem, 28 October 1999. Document available at PCATI office.

'necessity' would be at the interrogator's disposal, and he or she would be exempt from criminal liability; if not, he or she would be tried, at which point he or she would also be able to invoke the 'necessity' defence.

This approach is problematic from a number of perspectives. From a legal-theoretical perspective, the ruling creates a situation where every state is able to violate its international obligations, while granting the agents who carry out the violations on its behalf legal protection, even if only retroactively. From an ethical perspective, the permission to torture a person – even if only under extreme circumstances – grants legitimacy to one of the most abhorrent of crimes, which should cease to exist, and has no justification under any circumstances. From a practical perspective, the ruling leaves an expansive 'grey area' in which the law does not explicitly stipulate whether or not one may torture and ill-treat humans. The Supreme Court leaves the decision on this matter, which requires a principled decision of society, based on its basic values, in the hands of the interrogator, who is in the throes of an urgent and difficult interrogation. On the one hand, the interrogator lacks a priori permission to apply methods of torture, meaning that he or she has not been trained to use them in an 'effective' manner. On the other hand, the court signals to the same interrogator that torture may be the right thing to do. Leaving the decision to the improvisation of the 'simple soldier' is appropriate for unexpected situations, but if the state claims that 'ticking bomb' situations occur often, then it is fitting that the necessary tools be given to whoever deals with them, and that this person be given appropriate instructions. The Court passed the problem on to the lowest ranks instead of solving it itself.

A ruling consistent with the spirit of international law would determine that: torture and ill-treatment are in absolute violation of the laws and principles of the state and its values, as well as of international law. Torture and ill-treatment are forbidden in any situation, and anyone who tortures or ill-treats detainees is committing a serious, punishable crime, for which there are no a priori permission and no *ex post factum* exemptions.

Such a ruling would have placed Israeli law in line with the most enlightened nations in the world, would have eliminated any legal or practical ambiguity, and would have instructed the GSS and its interrogators unequivocally to cease looking for ways of inflicting pain on interrogees and degrading them, and instead to carry out its work in a manner appropriate to the GSS's role as an intelligence unit operating at the beginning of the third millennium, in a country that declares frequently that it is democratic, committed to the rule of law and upholding human rights.

Lacunae that beckon: sleep deprivation and prolonged tying

The Supreme Court outlawed the systematic use of 'most of the physical means of interrogation' permitted by the Landau Commission. The prohibition, however, is not absolute regarding two of these methods – sleep deprivation and shackling during the interrogation.

The Supreme Court did limit in both cases the use of these methods, and in practice disqualified them as methods of interrogation. Regarding sleep deprivation, the court ruled that 'prolonged' interrogation is allowed, even if it involves sleep deprivation, but this is only on the condition that lack of sleep is a 'side effect' of an interrogation and not a means employed 'for the purpose of tiring him out or "breaking" him'.

Regarding shackling, the Supreme Court ruled that interrogators are authorized to use this method, 'but only for the purpose of preserving the investigators' safety'. In contrast, 'Cuffing causing pain is prohibited'. The court added that, 'moreover, there are other ways of preventing the suspect from fleeing from legal custody which do not involve causing the suspect pain and suffering'.

Yet given the poor record of the GSS in all that involves turning 'security methods' into methods of torture, the HCJ ruling is wanting in that it fails to place clear and firm limitations on the use of these methods. What is the meaning of a 'prolonged' period for which the detainee is questioned by the interrogator? Ten hours? Twenty hours? Two days? Who determines when 'handcuffing' becomes 'painful handcuffing' – the detainee, the interrogator, or perhaps a medic or a physician?

The court failed in that it refrained from fixing, at the very least, minimum periods of rest and sleep which must not be denied under any circumstances, and which ensure that the detainee's physical and mental health is not harmed, whether intentionally or as a 'side effect'; ordering measures to ensure that 'cuffing' indeed does not cause pain and suffering; and ordering that monitoring mechanisms be placed to ensure that such orders are strictly adhered to.

The practical result of the ruling in these matters is that the GSS holds people in the interrogation rooms for many hours, sometimes days, while they are shackled to a chair. The explanation offered by the State Attorney's Office is, for example:

> The manner and form of his interrogation derive from the assessment of security officials, according to which your client harbors even today information that can enable the foiling of [terrorist] attacks in the near future ... regarding your claims about his shackling during his interrogation – this arises solely from the need to assure the security of the interrogators. (...)[28]

The style is almost identical to that previously assumed by the State Attorney's Office in response to claims raised by interrogees and their attorneys regarding the 'shabeh' method. As explained below, the Public Committee Against Torture in Israel has concluded, based in its study, that sleep deprivation and prolonged, painful shackling have been turned by the GSS into means of torture and ill-treatment *par excellence*, in complete contravention of the HCJ ruling. Yet because GSS interrogators are protected, as explained below, in a shroud of isolation and disconnection from the outside world, and the person sent by the State Attorney's Office to investigate individual complaints against them is no less than a GSS agent, the result is that the word of the 'terrorist' detainee, claiming that he or she was tortured, is again, as in the days of the 'shabeh', pitted against that of the state's dedicated guardians, according to whom shackling and sleep deprivation are only 'side effects' and 'security measures'. The results are clear.

The above is not intended to detract from the importance of the HCJ ruling or from the weight of its positive aspects – the ruling constitutes, as stated, a most significant step in the right direction. It puts an end to permitted and authorized mass and routine torture, limits the authority of GSS interrogators in interrogation (or the means of interrogation at their disposal), and largely limits, at least in theory, the field of play within which GSS interrogators can torture and ill-treat Palestinian detainees.

28 Letter of Attorney Shai Nitzan, Official in Charge of Security Matters in the State Attorney's Office, to Attorney Andre Rosenthal, on the matter of 'Arguments regarding interrogation methods used against Nasser 'Iyad', 20 March 2001, paras 'a' and 'b'.

This notwithstanding, the Supreme Court did not muster the courage to fall into line with the provisions of international law. The court avoided calling the interrogation methods recommended by the Landau Commission by their proper name – torture – even though it clearly indicated that this was its position. The court avoided adopting the position of international law that rejects torture in any situation, and left intact the applicability of the 'necessity defence' for torturers during a 'ticking bomb' situation, thereby both creating an opening for the existence of torture in practice, and lending legal and ethical legitimacy to this deplorable crime. The court allowed, under limited conditions, sleep deprivation and prolonged tying of detainees, creating cracks into which the GSS hastily squeezed through to find ostensibly legal methods of torture and ill-treatment. The result is that protection for Palestinian detainees from torture and ill-treatment is still lacking.

Torture and ill-treatment during interrogations by the GSS

This section describes in detail the means of torture and ill-treatment practised by the GSS against Palestinian interrogees. It is important to recall that no method is used on its own – one method connects to the next, accumulating into pressure that increases steadily with time, so that the suffering caused to interrogees also increases steadily.

The shroud of isolation and disconnection which facilitates torture and ill-treatment

The system of torture and ill-treatment in GSS facilities is based on a shroud of isolation and secrecy that encompasses the physical facilities. This shroud, on the one hand, denies Palestinian detainees basic rights of contact with the outside world, first and foremost with their family, attorney and any other friendly person to whom they can complain and who can defend them in 'real time' from the GSS. On the other hand, this shroud of isolation and secrecy protects GSS interrogators from any critical and independent eye, and thus from the need to justify their illegal actions, granting them broad freedom of action to do as they please with Palestinian detainees, at least during the initial period of interrogation.

ISRAEL

Incommunicado detention of interrogees as a means of ill-treatment

The provisions of article 78 of the Security Regulations Order, issued by the military commanders in the Occupied Territories, grant a police employee with the rank of officer the authority to detain a Palestinian for up to eight days prior to bringing him or her before a judge, grant a military judge the authority to extend the detention by three periods of up to 30 days, and allow a military judge in a military appeals court to add up to three additional months to this period.

At the same time, the official 'in charge of the interrogation' is authorised to deprive detainees of their right to meet with their attorney for a period of up to 15 days. An 'approving authority' may extend this period by 15 additional days. The military judge may extend it for additional periods of up to 30 days each time, for a total of up to three months. The president on duty at the military appeals court has the authority to extend it (at the request of the state attorney) to a period of up to 30 additional days. In total, a resident of the Occupied Territories can therefore be held for six months under detention order, without the privilege of meeting with his or her attorney. (...)

The authority to deprive detainees of their basic human right to contact with their families, to legal counsel, and to legal scrutiny for prolonged periods, which the military orders intended, presumably, for extreme cases, is in practice used routinely with Palestinian interrogees. From the beginning of the al-Aqsa Intifada through the end of August 2001, the Public Committee Against Torture in Israel processed the cases of hundreds of Palestinian detainees subject to GSS interrogation, whose right to meet with their attorney was denied for days and weeks. Many contacted other human rights organisations or attorneys. In addition, many Palestinian detainees whose families did not hasten to procure them an attorney remained without legal representation even when no order was issued against them preventing meeting with their attorney.

Unfortunately, the Supreme Court is a full participant in this glaring violation of basic human rights. The justices of the court often try to reach an arrangement or compromise between the parties, such as an agreement not to renew the order preventing detainees from meeting with their attorneys, and sometimes, during the trial, recommend the cancellation of the order. However, the court has not acquiesced even to a single one of the

[122]

hundreds of petitions submitted by attorneys on behalf of the
Public Committee Against Torture in Israel, on behalf of other
human rights organisations, or independently, during the past two
years. In other words, it has always refused to rule that such an
order be annulled. The routine and laconic response of the Court
justices to such petitions is of the following sort: 'We are convinced
that preventing a meeting between the petitioner and his attorney
is necessary for the interrogation to continue, as well as for the
security of the area.'

The Supreme Court was not even deterred from leaving a
detained 17-year-old Palestinian minor incommunicado for three
weeks.[29] In another case, the Court went so far as to refuse to order
the GSS to inform a Palestinian detainee that such an order had
been issued against him preventing him from meeting with his
attorney, this too 'for reasons of state security'. If it is not enough
that in Israel it is not compulsory to apprise detainees of their
rights, as is the practice in most democratic countries, even
informing detainees that they are being denied their rights constitutes, according to the Supreme Court, harm to the security of the
state.

Needless to say, visits by family members of Palestinians under
GSS interrogation are, mildly stated, extremely rare occurrences.

It is important to understand that in terms of international
law, denying detainees contact with the outside world is not only
a violation of legal rights, but also constitutes a violation of the
right to freedom from torture and ill-treatment. The Public
Committee Against Torture in Israel has no doubt that one of the
goals of denying these rights is to place emotional pressure on
detainees.

In specific reference to the policy of incommunicado detention
of Palestinian detainees in Israel, the UN Special Rapporteur on
Torture, Professor Sir Nigel Rodley, stipulates explicitly in a report
he submitted in 2001 to the UN Commission on Human Rights,
that 'the government continues to detain persons incommunicado
for exorbitant periods, itself a practice constituting cruel, inhuman
or degrading treatment'.

This means that the ill-treatment of Palestinian detainees begins
with depriving them of the right to contact with the outside world
– mainly with their lawyers and family members – for a period of

29 HCJ 5242 Muhammad Ibrahim Huhammad al-Matur and the Public Committee
Against Torture in Israel *v.* Erez Military Court, decision of 15 February 2000.

days or weeks. The study conducted by the Public Committee Against Torture in Israel reveals methods of torture and ill-treatment that are routinely implemented by the GSS in the interrogation rooms, and others that are applied in more rare situations.

Description of routine techniques

Sleep deprivation

As stated, the Supreme Court ruled that 'prolonged' interrogation, involving sleep deprivation, is permitted only on the condition that the lack of sleep is a 'side effect' of the interrogation and not a means employed 'for the purpose of tiring him out or "breaking" him' (article 31). The study conducted by the Public Committee Against Torture in Israel shows clearly that the GSS has ignored this condition set by the Supreme Court, and uses various methods that deprive detainees of sleep as a means of pressuring them during their interrogation.

The GSS holds Palestinian interrogees, as a matter of routine, shackled to a chair in the interrogation room for long and contiguous periods, excepting short pauses for meals, and sometimes pauses (even shorter ones) for using the toilet.

The study conducted by the Public Committee Against Torture in Israel reveals that shackling detainees in the interrogation rooms for 15 and even 20 hours a day, for a number of consecutive days, is a matter of routine. On more than a few occasions, detainees have been shackled in the interrogation rooms for more protracted periods – for a number of consecutive days. As becomes clear in what follows, various means of sleep deprivation are also employed in the isolation cells.

The study reveals that in most if not all of the cases, these protracted periods are not used fully for the purpose that they were ostensibly intended – for questioning interrogees regarding information they may possess. The interrogators sometimes 'spend' hours in idle conversation; repeat the same exact question over and over, sometimes for many hours; and in many cases do not speak with the interrogees and even leave the interrogation room for hours, while assuring that the interrogee will not be permitted to sleep while they are gone. The 'protracted interrogations' are therefore intended, first and foremost, to 'kill time' while the interrogee becomes increasingly tired – that is, to exhaust interrogee and 'break' them, in contravention of the HCJ ruling.

Shackling to a chair in painful positions

The GSS has interrogees sit for many hours, sometimes for a number of consecutive days (with the exception of short breaks for meals, and even shorter breaks for going to the toilet), on an ordi-nary-sized or low unupholstered wooden or metal chair (although they no longer use a tilted child's chair), with their hands shackled behind their backs in handcuffs and linked to the chair using an additional handcuff.

The chairs are not particularly comfortable even for sitting for short periods. The detainees sit for long periods, with no possibil-ity of even changing position, let alone a stretching break, leading sooner or later to pains in the back, arms, shoulders or all of these. The shackles are not intended for prolonged tying, and even when they are not tightened intentionally, the prolonged handcuffing eventually leads to pain and swelling in the wrist.

GSS agents and the State Attorney's Office insist that shackling is not intended to inflict pain, but is used for the 'security of the interrogators'. These questionable explanations recall the claims made for many years by the State Attorney's Office, that the 'wait-ing' method mentioned above was intended only to prevent communication between detainees and to protect interrogators from attack. Only during discussions before the special panel of judges convened for HCJ 5100/94 did State Attorney's Office attorneys admit that it was by all means a method of applying pressure ('passive', they claimed).

The study conducted by the Public Committee Against Torture in Israel reveals clearly that shackling detainees causes them suffering and pain, and is in contravention of the HCJ ruling, which stipulated explicitly that 'cuffing causing pain is prohibited' (para. 26). The study also reveals that painful tying is used to apply pressure on the interrogee, in conjunction with other meth-ods of pressure, and is thus in violation of international law and the HCJ ruling.

This conclusion is not unique to the Public Committee Against Torture in Israel. Magistrates court Justice Haim Lahovitzki reached the same conclusion, commenting as follows at the end of his decision regarding extending the detention of Jihad Shuman:

> As an aside, let the following be said: the Respondent claims, through his attorney, that even today, during his

interrogations, his interrogators regularly shackle him with his hands behind his back. Regarding the question of Attorney Tsemel to the police representative on this matter, the latter responded that it was done for reasons of his [Shuman's] interrogators' security. I tend to doubt this argument and yet, if there is indeed a danger to the well-being of the interrogators – and I leave that solely to their discretion – it appears to me that it is possible to assure their security in another manner. On the other hand, if the shackling is performed in this manner as a means of pressuring the respondent, it seems to me that there is no point to it and I do not believe that such a means will further in any way the goal of the interrogation. I say these things based on what I saw and what has been presented to me up to now. (…)[30]

It should be stated that while Justice Lahovitzki did well in confuting the far-fetched explanations of the interrogators and their spokespersons regarding the reason for shackling interrogees, he failed in not drawing the necessary conclusion, namely that GSS interrogators violated the Supreme Court decision, and in so doing committed a criminal offence deserving of an investigation at the very least.

The Supreme Court itself, in a manner similar to Justice Lahovitzki, commented as stated in its ruling that 'there are other ways of preventing the suspect from fleeing from legal custody which do not involve causing the suspect pain and suffering'. The fact that the GSS chose to disregard these comments and to stand by the use of shackles also bears witness that the aim of shackling should be sought in the realm of torture and ill-treatment, rather than in the realm of security.

Beating, slapping and kicking

During the 'interrogation', interrogators often beat detainees, slap them on the face, kick them and employ other violent means – all with various degrees of intensity. The study carried out by the Public Committee Against Torture in Israel indicates that the use of these means has increased during the period following the HCJ ruling, and particularly during the al-Aqsa Intifada.

---

30 Jerusalem Magistrates Court, before Justice Haim Lahovitzki, M 007453/01, Regarding Israel Police *v.* Shuman Jihad, 2 February 2001, p. 9 of the decision.

Threats, curses and insults

This method was used routinely prior to the HCJ ruling as well. While the Supreme Court ruled that 'a reasonable investigation is necessarily one free of cruel, inhuman treatment of the subject and free of any degrading handling whatsoever', and it is clear that these means fall under at least one of those categories, the ruling did not relate specifically to these means, and in all likelihood the GSS believes that this fact gives a 'green light' to their continued use.

The curses, threats and humiliations are often of a racist or sexual nature. The interrogators, who supposedly represent the law of the State of Israel, threaten interrogees that they will perpetrate acts against them or their families (usually women) that are considered serious criminal offences, such as rape. In many cases, they threaten to perpetrate acts against interrogees or their families that are prohibited by international law but acceptable in Israel, such as protracted and arbitrary administrative detention, or summary execution (referred to in Israel as 'elimination', 'interception', 'focused prevention', and so on).

There follow a number of examples of what is described above.

From the testimony of 'Abir Abu Khdeir (a woman)

> In the beginning they did not tie me at all. I would take advantage of the periods when they left the interrogation room to lie on the sofa and sleep. In response, they began – starting on Monday – to tie me to the chair. Afterwards, I managed to draw myself slightly closer to the table and I fell asleep on it each time that they left, so they moved the table far away. Physically speaking, I was extremely exhausted. I lost maybe 8 kilos during the first week. I would fall asleep on the chair during interrogation, but each time the interrogators would yell at me and kick the wall behind me hard. My back also hurt a lot from the prolonged sitting – therefore I barely fell asleep on the first night. (...) The curses that they used against me: Allah will curse you. You whore, fuck your mother. Robert said, 'If you don't talk, maybe we'll bring your children and interrogate them.' I knew that wasn't serious. I said, 'Please, bring them.' They also said, 'Don't dream of leaving here in less than two years.'
>
> The court extended my detention five times, and the interrogators threatened, 'We will extend your detention by

another 30 days, and then for another 30.' That did scare me, because I knew that they were capable of doing it.

From the testimony of Walid Abu Khdeir

Each interrogator would come and say, 'Tell me a story.' If one got tired, another would come. If I said, 'I already told it', he would say, 'Tell it again.'

Sometimes they would leave me – sometimes for two or three hours – in the interrogation room alone. But every ten minutes someone would open the door to make sure that I wasn't sleeping'. (...)

Examples of special techniques

From the affidavit of Muhammad Abu Daher

The names of the interrogators were General Abu Sharif, Colonel Shalom, Captain Oscar and Captain Mikki. It should be noted that I asked them to take off the [plastic, disposable] handcuffs because I felt excruciating pain, but they ignored my requests.

The interrogators immediately began interrogating me. My interrogation was only about my relationship with Mr Muhammad a-Sinwar, and when I answered that I did not know him, General Abu Sharif slapped me hard across the face three times. Abu Sharif had a hammer. He began waving it about in the air, turned to Shalom and said to him, 'This – later.' As a result of the tight plastic handcuffs, my hands swelled up and they turned black. At that moment, I was no longer able to bear the intense pain, and so I begged the interrogators, 'Look at my hands.' When they saw them, they cut off the plastic handcuffs and brought me others in their place.

(...) Shalom and Oscar left and the two other interrogators stayed with me, but they didn't interrogate me. They told stories so that I would stay awake. Qiss [an interrogator] told me about his good relations with Arabs [until the morning]. Even though I wasn't being interrogated, they didn't let me sleep. (...)

In the morning, during my interrogation, Abu Sharif slapped me hard across the face and Qiss pressed hard on my shoulders. During my interrogation, my feet and hands were in shackles, and my arms were stretched backwards. The interrogator [called] Shalom sat across from me, separated my legs, pushed hard against them, and put his hand on my chest and pressed on my body. I felt excruciating pains.

In the afternoon, an interrogator named Udi interrogated me. Udi also tortured me using the same method.

In the evening, William and Shaki interrogated me until late. I was tired and tried to sleep, but William ordered me, 'Now you will sit *qambaz* style. What, you don't know how to sit in *qambaz*? Squat on your toes.' My hands were shackled in front of me, and the foot shackles were tight, and when I tried to shift positions, I met with yelling. 'What, you're not a man. Sit properly in *qambaz*.' This went on for about ten minutes.

It should be noted that while I was squatting, they pressed on my legs and my shoulders. Afterwards they returned me to the chair and when I tried sleeping, they ordered me to stand. A few minutes later, I told them that I did not want to sleep, and then they sat me back on the chair. (...) I was seated on the chair, with hand and leg shackles, with my arms stretched backwards. Shalom sat across from me, and Mason was alongside me. Shalom separated my legs and pressed his legs hard against them, and with his hand pressed against my chest, so that my back was stretched to the side and was in the air. My stomach shook from all that pain, and I felt that I would become paralysed. When I tried putting my hands on the floor, Mason kicked me. This went on for about ten minutes. I was interrogated for about 23 hours a day, a continuous and non-stop interrogation. (...)

From Attorney Leah Tsemel's letter of complaint to the State Attorney (signed by Jihad Shuman)

Upon detention, he was not notified of having any rights at all. When he asked his interrogators what his rights were, they told him that he had no rights, and that in Israel every interrogee is obligated to confess to all the crimes.

He demanded that he speak with an attorney and meet with the [British] Consul. A man arrived and said 'I am the consul', and afterwards a man came and said, 'I am the attorney', but the detainee was convinced that they were interrogator impersonators.

He was physically beaten by his interrogators. Among other things, they kicked him, slapped him on the face with great force many times, to the extent that his nose was bruised and he was bleeding from the nose. Since the beginning of the interrogation, his nose has been congested and he has experienced difficulty breathing.

Since the beginning of his interrogation he has been placed for extraordinarily long hours on a tiny chair, with his legs pushed in and pressed behind the legs of the chair. He was tied, with his back pressing against the side of the back of the chair (the chair was placed sideways). His interrogators forced him to bend backwards with his entire body pressed and his muscles hurting to the limits of what he could endure. They forced him to remain in this painful position, and did not allow him to get up. Following continued efforts to remain seated, he would collapse to the floor. The interrogator would grab his chest and lift him up to the same painful position. He was forced to do this for a number of days in a row, and many times for what seemed to him for entire days. His back hurt tremendously as a result of these acts, and he felt that his back had been broken.

For days on end he was not allowed to sleep. He remembers at least three consecutive days during which he was tired and exhausted 'to death'. Every time he showed signs of fatigue, the prison guard would take him by force to the shower and pour cold water on him, and he would be forced to sit for hours in the freezing cold, wet all over.

The interrogation included threats and insults of every type. First and foremost, sexual threats such as that he would be raped or that they would rape his mother. In addition, they threatened him with electric shock and that they would cut off his nerves. They made ample use of curses against his family and his mother. (...)

Summary and conclusions

For the GSS and the politicians responsible for it, the HCJ ruling could have served as a watershed. Their response to the ruling should have been like the one of farmers forbidden to use slaves, or judges after legislators have prohibited them from sentencing to lashes, stoning or hanging: to accept the fact that methods of torture and ill-treatment are no longer at their disposal, and to find humane ways of achieving their goals. The security services of many democratic countries, among them those who deal with cruel terrorism, implemented this change decades ago, without detracting from their ability to fight various types of crime, including murderous terror.

But the GSS and those responsible for it did not manage to shake free of the concept that has been guiding them for decades – that the most effective way of eliciting information from an interrogee is by causing mental and physical pain, exhaustion and degradation.

It is disappointing that the HCJ ruling, while constituting an important step in the right direction, did not succeed in disposing of torture and ill-treatment in Israel once and for all in their appropriate place – the trash bin of history. The Supreme Court let stand the legal and ethical conception according to which an interrogator is authorized to consider torture, even if only in extreme situations, as a legitimate option. The court justices did not fully rise to the occasion, and failed to apply to Israeli law the position of international law, namely that torture and ill-treatment are an absolute evil – like slavery, genocide or the use of cruel means of warfare – which is neither permitted nor justified under any circumstances.

The Supreme Court also left more practical openings for the GSS – sleep deprivation and prolonged shackling – through which it continues to implement this same violent concept. The result is that the wall of defence erected by the court with the goal of protecting the basic rights of Palestinian interrogees has not proven itself to be sufficiently effective.

The following conclusions emerge from the study conducted by the Public Committee Against Torture in Israel two years after the HCJ ruling:

• The Public Committee Against Torture in Israel estimates, based on accumulated information in its possession, that each month, dozens of Palestinians interrogated by the GSS are exposed, to one extent or another, to methods of torture and ill-treatment. These include the shroud of isolation and disconnection from the outside world, as well as an assortment of methods used both in the interrogation rooms and in the isolation cell.

- Ill-treatment of Palestinian detainees begins with the denial of their right to contact with the outside world, and particularly with their lawyers and relatives (incommunicado detention) for days and weeks.
- The methods of torture and ill-treatment implemented in the interrogation rooms. Routine methods include sleep deprivation, shackling to a chair in painful positions, beating, slapping and kicking, threats, curses and insults. Special methods include bending the body in contorted and extremely painful positions; intentional tightening of handcuffs; treading on shackles; applying pressure to various body parts; shaking the interrogee's body in various ways; forcing the interrogee to squat ('qambaz').
- Methods of torture and ill-treatment used in the isolation cell include sleep deprivation; exposure to extreme heat and cold; continual exposure to artificial lights; detention in sub-human conditions.
- GSS interrogators are protected from external scrutiny, and from the possibility of criminal investigation and criminal charges, through the shroud of secrecy and isolation surrounding GSS interrogation facilities. Complaints by interrogees are investigated by a GSS agent (the 'official in charge of investigating interrogees' complaints') who questions, on behalf of the State Attorney's Office, both his interrogator colleagues and the detainee. Many of the detainees who have complained of torture and ill-treatment by GSS agents naturally do not cooperate with this GSS agent, who conducts an investigation without informing the detainee's attorney or the attorneys of the Public Committee Against Torture, and in their absence. This agent naturally tends, in any case, to prefer the version of his or her colleagues. As a result, not a single GSS interrogator has been criminally charged since the investigation of complaints against the GSS was transferred to the State Attorney's Office in 1994.

The picture emerging from this report is harsh and disappointing, particularly in light of the expectations raised by the HCJ ruling. It appears that despite the great achievement that this ruling constitutes, for the Public Committee Against Torture in Israel, and other organisations and entities that deal with the protection of human rights of detainees in Israel, a difficult and protracted struggle lies ahead.

The Public Committee Against Torture in Israel is concerned that in the heat of the struggle against acts of terror, which are totally condemnable themselves, Israel is opting for condemnable and manifestly illegal methods. The many years of widespread use of torture and ill-treatment against Palestinian detainees have not brought Israel peace and quiet – quite the opposite. It is time to try another path, the path of respecting human rights in general, and the rights of detainees under interrogation in particular.

This conclusion is just as sound after the dreadful terrorist attacks in the USA on 11 September 2001. Enlisting cruelty for the war against the cruel, or the use of terrorism in order to fight terrorism – whether through torture or through such means as targeting civilians and civilian infrastructure or collective punishment – are not only illegal and inefficient, they also constitute a victory for terrorist morality and the terrorist way.

10 The status of the Palestinian minority in Israel[31]

International Federation of Human Rights Leagues (FIDH)

History of the Arab population in Israel

On 29 November 1947 the General Assembly of the United Nations adopted a Partition Plan foreseeing the creation of two states, one Jewish and the other Arab. Jerusalem would be given a special status outside the sovereignty of either state. The Jewish authorities accepted this but the Arab states refused, considering it very unfair, as one-third of the population would be granted 60 per cent of the territory. The day after the declaration of the State of Israel on 14 May 1948, Israel was invaded by military troops from the Lebanon, Syria, Transjordan and Egypt. This first war came to an end with the successive Armistice agreements signed under the aegis of the UN in 1949 with Lebanon, Syria, Jordan and Egypt. In accordance with these agreements, at that time the Israeli territory extended over 20,000 square kilometres, almost four-fifths of the former Palestine under British mandatory rule. However no more than approximately 130,000 Arabs remained within Israeli borders, compared with 850,000 previously.

Recent historic studies, and especially those carried out by those we would call 'new Israeli historians' such as Benny Moris, Tom Segev and Ilan Pappe, have shown that their departure was largely caused by the attitude of the Israeli army, which acted with impunity (expulsions, harassment, massacres counted by Benny

31 Excerpt from *Investigative Mission. The Status of Israeli Arab Citizens. Foreigners Within: The Status of the Palestinian Minority in Israel*, July 2001.

Moris to number 80 between 1947 and the end of 1948, especially that of Deir Yacine; terrorising the population and inciting them to leave their land, and so on).

Today, Arabs living in Israel make up a population of around 1,050,000, a little less than 19 per cent of the population of the State of Israel, which is generally estimated at 6,100,000. The Arab population is mainly concentrated in three areas: Galilee in the north, a little triangle in the centre, and the Negev. Approximately 100,000 people live in mixed towns (Haïfa, Jaffa, Acre, Lod, Ramallah), half a million in rural towns, of which 135,000 are Bedouins living in the Negev and Galilee, and the rest of this population live in former villages which have now become towns, such as Tamra, Sakhanine and Taybe. Nazareth was the only remaining Arab town after 1948. Within this Arab population, the Druze number approximately 100,000, Christians 150,000, and the majority of 800,000 are Sunni Muslims.

The events of October 2000

Following a visit by Ariel Sharon on 28 September 2000 to Temple Mount – the Esplanade of Mosques for Muslims – and the brutal repression by the Israeli army of Palestinian demonstrators denouncing this visit as an act of provocation, on 30 September the Follow-Up Committee for Israeli Arab Citizens called for a general strike in all Arab towns on 1 October 2000, coinciding with the Jewish New Year, and for demonstrations 'to denounce the massacre' of Palestinians. The usual spiral of violence accompanied these demonstrations: stones thrown by demonstrators at police and Israeli border police, and their response by firing rubber bullets (in theory) and tear gas.

In total there were 13 deaths of Israeli Arabs, 700 injuries and 1,000 arrests. Analysis of the events in October 2000 leads to serious questions about the responsibility of the Israeli authorities, first of all with regard to the police. The brutality of the repression shows excessive use of force: in addition to provocative and discriminatory behaviour, the police forces resorted to using live rounds of bullets. It has been pointed out that in several towns when the police did not intervene, demonstrations took place and dispersed calmly. Furthermore, and in particular in Nazareth on 8 October 2000, one could question the strange passivity of the police forces during violence by Jewish extremists towards the Arab population, and the unilateral repression of the Arabs by the police on this same day.

[135]

Access to the political system

Article 25 of the International Covenant on Civil and Political Rights (ICCPR) states that without discrimination and unreasonable restriction, everybody should be able to 'take part in the conduct of public affairs, directly or through freely chosen representatives'. However, the Israeli political system excludes from electoral competition any grouping that may bring into question the Jewish nature of the State of Israel: that is, contest that the State of Israel is the 'Jewish state' (article 5 of the Political Parties Law; and article 7(a) of the Basic Law: Knesset). On several occasions Arab lists have been threatened with being unable to present candidates for election because it was suspected that their programme could lead to their contesting the State of Israel as the 'Jewish State'. According to Supreme Court jurisprudence – fixed in 1988 in the case of Ben Shalom *et al. v.* Central Elections Committee for the Twelfth Knesset *et al.* – if a political formation brings into question either the demographic composition of the State of Israel as a state with a Jewish majority population, or the preference given to Jews in the return to Israel, or even the existence of privileged links between the State of Israel and the Jewish diaspora all over the world, these three elements being the central elements of the definition of the Jewishness of the State of Israel, then this political formation may be excluded from the election. This jurisprudence in particular means that any discussion relating to the Law of Return is excluded from political debate, as is also debate on the return of the 1948 Palestinian refugees to Israel.

Cultural, religious and linguistic rights of the Arab minority

According to article 27 of the ICCPR:

> In those states in which ethnic, religious or linguistic minorities exist, persons belonging to such minorities shall not be denied the right, in community with the other members of their group, to enjoy their own culture, to profess and practise their own religion, or to use their own language.

Respecting this measure is particularly difficult in Israel because of the founding ideology of the State, Zionism, which grants it the vocation of being the national home for Jews all over the world. The Jewish nature of the Israeli state, a nature that represents not only its sociological composition but also, as stated earlier, the very foundation of the state, explains why on issues such as the calendar for holidays, religion or language, the Arab minority struggle to have their rights recognised.

Indirect discrimination

Even more worrying than open discrimination towards Israeli Arabs, which results from granting certain privileges to only Jewish citizens of Israel, is the indirect discrimination that they must undergo: that is, the disadvantages that stem from the general structures of Israeli society. This indirect discrimination is in fact more difficult to identify because of its very nature: it is present mostly in practice rather than in regulations. It can be attributed for the most part to the close link between the State of Israel and economic institutions, to the point where an observer noted that the Israeli economy did not really correspond to the rules of the market economy, the main decisions on an economic level being taken by government bodies – a characteristic that is of course to the detriment of the Arab minority.

The lack of funding for Arab local authorities

The fight against this discrimination, which is mainly situated in the socio-economic field, requires more than simply making laws conform with the demand for equality. Factual differences between the communities must be taken into account, by adopting programmes that aim to place the Arab minority in the situation it would have been in had there been no discrimination in the past. Furthermore, the fight requires investment which could be significant, as many of the disadvantages suffered by Israeli Arabs originate in the relatively small funds available to Arab local authorities for basic services for their residents, especially in areas such as primary and secondary education and basic health care.

This is the road that Prime Minister Ehud Barak's government chose to go down, albeit belatedly, when it announced at the end of October 2000 a development programme worth 4 billion Israeli shekels (ILS) (455 million euros) over four years. This is a considerable sum, which must however be put into perspective by taking three factors into account. First, this amount only compensates very partially for the structural inadequacy of investment in the development of Arab towns, and the suffering they have consequently felt for many years. For example, in the 2000 budget, despite 13 billion ILS being allocated to town councils, only 500 million ILS was given to Arab local authorities: approximately 4 per cent of the total, for local governments providing basic social services to, according to the lowest estimates, 12 per cent of the overall population.

Second, the needs of Arab local authorities were assessed in 1999 at 14 billion ILS, following the discussion begun in 1997 between Prime Minister Netanyahu's government and the National Committee of Chairs of Arab Local Authorities. Finally, this investment programme in the development of Arab local authorities is yet to be implemented, despite being announced by the new government formed by Ariel Sharon.

The findings of the FIDH mission should encourage progress in that direction. All the facts show that the Arab local authorities have the greatest needs in terms of development. Ten years ago, a study showed that Arab municipalities received only 2.3 per cent of the total budget allocated to local governments, while Arab towns represented 12 per cent of Israel's overall population. Per capita, the budget for Arab local authorities was then between 25 to 30 per cent of the average budget per capita for Jewish local authorities; the budget allocated to development is on average three times greater for Jewish local authorities than for Arab ones.

This situation has not greatly changed since. Therefore according to Sikkuy (the Association for the Advancement of Civic Equality, an Israeli association with Arab members, which receives large amounts of funding from the Jewish community), whereas 78 Arab local authorities out of 82 face socio-economic conditions termed 'very bad', only 29 out of the 183 Jewish ones do.

However, despite these facts, Arab local authorities have not been amongst the priority development areas in which successive Israeli governments have made their main investments. The Sikkuy association notes therefore that while the 18 communities with the highest unemployment (between 11.5 per cent and 27.5 per cent) are Arab communities, only one Arab community (Tel Sheva) has been chosen as a priority development area in the government's three-year development plan, which targets eleven communities for preferential treatment.

This phenomenon is not new. Since the beginnings of the state, Israeli government development policies have in reality operated systematic discrimination against Arab local authorities. A notable feature of the discrimination is that 'certain Arab areas, more underdeveloped economically than others in Israel, are excluded from the development zone'. This phenomenon had already been spectacularly brought to light by a report drafted in 1972 by an Arab sociologist, Sami Jerisi, commissioned by the Israeli Ministry for the Interior to examine the differences in treatment from which Arab local authorities suffered compared with Jewish ones. Although the results of this investigation were never officially published, the information that emerged made it possible to amply confirm, and put figures on, the structural discrimination suffered by the Arab people.

The lack of funding for Arab local authorities is increased because part of their funds, comprising the operational budget for the provision of local services (education, social work, help for those in need, public hygiene) derives from local taxes, which obviously generate less money because the socio-economic condition of the population is poor and it is rare to find companies based in these areas.

Mayor Shawki Khatib, who presides over the Yaffia local council, gave the FIDH mission examples from both Arab and Jewish areas of Nazareth, a town that includes his local authority area. Whereas in the Arab sector 88 per cent of local taxes are paid by individuals residing there (and 12 per cent by companies), in the Jewish sector these figures are 30 per cent (individuals) and 70 per cent (companies). These figures correspond with those provided by al-Haj and Rosenfeld in their 1990 study of Israel's Arab municipalities, where they reject the Israeli government's argument that the low level of social and economic development in Arab municipalities is due to a lower level of tax contributions by the inhabitants in these municipalities.

Using a memorandum on the financial situation of Arab municipalities presented to the Israeli government on 13 December 1985 by the National Committee of Chairs of Arab Local Authorities, these authors find that according to this Committee:

> The argument that Arabs do not pay taxes is groundless. Property taxes make up 18 per cent of the budget in the Jewish municipalities and 15 per cent in the Arab municipalities; but in reality 12 per cent of municipal income is collected in this manner in the Arab sector, compared with 11 per cent in the Jewish sector.

This does not therefore mean that residents in Arab municipalities pay less – that is, that they are in a situation of greater dependence on the state – but rather that the authorities have less money, given the relatively low average socio-economic status of the people living there. The fact that despite their great need, Arab municipalities have been systematically discriminated against in the formulation of municipal development policies does not mean that the backwardness in these municipalities is wholly due to this discrimination.

There are also reports of budget misuse on the part of Arab municipalities, which some FIDH speakers would attribute to local politicians being tempted to favor family solidarity over healthy management of public finances. It still remains that while discrimination is not the only explanation for the backwardness of the Arab people, it is the main reason for it, and for the difference in their socio-economic situation from the Jewish majority.

Only recently has discriminatory implementation of public development policies, to the detriment of Arab municipalities, been punishable by justice, and highly significantly so, in the field of education. However, this recent tendency is yet to be confirmed. We still lack sufficient distance from events to evaluate the consequences. However, what is needed, more than the acknowledgement of a ban on discrimination, as the facts of a case judged by the Supreme Court in July 2000 show, is the implementation of 'positive discrimination' programmes to compensate for underdevelopment in the Arab community in relation to the Jewish community, especially in education and also in developing infrastructure and public health facilities.

Access to employment within the civil service

The difficulties that the Arab minority faces when trying to gain work within the Israeli civil service can be corroborated by a few figures. Arab citizens in Israel account for 18.6 per cent of the overall population. However, they provide the following percentages of employees within the administrations of the ministries of:

- the Environment, 2.5 per cent (10 out of 400)
- Health, 6.3 per cent (1,731 out of 27,330)
- Domestic Security, 0.7 per cent (1 out of 150)
- Construction and Housing, 1 per cent (3 out of 300)

- Education, 4.4 per cent (118 out of 2,700)
- Agriculture and Rural Development, 4.2 per cent (60 out of 1,410)
- Science, Culture and Sports, 4.3 per cent (8 out of 185)
- Justice, 1.8 per cent (32 out of 1,797) (within the judiciary, 19 out of 426 judges are Israeli Arab citizens, that is, 4.5 per cent)
- Employment, 4.8 per cent (170 out of 3,525)
- Religious Affairs, 7 per cent (42 out of about 600)
- Home Affairs, 2.7 per cent (41 out of about 1,500)
- Transport, 0.9 per cent (6 out of 640)
- Tourism, 3.1 per cent (5 out of 160)
- Industry, Commerce and Trade, 0.76 per cent (4 out of 520)
- Communication and Media, 0 per cent (out of 180).

These figures bear even more witness to the discrimination Israeli Arab citizens suffer within the civil service if it is taken into consideration that they hold nearly a third of these posts because of their specific characteristics (that is, they are posts especially created for the provision of services to the Arab communities within the Departments of Finance, Religious Affairs, Education, Employment and Social Affairs).

Furthermore the situation within state-owned companies, numerous in Israel and important for the Israeli economy, is not much better for Arab citizens from an employment viewpoint. The National Electric Company, which had 13,000 employees in 1998, only employed six Arabs. According to the company's board this was because applicants were required to produce a security certificate; these are handed out with great parsimony to Arab citizens. Recently (in December 2000) a law was passed that is designed to ensure fair representation of Arab citizens on state-owned companies' boards of directors. Efforts have also been made to employ more Arab citizens within the civil service. These consist of a policy of outreach, for example publishing notices of competitive entry examinations in Arabic newspapers; they should be increased.

Access to employment within the private sector

The employment of Arab citizens within the private sector is characterised on the one hand by their de facto exclusion from a large number of companies. (According to a study published in 1998 half of the industrial companies had no Arab employees in their workforce.) On the other hand there is strong segregation, to the detriment of Arabs, who are over-represented in the secondary employment market (of precarious and less well-paid jobs), at the lowest level of the professional hierarchy, and in companies in declining industrial sectors.

Professional segregation increased from 1967 onwards, because of the entry into the Israeli labour market of numerous workers from the Occupied Territories of the West Bank and Gaza, leading to overall reductions in pay levels for Israeli Arabs. To discrimination in access to employment we must add discrimination in pay, partly caused by the professional segregation that Arab citizens suffer, but also comprising a separate form of discrimination. The average pay per hour of a Jewish woman is 28 per cent higher than that of an Arab woman, and 47 per cent of this difference cannot be explained by objective factors: that is to say, there is real inequality in payment for comparable jobs. The average pay per hour of a Jewish man is 33 per cent higher than that of an Arab man, and 41 per cent of this difference cannot be explained by objective factors.

If lack of funding for Arab municipalities constitutes one of the explanations for Arab citizens' low employment rates, making it even more difficult for them to acquire skills welcomed by employers, the lasting presence of anti-Arab racism is another explanation. Opinion polls indicate that a third of Jewish youths declare themselves to be racist or to hate Arabs; two-thirds are opposed to the granting of equal rights to Arabs, and would support the banning of Arab representatives from the Knesset.

Within the Jewish population in general, in 1994 60.1 per cent were opposed to any legislation forbidding discrimination against Arabs within the employment and labour sector; and 68.2 per cent of Jews declared that they would find it unacceptable to be under the authority of an Arab at their workplace.

The weakness of legal protection against these discriminations allows these attitudes to grow, in most cases unpunished. The decisions of the Supreme Court of Israel with regard to equality only constitute a partial solution. On the one hand, these decisions only impose non-discrimination on state organisms and not on individuals (such as financial backers and employers). No law offers guarantees against discrimination within the private sector, except where it concerns employment (covered by the existing equal employment opportunities law) and more recently, access to establishments open to the public. On the other hand, as they fail to raise the value of equality to a constitutional level, these decisions impose respect for the rule of nondiscrimination only when there is no legislative ruling that legalises a difference in treatment.

With regard to recruitment in the private sector, among the essential causes of the indirect discrimination Arabs suffer is the criterion that applicants must have completed their national service. This is even used for jobs for which no such requirement is relevant. Moreover, to our knowledge, authorities within the Enforcement Division of the Ministry of Labour and Social Affairs, who are in charge of monitoring the law on equal opportunities, have never taken steps to forbid the use of this criterion. It is however clear that this criterion is generally used only to exclude Arabs: the requirement of national service serves as a poor and partial mask for discrimination based on ethnic origin. This example is only one indication among many others of the lack of effort put into enforcement of the equal employment opportunities law by the Ministry of Labour and Social Affairs.

The land issue

Already a decisive issue in the Palestine of the British Mandate before the creation of the State of Israel, the distribution of land in Israel has always depended on demographic and strategic interests. Before 1948 the acquisition of land by Jews was considered a preparation for the creation of a national Jewish homeland in Palestine. After 1948, the close relationship between the sovereignty of the State of Israel and the control of Zionist institutions over the distribution of the land continued. Not only did the policy continue that only the Jewish population could use the land acquired by the Jews, in addition the creation of the State of Israel made available another instrument, which naturally had not been available to the Zionist movement under the British Mandate: confiscation by the state of land owned by private individuals. Overall, to the old aim of affirming Jewish presence in the land of Palestine in order to facilitate the establishment of the Jewish State of Israel were now added new aims. The management of owned land, largely guaranteed since the creation of Israel by state institutions, on the one hand fulfilled the needs of the Jewish immigrants benefiting from the Law of Return, and on the other helped to establish Jewish control over the largest possible amount of land, including those areas with a majority Arab population, such as Galilee and the Negev Desert.

This issue is pivotal to the relations between the ethnic communities within Israel. It is not by chance that the events surrounding the observance of 'Land Day', 30 March 1976, followed the government's decision to expropriate 20,000 *dunam* of land, including over 6,000 *dunam* belonging to Arabs, in order to ensure development in Galilee. This has been the most important issue for Israeli Arabs since the creation of Israel. What we are witnessing is a carefully orchestrated policy, coordinated at state level, to colonise the land in the interior of the state to the detriment of the remaining Arab population.

In Israel 93 per cent of the land is owned by the state, by the National Jewish Fund (Keren Kayemet Leisrael) or by the Development Authority; only 7 per cent of the land is privately owned (4.2 per cent by Arabs, 2.8 per cent by Jews). The management of land owned by the state is carried out by the Israel Land Authority (ILA) on behalf of the three bodies: the state itself (80 per cent), the Jewish National Fund (10 per cent) and the Development Authority (10 per cent).

This ownership system therefore gives a large role to state-owned properties. In virtue of the 1960 Basic Law: Israel Lands, land that is the property of the state, of the Jewish National Fund or of the Development Authority cannot be handed over to individuals as their full property. What we incorrectly define as land transfers are in reality transfers of long leases: for 49 years, or more rarely for 99 years.

The management of this property is influenced by various organisations linked to the Zionist movement, which existed before the founding of the State of Israel. It is here that we can see the source of the considerable discrimination that Arab citizens in Israel suffer with regard to access to land. This discrimination is also based on massive expropriation from Arabs residing in the mandated Palestine. In particular, this took legal form with the adoption of the Absentee Property Law in 1950.

This law declared as 'absentees' all the Palestinians who had left Israel during the war of 1948, including those who later returned to their villages, and even those who had migrated within the country, that is, Palestinians who remained within the frontiers of Israel (as set out on 19 May 1948), if the migration had been to areas occupied by enemy armed forces. According to the law (section 1), in effect the 'absentee' was usually a Palestinian who had 'left his ordinary place of residence in Palestine (a) for a place outside Palestine (before 1 September 1948) or (b) for a place in Palestine held at the time by forces that sought to prevent the establishing of the State of Israel, or that fought against it after its establishment'.

This is how the category of 'present absentees' emerged: that is, people expropriated of their lands because of internal migration during the war of 1948. More than 75,000 Arabs are estimated to have been legally expropriated of their lands in this way during the period that immediately followed the declaration of independence. Even if it is the most notable law facilitating land transfers to the benefit of the state after its founding, the 1950 Absentee Property Law has not been the only one contributing to this process. In 1953, the Land Acquisition (Validation of Acts and Compensation) Law set out that essentially all property that was certified to not be in possession of its legal owners, and that had been requisitioned either for security purposes, for military use, or for development purposes such as to establish Jewish settlements, could definitively be expropriated.

As is also underlined for example by Ian Lustick, this law allows *a posteriori* legalisation of the de facto expropriations that took place during the conflict of 1948 and the years that immediately followed. The current system of housing ownership, which grants enormous importance to the State of Israel and to organisations closely associated to the Zionist project, is derived from these laws, even more than from the systematic acquisition of land by Jews before the establishment of the State of Israel. As the FIDH's mission witnessed by visiting areas surrounding the village of Umm al-Fahm (an Arab town of 35,000 inhabitants), the land occupation policies conducted by the ILA, but also following the initiative of the Jewish Agency, its Settlement Department in particular, which the state entrusted with the task of developing infrastructure and building new housing areas for the Jewish population, consist of monopolising the largest perimeters possible, even with a limited number of Jews, in order to limit as much as possible the expansion of Arab localities. Consequently the Arab village of Umm al-Fahm cannot expand farther than its current perimeter despite the needs of its population. Meanwhile the surrounding Jewish population, literally spread out like a belt surrounding the village, consists of no more than 11,000 inhabitants.

It is only by keeping this context in mind that we can measure the potentially considerable importance of the Supreme Court's March 2000 decision regarding Katzir. This town had been established in 1982 on state-owned lands managed by the Jewish Agency. An Arab couple wanted to acquire some land in Katzir in order to build, and found their petition rejected because of the desire to preserve the Jewish nature of the Katzir settlement. The Supreme Court ruled that the State of Israel was not authorised to delegate to the Jewish Agency the distribution of the lands of Israel, and that this private organisation was guilty of discrimination against non-Jews.

The ruling constitutes first a prohibition, in principle, on public authorities treating citizens differently on the basis of their nationality or religion. Quoting the US Supreme Court's Brown *v.* Board of Education ruling, which put an end to the segregation of blacks in American schools in 1954, the Court classed as discrimination the simple fact of separating communities within specific perimeters ('separate is inherently unequal'). This discrimination is not excluded, according to the court, simply because while some areas are reserved for Jews, others are reserved for Arabs. The ruling confirms that what the state cannot do directly, that is, discriminate against the Arab minority in the country, neither can it do indirectly, by assigning the task of distributing land to a private organisation, in this case the Jewish Agency, which has a policy of distributing it in a discriminatory way. In conclusion, the court forbids the State of Israel to transfer the land through the Jewish Agency 'for the purpose of establishing a new municipality on the basis of discrimination between Jews and non-Jews'.

The Court specifically took care to clarify that its decision was based on particular circumstances, and that the ruling could not be interpreted as a condemnation of all forms of communities founded on membership of an ethnic or religious group. Nevertheless this clarification does not take anything from the importance of the principle that was affirmed: for the first time to our knowledge, the Supreme Court decided to penalise open discrimination against the Arabs, and rejected the argument that the difference of treatment presented in court could be justified by the Jewish nature of the State of Israel.

Even if it is too early to evaluate the consequences that may result from the decision, especially when its implementation still seems quite problematic one year later, this step forward deserves to be underlined.

Discrimination stemming from the advantages linked to completion of military service

Among the sources of discrimination that Arabs in Israel suffer, one results from the link certain regulations establish between the completion of national service within the Israeli Defence Force (IDF) and the granting of various social benefits. Even if Palestinians are formally supposed to do national service in the armed forces, with the exception of the Druzes (9 per cent of the Arab minority), they are discouraged from doing so by their own community, and the exemptions requested by them are automatically granted by the Israeli authorities. Even more than the Palestinians do not wish to serve in the armed forces of a state that, even if it is theirs, is still perceived with hostility by their community and by the exiled Palestinians with whom they feel solidarity, the Israeli army does not want to run any risk, or anything that could be perceived as a risk. It perceives a risk in having among its ranks people who could betray the cause of the state's defence, and introduce insubordination when the Israeli army is assuming national defence missions, such as law enforcement missions, especially in the Occupied Territories of the West Bank and the Gaza Strip.

The exemption of Palestinians from national service suits both parties; however, it also brings about two difficulties. First, because of this exemption, Arab citizens of Israel are in fact excluded from an institution that cements the national unity of their state. National service plays a central role in the life of the Israeli state, which has continually faced external threats since its creation. Men perform three years' service, and women one year. That Palestinians, with the exception of the Druze, are treated as exempt is clearly not helping the integration of the Arab minority within the state. Furthermore, army service constitutes an important period for young Israelis, and influences many later stages of their life; a clear example of this is the over-representation of people with a military career within the Israeli political class.

Second, linked to national service are a series of social benefits denied to the Palestinians because they do not carry it out. These benefits concern access to mortgages, partial payment of registration fees for some of the professional training courses organised by the state, grants and student accommodation. There is a specific law aiming at supporting the integration of former army recruits into civilian society (Absorption of Former Soldiers Law 1994). This law, which in particular consists of grants for finishing

[147]

secondary-level studies with a view to later access to university or professional training, as well as mortgages and loans for the creation of companies, cannot by definition benefit Palestinians, including those who may have the same needs.

Even if it does not specifically constitute discrimination to grant specific benefits to those who have completed their national service, in order to recompense the sacrifice made for the nation, one can fear that the extent of these benefits goes beyond what is justifiable on such grounds. When this is the case, the national service criterion only serves to legitimise a difference of treatment to the detriment of the Arabs, which has no reasonable or objective justification.

Suspicions surrounding the granting of benefits linked to the completion of national service stem from the fact that, until recently in any case, the exemption of *haredi* students of *yeshiva* (orthodox Jews) from the service for religious reasons did not deprive them of the benefits granted to those who had fulfilled their service. Is it conceivable to allow the Arab minority of Israelis, including those who have not completed national service (the majority of them), to benefit from advantages that require completion of this service? The Israeli population overall considers that the advantages linked to national service are legitimate. Nonetheless, as long as the State of Israel maintains conflictual relations with its Arab neighbours in the Middle East, and as long as the Israeli–Palestinian conflict is not resolved, it will remain inconceivable that Palestinians should be integrated into the forces of the Israeli army, despite former Prime Minister Ehud Barak's efforts. However a replacement national community service (proposed in 1998 by Prime Minister Binyamin Netanyahu) also received a particularly cold reception from representatives of the Arab minority. They view the imposition of any compulsory national service as unacceptable: what do they owe to a state that treats them as second-class citizens, upholding discriminatory practices that make them feel foreign in their own land? Even the proposal of a volunteer civilian service seems impossible: such a proposal could create splits within the Arab minority, when they should preserve their unity in order to obtain the lifting of the discrimination to which they consider they are subject. Even the idea of subordinating to the requirement that a form of service be rendered to the nation, the right of non-discrimination between Arabs and Jews (with regard to the benefits mentioned) is seen as highly questionable. Should not the recognition of equal rights precede the demand of a counterpart, instead of being subordinate to it? (...)

PART II

PALESTINE

11 Killings committed by Palestinians[32]

Amnesty International

(...) There is no army under the Palestinian Authority (PA), although there are at least eleven armed security forces, said to amount to 43,000 personnel in total. The attacks on Israelis by members of the Palestinian security forces appear to have been carried out as a result of the members' affiliation to an armed group rather than in response to any orders from above. Palestinian members of armed groups have attacked Israeli military personnel and civilians.

The main armed groups that have been involved in attacks on Israelis are Fatah, which is the dominant political force of the Palestine Liberation Organisation (PLO) and thus of the PA, and Hamas and Islamic Jihad, which have opposed the peace process and been highly critical of the PA.

Fatah has attacked Israelis anywhere in the Occupied Territories. According to statements of Fatah's General Secretary Marwan Barghouthi to Amnesty International delegates in July 2001, Fatah considers itself bound by the PLO's recognition of Israel and has not attacked Israelis in Israel.

Hamas and Islamic Jihad have killed Israeli civilians by bombs which have usually been placed within Israel. The Popular Front for the Liberation of Palestine and the Democratic Front for the Liberation of Palestine also carry out attacks. Other victims have been killed by new groups whose political organisation remains vague, or by individual Palestinians unconnected with armed groups.

Fatah is headed by Yasser Arafat, who also heads the PLO and was elected President of the PA in January 1996. The degree of control that President Arafat has over members of Fatah, or its military wing

---

32 Excerpt from *Israel/Occupied Territories/Palestinian Authority: Broken Lives – A Year of Intifada*, AI Index : MDE 15/083/2001, November 2001.

Tanzim, who shoot at Israeli soldiers or civilians is unclear, and alters according to the political situation at the time. For instance, a respite in the shootings and bombings (but not in riots) by Palestinians occurred, apparently as a result of pressure from President Arafat, during peace talks such as those at Taba in January 2001.

On other occasions President Arafat has called for the cessation of violence, but shooting or bomb attacks have continued. Attacks by Palestinian armed groups continued after a ceasefire declared by President Arafat on 17 September 2001. PA security services tried to stop the shooting but three PA security service stations in Rafah were reportedly set on fire by angry crowds.

Israel has frequently called on the PA to arrest individuals who are said to have ordered the killings of Israelis, and Israeli authorities have stated that their 'targeted killings' are a result of the failure of the PA to arrest the perpetrators of crimes. The Israeli government has frequently given President Arafat lists of 'terrorists' to arrest. On 27 July the PA responded by offering Israel a list, apparently of 50 settlers and others wanted for attacking Palestinians. On 5 August the Israeli Ministry of Defence publicly named seven people wanted for bomb attacks, and asked the PA to arrest them, declaring that the IDF would push ahead with its policy of killing 'the terrorists and their leaders'.

Later the PA arrested three alleged Hamas activists in Ramallah. However, the PA has signally failed to carry out proper investigations into the killings of Israelis by Palestinians. On the rare occasions when Palestinians have been arrested in connection with killings of Israelis, they have apparently been released within a few hours or days. No one is known to have been brought to justice for any of the killings.

The PA has an obligation to arrest and bring to justice those who are suspected of committing recognisably criminal offences, including those who may have ordered or committed unlawful killings. In the past the PA has arrested opponents and held them in detention without charge or fair trial. Between 1995 and 2000 the PA held scores of alleged opponents of the peace process, including suspected members of Hamas, Islamic Jihad and other opposition groups, in detention without charge or trial. Anyone who is arrested should be treated in accordance with international human rights standards, properly charged and brought promptly to trial in accordance with internationally recognised standards of fair trial.

Amnesty International condemns all attacks against Israeli civilians. Israeli settlers are civilians and should not be targeted unless they are threatening the lives of others. Attacks by Palestinian armed groups on civilians within Israel or the Occupied Territories are a gross abuse of the right to life.

Hamas and Islamic Jihad

Hamas and Islamic Jihad have frequently placed bombs in public places, usually within Israel, in order to kill and maim large numbers of Israeli civilians in a random manner. Both organisations have fostered a cult of martyrdom, and frequently use suicide bombers. In Gaza, Hamas has been accused of training children as young as nine to become suicide bombers, or at least to welcome the idea of suicide bombing. No child under 18 has yet been sent on a suicide mission.

Amnesty International has frequently raised its concerns, especially with Hamas, about the killing of civilians. The organisation has in recent years met leaders of Hamas in Jordan and in Gaza, and in July 2001 met Shaykh Ahmad Yassin, the founder and spiritual leader of Hamas, to express such concerns. Amnesty International stressed that the deliberate killing of civilians is never justified, and that the absolute prohibition on deliberate killing of civilians must be respected by armed groups as well as states.

Al-Fatah and Tanzim

Al-Fatah, Tanzim and other apparently allied armed groups have carried out a number of deliberate shootings at cars with Israeli number plates travelling along roads in the West Bank. These

---

Bomb attack on pizzeria

Sixteen people, including seven children, were killed and more than 100 injured in a suicide bombing on 9 August 2001 in the Sbarro pizza restaurant on Jaffa Road in Jerusalem. Those killed included five members of the same family. Mordechai and Tzira Schijveschuurder of Talmon settlement took five of their eight children for a day out in Jerusalem; they and three of the children, Ra'aya, aged 14, Avraham Yitzhak, aged four, and Hemda, aged two, were killed in the attack. The suicide bombing was carried out by a member of the 'Izz al-Din al-Qassam Brigades, the armed wing of Hamas.

---

[153]

The Dolphinarium bombing

A total of 21 people were killed and 84 injured when a Palestinian suicide bomber blew himself up among a group of young people waiting outside a disco near the Dolphinarium in Tel Aviv on 1 June 2001. Most of the victims were immigrants to Israel from the Commonwealth of Independent States; the youngest, Maria Tagilchev from Netanya, was 14. Two sisters, Yelina and Yulia Nemilov, aged 16 and 18, from Tel Aviv, were also killed. The suicide bombing was claimed by Hamas.

shootings target settlers. They frequently appear to be directed towards the car on the basis of its Israeli number plate, whether the occupants are Jewish men, women and children, or – since they may drive Israeli-registered cars – Palestinian citizens of Israel or residents of East Jerusalem. Fatah rarely claims direct responsibility for any individual killing, but does not deny the targeting of settlers in drive-by shootings.

In July 2001 Amnesty International delegates raised the deliberate killing of civilians with Marwan Barghouthi, member of the Palestinian Legislative Council and Secretary General of Fatah. Again, Amnesty International stated the prohibition under international law against killing any civilian, and stressed that settlers were considered as civilians under international law unless they were participating in an attack.

Sarah Blaustein and Esther Alban

Sarah Blaustein, aged 53, and Esther Alban, aged 20, both from Efrat settlement near Bethlehem, were killed on 29 May 2001 when the car they were driving in was targeted by gunfire from a passing car near Neve Daniel. A Palestinian group calling itself 'the Popular Army Front, Battalions of Return' claimed responsibility for the killings in a statement sent to Agence France-Presse (AFP). The group said the attack 'is in answer to the murders of officials from Fatah and a warning to the leaders of the settlements'. Four other people, including the husband and son of Sarah Blaustein, a US citizen, were wounded in the attack.

Ekaterina Weintraub

Ekaterina (Katya) Weintraub, aged 27, was killed and another woman, Yehudith Eliyahu, was seriously injured by shots fired from a car waiting by the side of the road at a roadside junction near Jenin on 28 June 2001. The two women were travelling in convoy from Ganim settlement in the West Bank The attack was claimed by an organisation calling itself al-Aqsa Brigades of Fatah, which said it was in retaliation for the assassination of Usama Jawabreh, an al-Fatah activist, in Nablus on 22 June 2001.

Killings committed by individuals

Many Israeli civilians have been killed by Palestinian individuals who may not have been connected with armed groups. The Israeli government has almost invariably reacted to such killings by carrying out reprisal raids against Palestinian targets; such reprisal raids are forbidden by the Fourth Geneva Convention (article 33). Although the PA has on many occasions condemned such killings, it has frequently failed to arrest and consistently failed to bring to justice those who have carried out the killings.

The death penalty

Since the beginning of the recent Intifada ten people have been sentenced to death and two executed after summary and unfair trials before the Higher State Security Court. Such trials have been summary. They take place before military judges and frequently only with state-appointed, military defence lawyers. There is no right of appeal. Sentences are subject only to ratification by President Arafat and may be carried out within hours or days of the trial.

Such unfair trials and executions without the right of appeal flagrantly breach the UN safeguards guaranteeing protection of the rights of those facing the death penalty:

> Capital punishment may only be carried out pursuant to a final judgement rendered by a competent court after legal process which gives all possible safeguards to ensure a fair trial, at least equal to those contained in article 14 [of the

Detained Israeli soldiers killed by crowd

On 12 October 2000 an angry Palestinian crowd in Ramallah killed two Israeli reservists, Yosef Avrahami and Vadim Norzhich, who were in the custody of the Palestinian police. The throwing of one reservist out of the window, followed by a youth waving bloodied hands at the crowd, was caught on film and televised worldwide.

Law enforcement officers have a duty to protect those in their custody. Article 1 of the Code of Conduct says that: 'Law enforcement officials shall at all times fulfil the duty imposed upon them by law, by serving the community and by protecting all persons against illegal acts.'

Amnesty International delegates who investigated the lynchings spoke to the head of the Ramallah police station and other members of the Palestinian police in the police station at the time. They said that the Palestinian police had tried to protect the lives of those in their custody by talking to the crowd, moving the reservists from room to room, and offering to disguise them by dressing them as police. The station head said he had tried to protect the reservists with his body but had been flung aside. The head of the Ramallah police told Amnesty International delegates that an investigation was being held into the killing. However, no report of any investigation has been made public and no arrests are known to have been carried out by the Palestinian police.

The Israeli authorities arrested at least ten individuals in connection with the killings, including at least one police officer said to have been inside Ramallah police station at the time. One of those arrested was reportedly beaten upon arrest; the then Minister of Justice, Yossi Beilin, announced the suspension of six policemen in connection with the beating.

ICCPR] including the right of anyone suspected of or charged with a crime for which capital punishment may be imposed to adequate legal assistance at all stages of the proceedings. Anyone sentenced to death shall have the right to appeal to a court of higher jurisdiction, and steps should be taken to ensure that such appeals shall become mandatory.

Amnesty International believes that all executions constitute violations of the right to life, and works for the worldwide abolition of the death penalty. The UN General Assembly has stated, in a resolution in December 1977, that: 'The main objective to be pursued in the field of capital punishment is that of progressively restricting the number of offences for which the death penalty may be imposed with a view to the desirability of abolishing this punishment'.

Extrajudicial executions

The extrajudicial executions allegedly carried out by the PA have not received the publicity of those carried out by Israel. This is partly because there appears to be a chain of command under which Israeli extrajudicial executions are carried out, whereas the level of command under which extrajudicial executions are carried out of alleged 'collaborators' and others is more obscure. Some extrajudicial executions are said to have been carried out by members of Palestinian security services; others by members of

---

Majdi Makkawi and 'Alan Bani 'Odeh

On 12 January 2001 the PA tried Majdi Makkawi, 28, before the Higher State Security Court in Gaza on charges of giving information to Israeli intelligence services that led to the killing of four Palestinians. Jamal 'Abd al-Razeq, a Fatah leader and nephew of Majdi Makkawi, had been extrajudicially executed by Israeli forces on 22 November 2000 together with three other people, including two bakery assistants who happened to be in a nearby taxi. Majdi Makkawi was arrested around 10 December 2000. He pleaded guilty in a summary trial, and was sentenced to death. At the time of the announcement of his arrest on 20 December and during his trial, crowds of Palestinians demonstrated, calling for his execution. Only one day after his trial Majdi Makkawi was executed by firing squad in Gaza Police Headquarters. On the same day 'Alan Bani 'Odeh was executed in Nablus prison. He was convicted of giving information used by Israeli security forces to extrajudicially execute Ibrahim Bani 'Odeh, his relative'. 'Alan Bani 'Odeh had been sentenced in Nablus Higher State Security Court on 7 December after a three-hour trial.

---

armed groups or individuals. The common factor is that the PA consistently fails to investigate these killings.

Since the beginning of the current Intifada at least 22 Palestinians suspected of 'collaboration' with the Israeli authorities have been killed or found dead in circumstances that suggest they were extrajudicially executed. Even when eyewitnesses have said they have seen the alleged killer, no investigations are known to have been carried out, and no one has been brought to justice. Amnesty International is concerned that the failure of the PA to bring to justice those alleged to have carried out these killings (who on some occasions are said to have been members of a Palestinian security service) may be interpreted as permission, if not encouragement, to individuals, including the security services, to commit extrajudicial executions. (...)

Ghial Sultan

On 17 December 2000 Ghial Sultan, aged 34, was killed outside his house in Hares village in the West Bank. According to eyewitnesses he was killed in the early afternoon by someone who walked up to him and shot him twice in the back of the head with no warning and no word spoken. The killer was reported to be a member of the Palestinian General Intelligence. The Palestinian authorities reportedly made no attempt to investigate this event, although the family urged them to do so.

---

12 Palestinian attacks on Israeli civilians[33]

Amnesty International

27 May 2002: Sinai Keinan, aged 18 months, and her grandmother Ruth Peled, 56, were killed when a suicide bomber blew himself up at the entrance to the Bravissimo café in Petah Tikva, Israel. Fifty other people were injured, many of them children. The al-Aqsa Martyrs Brigade claimed responsibility.

27 April 2002: three armed men attacked residents of Adora, an Israeli settlement in the West Bank. In the bedroom of one house a gunman killed five-year old Danielle Shefi as she hid under a bed and wounded her mother Shiri and her brothers Uriel, aged four and Eliad, aged two. Elsewhere in the settlement, they also killed three adults. 'Izz al-Din al-Qassam Brigades (the military wing of Hamas) claimed responsibility for what it described as a 'heroic and daring operation'.

29 March 2002: Tuvya Viesner, 79, from Tel Aviv and Michael Orlanski, 70, from Petah Tikva were stabbed to death while visiting relatives at the Israeli settlement of Netzarim in Gaza. Al-Quds Brigades, the military wing of Palestinian Islamic Jihad, claimed responsibility for what it described as a 'heroic and courageous assault'.

27 March 2002: Twenty-nine people – 27 of them civilians – were killed and 140 injured when an attacker exploded a bomb attached to himself in the dining room of a hotel in Netanya during a meal to celebrate the Jewish festival of Passover. Nineteen of the dead were aged over 70. The oldest, Chanah Rogan, was 90. 'Izz al-Din al-Qassam Brigades claimed responsibility.

---

33 Excerpt from *Israel/Occupied Territories/Palestinian Authority. Without Distinction: Attacks on Civilians by Palestinian Armed Groups*, AI Index: MDE 02/003/2002), July 2002.

27 January 2002: Pinhas Tokatli, aged 81, was killed and more than 100 people were injured when Wafa Idris exploded a bomb attached to herself in Jaffa Street, Jerusalem, an area of shops and restaurants. Wafa Idris was the first female Palestinian 'suicide bomber'. Al-Aqsa Martyrs Brigade claimed responsibility.

4 November 2001: Menashe Regev, 14 and Shoshana Ben-Yishai, 16, were killed by a gunman who shot at an Israeli bus in Jerusalem. Palestinian Islamic Jihad claimed responsibility.

These are just six of more than 130 attacks since 29 September 2000 in which civilians were killed by members of Palestinian armed groups and by Palestinian individuals who may not have been acting on behalf of a group. In many attacks, perpetrators deliberately targeted people, like five-year-old Danielle Shefi and 79-year-old Tuvya Viesner, knowing without any doubt that their victims were not members of the Israeli armed forces. Other perpetrators attacked large groups of people in a busy street, a bus, a café, a hotel or a market, knowing that many if not most of the victims would be civilians.

Amnesty International condemns unreservedly direct attacks on civilians as well as indiscriminate attacks, whatever the cause for which the perpetrators are fighting, whatever justification they give for their actions. The organisation has repeatedly condemned attacks on civilians in reports and statements, and in meetings and other communications with armed groups that have attacked civilians in Israel and the Occupied Territories and in countries around the world. Targeting civilians and being reckless as to their fate are contrary to fundamental principles of humanity which should apply in all circumstances at all times. These principles are reflected in international treaty law and in customary law (…).

Historical background

(…) In 1993, Israel and the Palestine Liberation Organisation (PLO) signed a Declaration of Principles (the 'Oslo Agreement') which envisaged a period during which Israel would gradually withdraw its forces and transfer some functions in parts of the West Bank and Gaza to an elected Palestinian Self-Government Authority. Negotiations on a permanent settlement were to be concluded by May 1999.

The Palestinian Authority was established in 1994 and was given certain responsibilities in designated areas of the Occupied

Territories. In the West Bank, three zones were defined. In Area A, in which 98 per cent of the Palestinian population in the West Bank lives, the Palestinian Authority was given responsibility for civil affairs and internal security, while Israel was responsible for external security. In Area B, the Palestinian Authority was given responsibility for civil affairs while Israel was given overriding responsibility for security. In Area C, Israel was given responsibility for both security control and civil affairs.

Israel and the Palestinian Authority have been unable to conclude a permanent peace agreement because of disagreements over key issues such as the respective territories of Israel and the proposed state of Palestine; the right to return of Palestinian refugees; the future of Jerusalem; and the future of Israeli settlements within the Occupied Territories. Alongside the collapse of the political process there has been a major increase in the incidence of violence, particularly since the start of the al-Aqsa Intifada (uprising) on 29 September 2000. In the seven years between the Oslo Agreement and the beginning of the al-Aqsa Intifada, approximately 385 Palestinians were killed by Israeli security forces and 262 Israelis (both civilians and security force personnel) were killed by Palestinian armed groups, individuals and security forces. Over 1,400 Palestinians and nearly 500 Israelis – including more than 350 civilians – have been killed in less than two years since the al-Aqsa Intifada began.

The first attack by a Palestinian armed group on a civilian target – a commuter bus – by a perpetrator who exploded a bomb attached to himself was in 1994. By September 2000 there had been 14 other attacks by 'suicide bombers' that caused civilian deaths. Since then, to 21 June 2002, there have been 27 lethal suicide bomb attacks on civilians. There have been reports of many other occasions when people who set out to kill failed: they wounded or missed their victims, blew themselves up, or were killed or arrested before they could attack.

The current situation

Among Palestinians and supporters of their cause, there is considerable support for armed resistance by Palestinians, aimed at ending the occupation of the territory occupied by Israel in 1967. Commonly, advocates express support for the use of violence by Palestinians against Israel in general terms, drawing no distinction between attacks against military objectives and against civilians.

[161]

In Palestinian media and in public displays, there has been considerable praise for those who have been killed in the course of attacking Israelis, even if the attacks were targeted against civilians. 'Suicide bombers' are commonly referred to as 'martyrs' and their actions as 'martyrdom operations'. Armed groups appear to find it relatively easy to recruit people prepared to kill themselves while committing attacks.

Palestinian armed groups and their supporters offer a variety of reasons for targeting Israeli civilians: that they are engaged in a war against an occupying power and that religion and international law permit the use of any means in resistance to occupation; that they are retaliating against Israel killing members of armed groups and Palestinians generally; that striking at civilians is the only way they can make an impact upon a powerful adversary; that Israelis generally or settlers in particular are not civilians.

The United Nations General Assembly has recognised the legitimacy of the struggle of peoples against colonial and alien domination or foreign occupation in the exercise of their right to self-determination and independence. However, international law requires the use of force to be in accordance with certain basic principles that apply in all situations. In particular, the parties involved in a conflict must always distinguish between civilians and people actively taking part in the hostilities, and must make every effort to protect civilians from harm.

Amnesty International has for many years documented and condemned violations of international human rights and humanitarian law by Israel directed against the Palestinian population of the Occupied Territories. They include unlawful killings; torture and ill-treatment; arbitrary detention; unfair trials; collective punishments such as punitive closures of areas and destruction of homes; extensive and wanton destruction of property; deportations; and discriminatory treatment compared with Israeli settlers. Most of these violations are grave breaches of the Fourth Geneva Convention and are therefore war crimes. Many have also been committed in a widespread and systematic manner, and in pursuit of government policy; such violations meet the definition of crimes against humanity under international law.

However, no violations by the Israeli government, no matter what their scale or gravity, justify the killing of Sinai Keinan, Danielle Shefi, Chanah Rogan or any other civilians. The obligation to protect civilians is absolute and cannot be set aside because Israel has failed to respect its obligations. The attacks against civilians by Palestinian armed groups are widespread, systematic and in pursuit of an explicit policy to attack civilians. They therefore constitute crimes against humanity under international law. They may also constitute war crimes, depending on the legal characterisation of the hostilities and interpretation of the status of Palestinian armed groups and fighters under international humanitarian law.

Many Palestinians who support armed resistance, as well as those who support non-violent action, believe that targeting civilians is morally and/or strategically wrong. A number have been outspokenly critical. But the critics have in general not been as open or prominent in public as advocates for armed attacks who support, condone or do not criticise attacks on civilians. As Palestinian political leader Dr Hanan 'Ashrawi has noted, Palestinians 'have remained silent or whispered in the privacy of closed-door discussions' about the morality and effectiveness of such attacks by armed groups, among other issues:

> Why and when did we allow a few from our midst to interpret Israeli military attacks on innocent Palestinian lives as licence to do the same to their civilians? Where are those voices and forces that should have stood up for the sanctity of innocent lives (ours and theirs), instead of allowing the horror of our own suffering to silence us?

In 1998, the ICRC surveyed public attitudes about the rules of armed conflict in 17 countries, including a number where there were current wars or recently ended wars. One of the sites studied was Israel and the Occupied Territories, and the findings of the study were bleak:

> A half-century of seemingly unremitting conflict in the Middle East has brought down the normative and behavioural barriers that are supposed to protect civilians and prisoners in war. Perhaps as no other place in the world, the conflict between Israelis and Palestinians, as well as the Arab states, has engaged entire societies and left the distinction between combatants and civilians in tatters. The consequences are evident in the depth of mobilisation in both societies, the scale of disruption and injury, the permissive attitudes towards the treatment of prisoners, and in the heightened willingness of all parties to put civilians at risk.

> The principle of separation between combatants and civilians during wartime has been all but demolished by 50 years of total engagement in conflict.(...) More so than in any other country studied by the ICRC, Israelis and Palestinians countenance attacks on civilians during wartime.

The research found that one of the key factors in the erosion of constraints by both Israelis and Palestinians was the perception that the other party did not respect limits. People on both sides took the view that if the other side broke the rules, retaliation was permissible.

The lesson of the ICRC's study is one that Amnesty International has drawn from in its work in the region and other conflict areas around the world: the cycle of violence can be contained and eventually broken only if all parties place respect for human rights at the heart of all efforts to achieve peace. A critical element of such respect is accountability: those who abuse human rights should be brought to justice.

> [Suicide bombings have] disfigured and debased the Palestinian struggle. All liberation movements in history have affirmed that their struggle is about life not about death. Why should ours be an exception? The sooner we educate our Zionist enemies and show that our resistance offers coexistence and peace, the less likely will they be able to kill us at will, and never refer to us except as terrorists.
>
> Professor Edward Said, May 2002

Terminology

Attacks against civilians. On the basis of international humanitarian law, in this report the term is used to describe:

- Attacks in which the direct object of the attack is the civilian population generally or individual civilians.
- Indiscriminate attacks. These include attacks that fail to distinguish between civilians/civilian objects and military objectives; and attacks that, though directed at a military target, cause disproportionate harm to civilians or civilian objects. Military objectives are combatants (members of the armed forces of a party to a conflict) as well as objects that by their nature, location, purpose or use make an effective contribution to military

action, and whose total or partial destruction, capture or neutralisation, in the circumstances ruling at the time, offers a definite military advantage.

'Terrorism'. This term is commonly used to describe violent acts by armed groups, particularly those in which civilians are targeted. Amnesty International does not use the term because it does not have an internationally agreed definition and in practice is used to describe quite different forms of conduct. States and commentators describe acts or political motivations that they oppose as 'terrorist', while rejecting the use of the term when it relates to activities or causes they support. This is commonly put as 'one person's terrorist is another person's freedom fighter'. The UN Special Rapporteur on terrorism has noted that 'the controversial issue of terrorism has (...) been approached from such different perspectives and in such different contexts that it has been impossible for the international community to arrive at a generally acceptable definition to this very day.' Recent attempts at the United Nations to finalise a comprehensive international convention on 'terrorism' stalled in part because of disagreements between governments about the definition.

An overview of attacks on civilians

> At 4 p.m. I went to eat something at the café. I only spent 15 minutes on the meal, and I went to the desk. I remember a potato fell on to the floor and I bent and then there was the explosion. I fell on my back. I regained consciousness after five minutes. I saw that I was burned all over my body and face. I looked to my right and left and saw many people lying on the ground. I can't remember being evacuated by the medical teams. For two weeks I was in intensive care. Such acts are not human acts, they have no fear of God.
> (Aviad Lasa, victim of a suicide bombing at the Netanya fruit and vegetable market, Israel on 19 May 2002. Three civilians were killed and 50 injured. Note of interview with Amnesty International.)

Palestinian armed groups and Palestinian individuals who may not have been acting on behalf of a group are estimated to have killed more than 350 civilians since 29 September 2000. The figure excludes the killing of around 30 Palestinians by Palestinian armed groups, individuals and Palestinian Authority forces because they were suspected of 'collaborating' with Israeli authorities.

The great majority of civilians were killed in direct or indiscriminate attacks on civilians and civilian objects (defined above): the perpetrator targeted someone who he or she knew was not a member of the armed forces, or attacked a group of people among whom there were clearly many civilians. Amnesty International examined reports of incidents in which civilians were killed between 29 September 2000 and 31 May 2002, and estimates that 128 of these involved attacks on civilians and civilian objects. A total of 338 civilians were killed in the attacks. An overview of these 128 attacks is provided below.

The victims

The youngest victim was Yehuda Shoham who was five months old when he was killed by a rock thrown through the windscreen of his family's car near the Israeli settlement of Shilo in the West Bank on 5 June 2001. Avia Malka was nine months old when she was killed by two men who shot and threw grenades at cars and pedestrians in Netanya on 9 March 2002. Shalhevet Pass was 10 months old when she was shot by a sniper on a hill opposite the entrance to Avraham Avinu Israeli settlement in Hebron on 26 March 2001. In total, twelve of the victims were aged nine or younger, and 49 others were under 18.

Sixty-four of the people killed were older than 60. The oldest was Chanah Rogan, aged 90, killed in the bombing of a hotel at the celebration of Passover on 27 March 2002. Of the civilians killed in the attacks, 123 were female and 225 were male. Among the victims were non-Jewish Israeli citizens and foreigners. They include:

- Suheil Adawi, 32, a Palestinian citizen of Israel. He was one of 15 people killed in a suicide bombing in the Matza restaurant in Haifa on 31 March 2002. Suheil Adawi worked as a waiter in the restaurant. The restaurant was run by members of his family, five of whom were wounded in the attack.
- Shahada Dadis, 30, a Palestinian resident of Beit Hanina in East Jerusalem. He was shot dead on 16 January 2002 while driving a rented commercial vehicle with Israeli licence plates in the West Bank. Shahada Dadis was a salesperson for a pharmaceutical company, and was travelling to Jenin for his company.

- Father Georgios Tsibouktzakis, a Greek Orthodox monk from the St George Monastery near Wadi Qalt in the West Bank. He was shot dead from a passing car while driving on the Jerusalem–Jericho road on 12 June 2001. His car had Israeli licence plates.

Eleven of the people killed were foreign workers or visitors. For example, Ling Chang Mai and Chai Siang Yang, workers from China, were among six civilians killed when a suicide bomber attacked people at a bus stop in Jerusalem on 12 April 2002.

The weapons

Twenty-five of the attacks against civilians were committed by people who had strapped explosives to themselves and died in the attacks. Suicide bombings were particularly lethal, claiming 184 victims. On six other occasions, civilians were killed by explosives that were planted or thrown.

Eighty-eight attacks involved shootings; six people were stabbed to death; one was beaten to death and one – Yehuda Shoham, whose killing is described above – was killed by a rock.

The places

The great majority of attacks on civilians (92) and most of the shootings (79) were in the Occupied Territories. While there were far fewer attacks within Israel (34), they claimed the majority of victims (210), reflecting the fact that 22 of the 25 highly lethal suicide bomb attacks occurred within Israel.

The perpetrators

Armed groups reportedly claimed responsibility for about half of the lethal attacks on civilians (65) of the 128 attacks surveyed by Amnesty International. Claims were commonly made in phone calls or faxed statements to the media and in messages posted on websites. Sometimes more than one group claimed an attack. The main groups involved were: 'Izz al-Din al-Qassam Brigades (Hamas) – 23; al-Aqsa Martyrs Brigade – 23; Palestinian Islamic Jihad – 11; and the Popular Front for the Liberation of Palestine (PFLP) – five. The following section provides a profile of these groups.

[167]

2ov

Palestinian armed groups

This section describes the main Palestinian armed groups that have claimed or been accused of responsibility for lethal attacks on Israeli civilians since 29 September 2000. Responsibility for some attacks has been made on behalf of other groups about which little is known. No one claimed responsibility on behalf of an armed group for many attacks; in some of these cases where perpetrators were caught or killed, it appears that they were acting on their own initiative.

The section sets out the views of various leaders or officials of the organisations to which armed groups belong and of groups themselves, as presented in personal and written communications with Amnesty International delegates, in documents published by the groups, and as reported by the media. The views of members of particular groups sometimes differ.

Fatah – Tanzim – al-Aqsa Martyrs Brigade

Fatah, headed by President Yasser Arafat, is a secular, nationalist organisation which is the dominant political force of the PLO and thus of the Palestinian Authority. It has a military wing called Tanzim. The al-Aqsa Martyrs Brigade was formed by Fatah members in late 2000 but – as described below – there are conflicting views as to whether this group is controlled by Fatah leaders.

Members of Fatah have attacked Israeli soldiers and civilians in the Occupied Territories. All the lethal attacks on civilians claimed by or attributed to Fatah (excluding those claimed by or attributed to the al-Aqsa Martyrs Brigade) have involved shootings, including shooting at occupants of cars with Israeli number plates travelling on roads in the West Bank. The occupants of the cars have included men, women and children, among them Palestinian citizens of Israel or residents of East Jerusalem. Fatah members may also have been involved in mortar attacks on settlements in Gaza and towns in southern Israel.

President Arafat has condemned attacks on civilians on a number of occasions, but it is uncertain whether his statements apply to attacks on all civilians throughout Israel and the Occupied Territories or only to attacks on civilians within Israel. A number of statements seem to cover all civilians, and President Arafat and other Palestinian Authority leaders have previously spoken out against attacks on settlers. However, President Arafat on 20 May 2002 presided over a meeting of Palestinian leaders who issued a statement urging 'our people and all our struggling forces to comply with its decision to refrain from carrying out any operation against Israeli civilians *inside Israel* [emphasis added] even if they were in reprisal for the crimes of the occupation against Palestinian civilians'. Fatah Secretary-General Marwan Barghouthi has stated to Amnesty International delegates that Fatah considers that Israelis in the West Bank and Gaza are not civilians because 'it is all an occupied country'. Similar statements have been reportedly made by other leaders: for example, the Palestinian Authority Minister of Social Affairs, Intisar al-Wazir, is cited as stating in a lecture at Sheikh Zayid Centre for Coordination in Abu Dhabi that 'martyrdom operations' inside the Palestinian territories occupied in 1967 are 'legitimate because they are meant to resist occupation'. Fatah's policy, as publicly displayed on its website, is that 'only when Israeli soldiers and Israeli settlers have sustained heavy casualties will the Israeli government decide it cannot, after all, afford the price of continuing the oppression of the Palestinian people'.

Al-Aqsa Martyrs Brigade claimed its first civilian victim in February 2001 – Lior Attiah, aged 23, was shot dead near the village of Jalame on the West Bank. Lior Attiah was from Afula and had gone to Jalame to pick up his car from a repair shop. Since the killing of Lior Attiah, al-Aqsa Martyrs Brigade is reported to have claimed responsibility for more than 20 lethal shooting and bombing attacks against civilians in the Occupied Territories and in Israel, about the same as the number claimed by Hamas. Attacks claimed by al-Aqsa Martyrs Brigade include:

- The gunman who shot dead three *yeshiva* (religious school) students – Netanel Riachi, 17, Gilad Siglitz, 14, and Avraham Siton, 18 – at Itamar settlement on the West Bank, on 28 May 2002.
- The suicide bomber who killed Ruth Peled and her 18-month-old granddaughter Sinai Keinan in Petah Tikva on 27 May 2002.
- The suicide bomber who detonated his bomb next to a group of women and their children waiting near a synagogue where their husbands/fathers were, in central Jerusalem on 2 March 2002. Ten people were killed, among them seven-month-old Ya'acov Avraham and his mother Tzofia Yaarit; 18-month-old Oriah Lian and her twelve-year-old brother, Lidor; Liran Nehmad, aged

three, her sister Shiraz, aged seven, and her parents Shlomo and
Gafnit Nehmad; and Shaul Nehmad, aged 15.

The Israeli government alleges that al-Aqsa Martyrs Brigade is
an integral part of Fatah and that President Arafat has been
'personally involved in the planning and execution of terror
attacks. He encouraged them ideologically, authorized them
financially and personally headed the Fatah al-Aqsa Brigades
organisation.'

President Arafat has denied the Israeli allegations. President
Arafat has also reportedly denied that al-Aqsa Martyrs Brigade is
involved in 'terrorism', and has stated that financial assistance
provided by the Palestinian Authority to its members was 'merely
providing help to people who lost their jobs because of the ongoing
struggle'.

Israel also alleges that Fatah Secretary-General Marwan Barghouthi has direct authority over the al-Aqsa Brigades. Israeli
authorities arrested Marwan Barghouthi on 14 April 2002 and
allege that he ordered numerous attacks against Israel, including
suicide bombings. At the time of writing he faced the possibility of
being tried before a military court, whose proceedings Amnesty
International considers do not comply with international fair trial
standards.

Al-Aqsa Martyrs Brigade members have given different
accounts about their links with Fatah, some indicating that the
group is an integral part of Fatah and obeys President Arafat's
orders, while others state that the group acts on its own initiative.

Hamas – 'Izz al-Din al-Qassam Brigades

'Hamas' is the Arabic acronym for Harakat al-Muqawamah al-
Islamiyya, 'the Islamic Resistance Movement'. It was formed in
1987 by Sheikh Ahmed Yassin, who resides in Gaza. Hamas
opposes recognition of Israel, stating in its mandate that 'Israel
will exist and will continue to exist until Islam will obliterate it'
and that 'Jihad for the Liberation of Palestine' is the duty of
every Muslim. However, Sheikh Ahmed Yassin is reported as
stating in May 2002 that he has 'in the past' offered a truce with
Israel if it withdrew from the territory it occupied following the
1967 war.

Hamas runs extensive educational, welfare and religious activities in the Occupied Territories, and has engaged in peaceful polit-

ical activity. It enjoys significant popular support. The military wing of Hamas is called the 'Izz al-Din al-Qassam Brigades.

Hamas claimed responsibility for the first suicide bomb attack on civilians in Israel, which killed five people on a bus in the Hadera bus station in 1994. It claimed responsibility for 23 attacks on civilians between 29 September 2000 and 31 May 2002. These include:

- A suicide bomber who attacked people in the Matza restaurant in Haifa on 31 March 2002. Fifteen civilians were killed.
- The gunman who killed Yael Ohana, aged 11 and her mother Miri Ohana, 50, in their house in Moshav Hamra, an Israeli settlement on the West Bank, on 6 February 2002.
- The suicide bomber who attacked people waiting to enter the Dolphinarium night club in Tel Aviv on 1 June 2001. Twenty of the 21 victims were civilians, and 10 were aged under 18: Maria Tagilchev, 14; Yael-Yulia Sklianek, Yevgeni Dorfman, Raisa Nimrovsky and Katherine Astaniyada-Talkir, all aged 15; Yulia Nelimov, Liana Sakiyan, Irina Nepomneschi and Anya Kazachkov, all aged 16; and Marina Berkovizki, aged 17.

Sheikh Ahmed Yassin and other Hamas representatives have given a number of justifications for killing Israeli civilians. Sheikh Ahmed Yassin told Amnesty International delegates in July 2001 that under international law 'we may defend ourselves against aggression by all means'. He also stated that Hamas was 'against' the killing of civilians, particularly women and children, but that it occurred 'by mistake or to implement an eye for an eye, a nose for a nose': that is, that it was legitimate as a form of reprisal. In his view, when Hamas killed Israeli children Israel was responsible, because by killing Palestinian children it provokes retaliation.

Sheikh Ahmed Yassin has told Amnesty International that Hamas is willing to stop attacks on Israeli civilians if Israel stops targeting Palestinian civilians. He has also reportedly suggested an internationally sponsored agreement similar to that between Israel and Hizbullah, in which the parties committed themselves not to attack civilians. Hamas official 'Abd al-'Aziz al-Rantisi has also described attacks on civilians as reprisals, stating in May 2002 for example that 'as long as Jews continue to slaughter Palestinians we will hit Haifa, Tel Aviv and Afula. If a Palestinian child is hit, we will hit back. This is the formula.'

Other Hamas officials are reported to have stated that 'martyr-dom operations' would continue because they are considered to be an effective and legitimate means of fighting the Israeli occupation. For example, when the Palestinian Authority condemned a suicide bombing that killed civilians in Israel in March 2002, Hamas spokesperson Mahmoud Zahhar stated that the Palestinian Author-ity's condemnation did not represent Palestinian and Arab opinion and would not dissuade Hamas from further actions. Mahmoud Zahhar claimed that according to Islamic scholars the attack was 'the highest degree of martyrdom' and 'nobody from the Palestin-ian side, especially from the resistance movement or even from the Arabic people, can condemn martyrdom operations justified by our scholars'.

Palestinian Islamic Jihad (Harakat al-Jihad al-Islami al-Filastini)

This was founded in 1979–80 by Fathi Shqaqi, 'Abd al-'Aziz 'Odeh and Bashir Musa, Palestinian students in Egypt. The organisation has a number of factions, of which the main one is that founded by Fathi Shqaqi, who was killed by unknown assailants in Malta in 1995. The stated aim of Palestinian Islamic Jihad is the creation of an Islamic Palestinian state and the destruction of Israel.

Since October 2001, Palestinian Islamic Jihad has claimed responsibility for a number of attacks on civilians, including:

- The suicide bomber who detonated a device on a bus in Afula central bus station on 5 March 2002, killing 85-year-old Maharatu Tanaga.
- The gunman who fired at a commuter bus in Jerusalem on 4 November 2001, killing 16-year-old Shoshana Ben-Yishai and 14-year-old Menashe Regev.
- The suicide bomber who attacked people in the Sbarro restau-rant in West Jerusalem on 9 August 2001, killing 16 civilians including two-year-old Hemda Schijveschuurder, Avraham Schijveschuurder, aged four, and six other children aged between eight and 16. Hamas also claimed this attack.

When Egyptian President Hosni Mubarak, Saudi Arabian Crown Prince Abdullah and Syrian President Bashar al-Assad issued a state-ment in May 2002 rejecting 'all forms of violence', Islamic Jihad leader Abdallah al-Shami reportedly responded that the organisation would 'stick to our resistance even if the whole world stands against it'.

Popular Front for the Liberation of Palestine (PFLP) – Abu 'Ali Mustafa Brigades

Founded in 1967 by George Habash, this is a group guided by 'Marxist interpretation and dialectical materialism'. Like Hamas and Islamic Jihad, its formal position is that it does not accept the existence of Israel in principle, though PFLP members with whom Amnesty International has spoken state that they would be prepared to accept a settlement of the conflict that involved recognition of Israel. The military wing of the PFLP is called the Abu 'Ali Mustafa Brigades, named after its Secretary-General who was killed by Israeli security forces who fired a missile into his office in Ramallah on 27 August 2001.

The first reported PFLP killing of a civilian in Israel since the start of the al-Aqsa Intifada was on 27 August 2001, after the killing of Abu 'Ali Mustafa, and claimed by the PFLP to be in retaliation. The victim was Meir Lixenberg, father of five children, who was shot while travelling in his car in the West Bank. On 17 October 2001, the PFLP assassinated Israeli Tourism Minister Rehavam Ze'evi and claimed that it had done so in retaliation for Israel killing Palestinians, including Abu 'Ali Mustafa.

The PFLP has claimed several other attacks, including:

- A suicide bombing in a pizzeria in Karnei Shomron, Israel on 16 February 2002, killing three civilians – Keren Shatzki, 14, Rachel Theler, 16, and Nehemia Amar.
- A suicide bombing in a Netanya market on 19 May 2002 that killed three civilians – Yosef Haviv, 70, Victor Tatrinov, 63, and Arkady Vieselman, 40. This attack was also claimed by Hamas.

Following the killing of Rehavam Ze'evi, the Palestinian National Security Council banned the military wing of the PFLP within the Occupied Territories. Israel demanded that the Palestinian Authority arrest those responsible and hand them over to Israel for trial. Five PFLP members, including its Secretary-General, Ahmed Sa'adat, were detained. They were subsequently held in President Arafat's compound along with him when he was put under siege by Israel in April 2002. On 24 April four of the men – Hamdi Qar'an, Bassel al-Asmar, Majdi al-Rimawi and 'Ahed Abu Ghalma – were convicted by a hastily convened Palestinian military 'field court' of charges relating to the killing of Rehavam Ze'evi. The proceedings fell far short of international fair trial standards.

[173]

Under a deal struck to end the siege, the men were detained in a Jericho prison with their detention monitored by officials from the USA and UK. Ahmed Sa'adat was also transferred to the Jericho prison and has not been charged or tried. In June 2002, the Palestinian High Court in Gaza ordered his release on the grounds that there was no evidence against him. However, the Palestinian Cabinet decided to continue to detain him, stating that 'not implementing the resolution (of the court) is due to the Israeli threats of assassinating Sa'adat as there was an overt announcement to that by Sharon's spokesman'.

The Palestinian Authority should respect the court's decision and release Ahmed Sa'adat from detention unless he is charged and brought to trial on recognisable criminal charges within a reasonable period. Amnesty International has also called on Israel to publicly guarantee that Ahmad Sa'adat will not be subjected to any extrajudicial measures, including assassination.

There have been conflicting reports about the PFLP's reaction to recent efforts by President Arafat and leaders of Arab countries to curb attacks on civilians. According to one account, the PFLP joined Hamas and the Palestinian Islamic Jihad in dismissing the recent rejection of 'all forms of violence' by President Mubarak, Crown Prince Abdullah and President al-Assad, stating that 'our legitimate and just struggle will continue until peace is achieved in Palestine with the establishment of an independent and sovereign state'. However *Al-Hayat* has reported that a meeting of leaders of Palestinian organisations split over the issue of 'martyrdom' operations – the representatives of the PFLP and other 'left-wing organisations' were said to have opposed further such attacks, while Hamas and Islamic Jihad representatives remained committed to 'continue the resistance in all its forms'.

13 Shortcomings of the Palestinian justice system[34]

Human Rights Watch

Many of the human rights abuses described in this report have their origin in fundamental shortcomings of the Palestinian justice system. The Palestinian Authority (PA) executive – the president, ministers, the police and the range of different security forces – has systematically undermined the authority and independence of the judiciary, the law and legal remedies. The separation of powers is not respected. By weakening the ability of the judiciary to hold the executive accountable, the executive has permitted officials to commit serious human rights abuses, including torture, unlawful killings, and prolonged arbitrary detention, with impunity.

A detainee who is arbitrarily detained can complain to the attorney general and petition the High Court to be released. However, the security forces systematically ignore orders of the High Court to release detainees who are being held arbitrarily. Although it is a criminal offence not to follow such court orders, no member of the security forces or other official has been prosecuted or convicted for such abuses. Despite his obligations under the law, the attorney general rarely intervenes when detainees complain of arbitrary detention or mistreatment, and in practice has little authority over the security forces, especially in relation to alleged collaborators and Islamists in detention. The institution of the attorney general has been weakened further by the creation in November 1999 of the post of state security attorney general.

Direct interference by the executive is further undermining the independence of the judiciary. On at least two occasions in 1996

34 Excerpt from *Justice Undermined: Balancing Security and Human Rights in the Palestinian Justice System*, November 2000.

and 1998, judges were removed without good cause. In June 2000, President Arafat established the long-awaited High Judicial Council, which has responsibility for appointing, promoting, disciplining and training judges. Yet in September 2001 the security forces arrested a judge allegedly for facilitating the sale of land to Israelis, ignoring the authority of the High Judicial Council to sanction the arrest of a judge.

President Arafat has still not ratified several laws passed by the Palestinian Legislative Council (PLC) that are essential for unifying and updating the laws throughout the territory under the administration of the PA and establishing the rights of all persons in the PA areas. These keylaws are the Draft Palestinian Basic Law (passed by the PLC in October 1997), the Draft Judicial Authority law (passed in November 1998), the Draft Ordinary Courts Law (passed in May 2000), and the Draft Penal Code (passed in June 2000).

At least ten different security forces operate in the PA. They tend to perform as autonomous units with ill-defined, overlapping and poorly coordinated functions. With little accountability, they often ignore the judicial system and the laws governing their actions. The three security forces most frequently mentioned in this report are the Military Intelligence Service (MIS or Istikhbarat), the General Intelligence Service (GIS or Mukhabarat), and the Preventive Security Service (PSS or al-Amnal-Wiqa'i).

The Palestinian justice system was weak and politicised after operating from 1967 until 1994 under Israeli military administration, which did not encourage an independent judiciary and neglected its physical infrastructure. Palestinian courts did not handle cases related to security or political matters during the period of Israeli military administration. Thus, the period from the inception of the PA in 1994 represents the first time a local Palestinian legal system has been required to deal with political or security cases since 1948.

The justice system has been further damaged by the PA's failure to give sufficient authority, respect, and financial and other resources to the judiciary. The system is plagued by an insufficient number of judges, and a lack of properly qualified and trained judges, prosecutors, lawyers, and court officials. The inadequate budget provided by the PA for the judiciary has meant poor salaries that encourage corruption, and result in further deterioration of buildings and infrastructure.

The fragile Palestinian justice system has been battered further by Israeli responses to the current Intifada. The policies of closures, blockades and other restrictions on freedom of movement have brought chaos to the day-to-day functioning of the courts. Judges, lawyers and witnesses have found it difficult or impossible to reach court buildings. Human Rights Watch has also noted instances of Israeli harassment of Palestinian human rights lawyers, which have affected their ability to represent and reach clients.

Over the past year, several police, security, and civil defence installations – including prisons and detention centers – have been damaged by Israeli shelling or air strikes, often carried out in reprisal for attacks on Israelis by armed Palestinians, for which Israel holds the PA responsible. While Israel has called on the PA to imprison individuals involved in the planning and carrying out of attacks on Israelis, such reprisal attacks on the installations of the very organs that should be conducting these arrests appear to undermine that outcome. PA officials have complained that such attacks are compromising their ability to maintain law and order, and have further cited the threat to the lives of detainees from such attacks as a reason for releasing large numbers of detainees.

Unjustified arrests and detention

Human Rights Watch estimates that, as of September 2001, the PA was holding more than 450 Palestinians without charge or trial, the majority of them for allegedly being informants for Israeli security forces, but some for alleged involvement in the sale of Palestinian land to Israelis. This report examines in particular PA administration of justice as it pertains to these detainees.

These detainees, like many activists detained before them, regularly experience violations of their internationally-recognised human rights. Palestinian security forces sometimes arrest alleged collaborators arbitrarily, without sufficient evidence, acting on rumours and popular denunciations. Detainees are commonly arrested without a warrant and not told the reasons for the arrest; their families are not informed of their whereabouts; and while under interrogation the suspects are denied access to lawyers and independent doctors. They are commonly not brought before a judge within 24 or 48 hours, as required by Palestinian law. In many cases extensions in police custody are not authorised, as required, by the attorney general. Once arrested, they can spend months in detention without charge or trial, and without judicial supervision or an effective remedy to secure their release, at risk of abuse by the security forces that hold them.

On October 31 2001 the PA entered a new phase by issuing administrative detention orders placing seven alleged members of Islamic Jihad and Hamas in untried detention, without charge, for periods of six months to one year.

Persistence of torture

Those detainees who undergo interrogation by Palestinian security forces are often tortured, especially if they are suspected collaborators and particularly if they are held by the MIS, the GIS or the PSS. They are generally not physically ill-treated after interrogation ends, when they are usually transferred to a prison. The techniques of torture include *shabah* (prolonged sitting or standing in painful positions), *falaqa* (beating on the soles of the feet), beating, punching and kicking, suspending from wrists, and threats of death. Five Palestinians are known to have died in police or security force custody since the current Intifada began, at least three in circumstances that suggest torture may have contributed to their death. This brings to 28 the number of detainees known to have died in custody since the PA was established in 1994.

At least five factors encourage the torture of detainees under interrogation. First, detainees are routinely denied access to the outside world and the protection this brings while they are under interrogation. Second, prosecutors in the State Security Courts rely heavily on uncorroborated, signed confessions as the only or primary evidence, so there is intense pressure on the security forces to extract information from suspects. Third, perpetrators enjoy impunity. Torture allegations are usually dealt with by individual security forces as a confidential and internal disciplinary matter, a practice that is inadequate as an effective deterrent. Fourth, the absence of clear instructions by security force commanders and proper training of all security forces personnel has impeded the development of a culture of respect for the human dignity of all detainees. Finally, there exists a general public attitude that alleged collaborators deserve whatever treatment they receive by way of punishment, exacting revenge and deterring others.

Grossly unfair trials

The State Security Court, a special tribunal whose procedures do not comply with international fair trial standards, has displaced and undermined the ordinary courts. Established by presidential decree in 1995, with the strong encouragement of the USA and Israel, the court is neither independent nor impartial. The president convenes the court on a case by case basis. He or she can decide which cases are referred to it, and appoint and dismiss its judges at will. The ordinary courts have been further undermined and marginalised as the president has transferred to the court jurisdiction over an increasing number of crimes, many of which have little to do with national security.

Since the current Intifada began, 16 defendants have been tried in the Higher State Security Court or military court as informants for Israeli security forces. Fifteen have been convicted. Eleven of the 15 were sentenced to death, and two executions have been carried out.

Although the authorities have rectified some of the abuses of trial procedures prevalent when the court was established, the trials are still inherently and grossly unfair. Many are held in a highly charged atmosphere which compromises the right of defendants to be presumed innocent until proven guilty. Some hearings seem to have been convened hastily in response to Israeli attacks and to assuage public anger. Most trials last only a few hours. Most defendants who deny the charges against them are convicted solely or principally on their uncorroborated signed confessions, obtained while they were held in incommunicado detention, and which they often retract in court. The court has consistently failed to investigate adequately defendants' allegations that their confessions were extracted under torture. In violation of international standards and usual procedures in Palestinian laws, those convicted by the State Security Court have no right of appeal to a higher court.

Except in rare cases, the accused are defended by court-appointed counsel who are not practising lawyers, but serving members of the security forces. They usually say little on behalf of their client, fail to present a proper defence, and sometimes use language showing they consider their client to be guilty. Little advance notice of a trial is given, usually only a day. Defence lawyers sometimes have a few minutes, or in some cases 24 hours, to prepare their defence. Some court-appointed defence lawyers have tried to challenge evidence and present elements of a defence, but they have usually been blocked by court rulings. For example, the court invariably rejects requests for adjournments to prepare a defence.

Murders of suspected collaborators

Since this Intifada began Human Rights Watch estimates that at least 30 Palestinians, mostly alleged or suspected collaborators, have been shot or stabbed to death by unknown attackers in execution-style killings. The real total may be higher. In one town alone, Tulkarem, a human rights fieldworker told Human Rights Watch there had been eleven such vigilante killings since September 2000.

With no semblance of due process, completely outside the justice system, some killings appear to have been motivated by personal grievances. Others have resulted in the mistaken killing of the wrong person. In many cases a clandestine group has claimed responsibility and denounces the victim as a collaborator. While President Arafat and other senior PA officials have condemned the killing of alleged collaborators, investigations by PA security forces have been perfunctory and not a single perpetrator has been brought to justice.

14 The right to free expression in Palestine[35]

Palestinian Centre for Human Rights

This is our second report of this kind, which aims at highlighting the exercise of the right to free expression and the right to peaceful assembly under the Palestinian Authority (PA) during the period of 1 January 1999 to 30 April 2000. In September, the Palestinian Centre for Human Rights (PCHR) published its first report studying the period from May 1994 to the end of December 1998 in the Gaza Strip. In an attempt to extend the scope of work, this report includes a review of the status of exercise of these rights in the West Bank in addition to the Gaza Strip. Thus, this report essentially relies on the observation and documentation of the Field Work Unit of PCHR, and the organisations and institutions of human rights working in the West Bank for cases in the West Bank.

During the period under study, the PA continued to impose restrictions on free expression and press, and took several measures to restrict citizens' right to express their viewpoints, and to receive information. It also arrested several citizens on the basis of their opinions or political backgrounds. In addition, it imposed restrictions on the work of the press, arrested or warned several journalists for covering certain events, and closed several press institutions for publishing certain news items. During the period under study, the PA took several measures that limit citizens' right to peaceful assembly.

Attacks on freedom of expression

Palestinian Authority measures against press freedom

This part of the report reviews the most flagrant violations by the PA of citizens' rights to a free press and free expression. The period

---

35 *The Right to Free Expression and the Right to Peaceful Assembly: The Case of the West Bank and Gaza Strip (January 1, 1999–April 30, 2000).*

of study witnessed attempts by the State Information Service to intervene in the jurisdiction of the Ministry of Information through declaring its intention to issue special cards for journalists, and considering the work of any reporter or journalist who did not apply for such a card illegal.

This contradicts the Press Law of 1995, which asserts that the Ministry of Information is the official body mandated to regulate the work of reporters and journalists with regard to their obtaining accreditation, getting press cards, and office licensing. Because the Ministry of Information rejected the declaration, and the Journalists' Union also contested it, it was annulled without being put into effect. On the ground, Palestinian security services continued measures that aimed at limiting the freedom of journalists.

Interrogation, detention and arrests of journalists

The period under study (1 January 1999 to 30 April 2000) witnessed several cases in which journalists were detained or arrested for covering certain events. On 11 March 1999 the Criminal Investigation Unit in its headquarter in Rafah arrested nine journalists and confiscated their photographic films, for trying to cover bloody clashes in the town between Palestinian security forces and citizens, in the aftermath of the trial of three persons accused of killing Captain Refa't Joudeh. The journalists arrested were Sawah Abu Seif, a Reuters TV photographer; Ahmed Jadallah, a Reuters photographer; Shams Eddeen Atallah, a Reuters photographer; Sami Ziada, a JCM photographer; Husam al-Titi, an APC sound technician; Adel Muhanna, an Associated Press technical photographer; Fayez Nour Eddin, an AFP photographer; Mohammad al-Jahjouh, a Mayadeen Institution photographer; and Zakaria Talmas, of German television and then responsible for the journalists in Gaza.

On 22 May 1999 the Political Investigation Unit of the Palestinian police arrested Dr Ghazi Hamad, editor of *Al-Ressala* (the newspaper of the Islamic National Salvation Party), after the newspaper published two news items on 20 May 1999. The first item concerned Ayman Mohammad Abdelqader al-Amassi, who was moved to Shefa' hospital by the Gaza Criminal Investigation Unit after being severely tortured. The second was about the tension between Fatah and the PNA after a Fatah leader was insulted by a member of the PNA. Dr Hamad was released in the evening of 22 May. On the following day, 23 May, the Criminal Investigation Unit arrested Wissam Afifa, journalist, and Salah al-Bardaweel, editor-in-chief, both of *Al-Ressala,* for the same reason. The two were released the following day, 24 May. Palestinian police then rearrested Ghazi Hamad and arrested a trainee journalist, Hussam Ba'loosheh. The two were interrogated over an interview Ba'loosheh had had with Attorney General Zuhair al-Sourani on the status of the judiciary system in the PA areas (published in *Al-Ressala* on 12 August 1999, issue no. 117) and were accused of mis-stating al-Sourani's statements in the interview.

On 15 September 1999 journalist Maher Disouqi, of the Arab Cultural House in Ramallah, was arrested by a force of the Preventive Security Service. It was commonly believed that the arrest was prompted by his television interviews with families of prisoners in PA jails on Jerusalem Educational TV. The families had criticised the PA. Disouqi was released on 4 October 1999.

On 28 October 1999 the Criminal Investigation Unit arrested two journalists, one of them working for *Al-Hayat,* the other a correspondent for *Al-Sharq al-Awsat* (published in London), and a photographer for *Al-Ressala.* The former was detained for one day at the office of Brigadier-General Talal Abu Zeid, chief of the Criminal Investigation Unit, while the latter was detained in the prison of the Criminal Investigation Unit in Gaza. The two were interrogated on a news item published in *Al-Sharq al-Awsat* on the extradition by Israeli police to the PA of four Palestinian officers who were suspected of immoral practices inside Israel.

On 29 October 1999 Fathi Sabbah, a journalist for *Al-Ayyam* newspaper and a correspondent for *Al-Sharq al-Awsat* (the London paper mentioned above), was summoned by phone by the chief of political security to the Criminal Investigation Unit. He was interrogated on the same subject. On the same day, a force of the Palestinian police raided the office of the Jazeera Satellite Channel in Ramallah in the West Bank, and took its manager, journalist Wael Abu Daqqa, to the city's police station. His interrogation lasted three hours. Then he was released on bail, on the condition that he return so the interrogation could be completed. In a statement issued by the Journalists' Union on the same day, the union stated that arresting journalists was harmful to a free press, and limited journalists' abilities to carry out their professional and national duties. The union also called upon President Arafat to intervene to release detained journalists. In the first official comment from police on the arrest of these journalists, Maj.-Gen. Ghazi El-Jabali, Chief of Police, stated on the same day that the journalists had been summoned, not arrested. He added that these summons were part of a police investigation into the source that had disseminated fallacious news aimed at discrediting the PNA.

On 4 April 2000 Emad El-Efranji, manager of the al-Watan Press Office, was summoned by the State Security Prosecution, together with a correspondent for the *Al-Quds* newspaper, because of a news item in *Al-Quds* expressing concern about a decision taken by the Palestinian High Court of Justice to release Emad El-Amassi.

Physical attacks on journalists

Numerous cases of aggression towards journalists carrying out their duties by the Palestinian Security Services (PSS) were noted during the period of study. On 21 December 1999 journalist Mohammad Mousa Atia Manasra was assaulted by a force of the Preventive Security Service for criticising the PSS during a television programme on Bethlehem TV.

In addition, some aggression against journalists was shown by civilians. On 30 September 1999 Alla' Saftawi, editor-in-chief of *Al-l Weekly*, was threatened by members of the al-Khodary family because of his article, published in the paper that day, on the crisis over educational fees at al-Azhar University in Gaza.

On 24 November 1999 dozens of youths, including a number of students from the Islamic University of Gaza, assaulted students from the Journalism and Media Department and injured some of them. This took place after two of the students had written an article about begging in the *Voice of the University* magazine, published by the department on 23 November.

The failure of the PA to take strict deterrent measures against those who are involved in such assaults is both astonishing and to be condemned. It has negative consequences for those carrying out the trade of journalism. Today the work of journalists has become a victim not only of the PA and its measures, but also of some other social forces. The restrictions imposed on journalists carrying out their work have become heavier and heavier. At the same time a freely operating press can contribute to the establishment of a healthy civil society.

Closure of licensed media

According to the Field Work Unit of the PCHR, the period under study witnessed one case in which a licensed press institution was closed. On 27 April 1999 *Al-Ressala*, the newspaper of the Islamic

National Salvation Party, was closed *sine die* by a force of the Bureau of Investigation – Political Security Branch of Gaza. Our enquiries suggest that this was done because the leadership of the party had refused to participate in sessions the Palestinian Central Council had convened to discuss the issue of declaring a immediate Palestinian state. The party made contacts with officials of the executive, in an attempt to reopen the newspaper. These efforts were successful: the PNA permitted the paper's offices to reopen a few hours after they had been closed.

Measures of the PA against the right to free expression of political beliefs

Assaults, detentions or arrests of citizens on the grounds of factional affiliation

During the period studied the Palestinian security forces continued to arrest citizens because of their political affiliations. On 4 March 1999 Palestinian security forces pursued an arrest campaign against 14 leaders and members of the Islamic National Salvation Party, because of a public statement issued on 2 March 1999, criticising the formation of a 'state security court' to prosecute those accused of killing Captain Refa't Joudeh in February that year. The statement said that the party considered the court to be illegal and in contravention of international law and human rights conventions. The 14 detainees were released on 7 March.

On 13 March 1999 members of the General Intelligence Service arrested Ahmed Mohammad Nemer Hamdan of Khaniounis, a Hamas activist in the Gaza Strip, for delivering a sermon at al-Huda Mosque in Rafah, in which he criticised the Palestinian security forces for firing on citizens during the clashes in the town in the aftermath of the trial of those accused of killing Captain Joudeh. On 6 August 1999 the Bureau of Investigation of Palestinian police arrested Ahmed Mohammad Nemer Hamdan, Isamil Abu Shanab and Dr Abdelaziz al-Rantisi, because of their involvement with Hamas.

On 17 August 1999 'Special Bureau' operatives arrested Sami Noufal, member of the political office and secretary of the Islamic National Salvation Party. He was severely tortured before he was released on 24 August.

On 16 January 2000 the General Intelligence Service arrested a resident of Zawaideh suspected of being a member of the Islamic opposition, and writing wall slogans demanding that the PA release political detainees. He was released on 18 January.

Between 2 and 7 February 2000, the GIS in Rafah summoned six students, activists of the Islamic bloc in the town, and interrogated them on the activities of the bloc in Beer Essaba' secondary school, Rafah, and the Islamic University in Gaza. They were also questioned about a statement signed by 'Giants of Islam', and distributed in Rafah, accusing an official of the PA of financial and administrative corruption.

On 18 April 2000 the Bureau of Investigation arrested Yehia Mousa, secretary-general of the Islamic National Salvation Party and a lecturer at the Islamic University of Gaza, for distributing a statement by the party about various events at the university.

These examples make it clear that the period under study witnessed several cases of arrest, detention and summons of citizens by the PA on the basis of their factional allegiance. However, restrictions of the freedom of expression and political opinion also affect those who are not members of a formal political grouping.

Assaults, detentions or arrests of citizens on non-factional political grounds

The period under study witnessed several cases of arrest on non-factional political grounds. The first case was on 14 June 1999, when six residents of the al-Bureij refugee camp were arrested by the Palestinian Bureau of Investigation, for distributing a statement, signed by 'Madmen of Gaza', accusing some officials of the PNA of financial and administrative corruption. On 19 June another resident was arrested on the same grounds.

On 10 July 1999 the GIS summoned Salah Eddin al-Ghandour and Tawfiq Khamis Abu Zoureiq, residents of Nuseirat, and interrogated them about those who delivered sermons at al-Rahman Mosque in the camp.

On 27 July 1999, Zaki Abdelhamid Fadel, resident of al-Bureij, was arrested by the GIS for criticising the PNA in his sermons in the mosque. On 31 July Abdelghani Mohammad Hamdan, chair of the committee of Jabalia refugee camp market, was arrested by Palestinian police. He was interrogated about some articles published in local newspapers, accusing police of failing to commit to providing necessary services for the market.

On 1 August 1999 Hussein Saleh Karim and Khaled Sha'ban al-Sharif, residents of al-Bureij refugee camp, were arrested by the GIS for criticising the PNA in sermons they delivered at mosques in the camp.

On 5 August 1999 Dr Eyad El-Sarraj, director general of the Gaza mental health programme, was arrested by Palestinian police. He was questioned about his article, 'The open battle', in *People's Rights*, the magazine of LAW (the Palestinian Society for the Protection of Human Rights and the Environment) in Ramallah. In this article Dr El-Sarraj reviewed the PA's campaign against NGOs in general, and human rights organisations in particular. He also criticised the performance of the PA.

On 25 December 1999 members of the GIS arrested Essam A'mira of Sour Baher in Jerusalem for delivering a sermon at a mosque in Hebron on the same day, criticising the PA and its practices. He was released on 13 January 2000.

Two events during the period under study led to the gravest infringements of the right to free expression. On 27 November 1999, a statement signed by 20 Palestinian national figures, including nine members of the Palestinian Legislative Council, criticised the PA and accused it of 'following a horrible policy of corruption, and abasing and exploiting the Palestinian people'. This statement has come to be known as the 'Statement of the Twenty'.

On 26 February 2000, during his visit to Bir Zeit University in the West Bank, French Prime Minister Lionel Jospin was assaulted by stone-throwing university students. They were protesting about his statement on 24 February 2000, that he considered Hizbullah's resistance against Israeli occupation in South Lebanon to be a terrorist action. The protests had started peacefully before Jospin's arrival, with students simply expressing their disagreement, but the situation escalated when the French Prime Minister repeated his description of Hizbullah as a terrorist organisation.

In the aftermath of these two events, the PA adopted several extreme and severe measures against those who were involved. It described the two events as a threat to, and betrayal of, Palestinian national aspirations. It will be useful to review in detail the measures the PA took.

Immediately after the publication of the Statement of the Twenty, the PA took several severe measures against its signatories On 28 November 1999, Palestinian security forces imposed house arrest on Bassam El-Shaka'a, ex-Mayor of Nablus, and Wahid El-Hamdallah, ex-Mayor of Anabta. On the same day, the GIS summoned and interrogated Esmat El-Shakhshir on the subject of the Statement. It also arrested Dr Abdelsattar Qassem, professor of history at an-Najah University in Nablus, Dr Abdelrahim Kettaneh, Dr Yasser Abu Safia, a member of the board of directors of the Union of Health

Work Committees, Dr Adel Samara, a researcher and expert in economics, Ahmed Qatamesh, a member of the political bureau of the PFPL, Ahmed Shaker Doudin, and Adnan Oudeh, a researcher at the Palestinian Parliamentary Reseach Unit. On 31 November 1999, the house arrest on El-Shaka'a and El-Hamdallah was lifted. On 18 December all the above detainees were released except for Abdelsattar Qassem and Ahmed Shaker Doudin, who were moved on the next day from Nablus prison to the GIS prison in Jericho. They were released several days later. On February 18, Abdelsattar Qassem was arrested again by the Criminal Investigation Unit of Nablus, and it was commonly believed that this arrest too was because of the Statement of the Twenty.

In addition Dr Ma'awia al-Masri, a member of the Palestinian Legislative Council (PLC) and a Statement signatory, was assaulted by three masked men, one of whom shot him. He was injured in the leg and was moved to hospital. The event occurred when he was returning to Nablus after a closed session of the PLC, which had been convened on 1 December to discuss the Statement.

On 16 December Abdeljawad Saleh, a member of the PLC, ex-Minister of Agriculture and one of the signatories of the statement, was severely beaten by members of the GIS in Jericho. Saleh had been participating in a peaceful sit-in in front of the GIS prison in Jericho, in protest at the continuing detention of a number of national figures arrested for questioning about the Statement. He had asked the chief of the GIS to allow him and the other partici-pants to visit the detainees. He was called to the prison in a way that gave him the impression his demand had been accepted, but was then taken to a room where he was beaten.

The assaults against PLC members al-Masri and Saleh were met with wide condemnation on both the official and public levels.

In a comment on the assault against al-Masri, PLC member Hassan Khureisha, chair of the PLC Monitoring Committee and one of the signatories to the statement, stated that 'this assault will not terrify us, and any kind of assault will strengthen our determination to continue our struggle to combat corruption, for an independent judiciary and the rule of law, and respect for human rights.' Khureisha also called for an 'immediate investigation to reveal those who committed the assault and prosecute them'. He believed that 'the attackers are ordinary Palestinians, but suspicion focuses on those who planned this attack'.

On 16 December the Council of Palestinian Human Rights Organisations issued a statement condemning the assault on PLC member Abdeljawad Saleh. The statement called on the attorney general to take immediate steps against those who committed it. It also called upon the PLC to give serious consideration to the security and protection of its members.

A number of NGOs in the Gaza Strip also condemned the assault in a statement, which called for the prosecution on those who committed it. However the Criminal Investigation Unit in the Gaza Strip responded by summoning for questioning several members of the organisations that had signed the statement. These were Mohammad Dahman, director of the Democracy and Workers' Rights Centre in the Gaza Strip; Maher Abu Amsha, chair of the board of the Taghreed Institution for Culture and Arts; Nasser Kafarneh, a representative of the Economic and Social Rights Centre; and Khalil Abu Shammaleh, director of the al-Dameer Association for Human Rights in Gaza. They were all interrogated about the content of the statement.

The events at Bir Zeit University were also followed by arrests. On 26 February 2000, 32 of the university's students were arrested on the campus by Palestinian security forces. They were detained in the GIS headquarters in Ramallah and in the PSS prison in Jericho. The university administration also decided to close the university for three days, with study being resumed on 29 February 2000. The administration then extended the closure to 1 March 2000, while allowing the teaching staff as well as the university employees to resume their work.

The arrests of university students were met by condemnation and denunciation on both the local and international levels. In a statement, human rights organisations protested about the arrests, which they considered to be a violation of relevant international conventions and covenants, especially those asserting the right to education. They called for an end to arrest campaigns and respect for academic freedom. The LAW Institution also expressed its deep concern about the closure of the university in a statement issued on 28 February. It considered that some of the students arrested on campus had not been involved in the demonstration against M. Jospin. It also called for the campus to be reopened, for a committee to investigate the events, cancellation of the dismissal of some students who had participated in the demonstration, the release of detained students, compliance with legal procedures of arrest, and an end to arrest campaigns against students.

In a statement issued on 29 February, al-Haq Institution considered the arrest of students to be an intervention by Palestinian

security services in academic and student affairs, and that the measures taken by the PA against students were part of the PA's series of
attempts to suppress opposition, and a violation of the right to free
expression. The statement also called upon the PA to stop arbitrary
arrests of students in connection with the Jospin demonstration, to
release detained students who had been arrested without compliance with legal procedures, to investigate their torture during interrogation and prosecute those involved in such cases of torture, to
respect free expression, and to respect academic freedoms and not
intervene into the affairs of universities such as Bir Zeit. Amnesty
International expressed its deep concern at the arrest of the students
in a statement it issued on the same date. It also expressed its fear
that detained students might be tortured by the PSS.

On 5 March 2000 the PSS released the detained students after a
presidential decision, as a result of the pressure it had faced on both
the international and local levels. Four students were released on bail
and their cases referred to the director of public prosecutions, while
the other 28 students were released without charge. In his testimony
concerning the treatment he received during his detention, Eyad
More'eb, a student of Bir Zeit University and spokesperson for the
released students, asserted that 'the treatment he received during his
detention at the GIS prison in Ramallah was bad and some students
were beaten, but in Jericho treatment was good'. He also added, 'I
wish that the mechanism of arrest were legal and not arbitrary, and
that the file of political arrests will be closed for good.'

In fact, one of the consequences of these arrests (following on
the Bin Zeit University demonstrations and the Statement of the
Twenty) was an expansion in the class of people arrested for exercising the right to free non-factional political belief. After the
arrests of academicians and human rights activists, the class was
extended in 1999–2000 to include university students and
members of the legislature, who must carry out the role of
lawmaking and reviewing the PNA's practices. Undoubtedly, this
is an expression of the PNA's refusal to allow citizens, whatever
their status, to exercise their right to free expression.

Following these events Palestinian security services continued
their measures aimed at restricting the freedom of individuals to
exercise their right to free expression. On 17 April 2000 members of
the PSS arrested seven people, including six students at the College
of Education in Gaza, accusing them of vilifying an official of PSS
through a statement distributed at the college and signed by 'Nobles
of the Youth Movement'. The students arrested were Fuad Abu Nar

and Mohammed al-Bayoumi, of Nuseirat; Mohammed Salem, of Sheikh Radwan; Mazen El-Sheikh, of Khan Yunis (not a student of the college); Nedal and Ahmed El-Sheikh Eid, of Rafah; and Hazem Farajallah of Jabalia. They were all released later. One of them stated that he had been beaten and tortured during his detention.

Measures against the right to free peaceful assembly

This right includes the freedom to convene and participate in public meetings, the freedom to demonstrate and organise marches, and other forms of mass expression.

Prohibitions or restrictions on peaceful demonstrations, marches, public meetings and conferences

The first case was on 23 January 1999, when a force of Palestinian police intervened to disperse a sit-in organised by the Drivers Union in the Gaza Strip. The sit-in was in protest at a decision of the director general of the Ministry of Agriculture to use Jordanian trucks, instead of Palestinian trucks, to transport about 35,000 calves and sheep, imported from Australia through the Israeli Eilat seaport, to the Gaza Strip.

January 1999 witnessed an important development regarding the right to free peaceful assembly. On 27 January the Law on Public Meetings was put into effect. It had been approved by the PLC on 30 September 1997, and submitted on the same day to the chair of the executive, who ratified it on 28 December 1998. A review and analysis of this law reveals the legal context, in which it was expected to reinforce the right to convene public meetings and organise peaceful demonstrations and marches, and outlines the extent to which the PA complied with the law in letter and in spirit.

Law (12) of 1998 on Public Meetings

The law consists of nine articles that deal with the procedures for convening public meetings, beginning with the concept of a public meeting, moving on to an emphasis on the necessity of submitting a written notice to the governor or chief of police of a region in which a meeting is intended to take place, and ending with the penalty for violating the provisions of the law. In short, the law represents an attempt to provide a fairly wide scope for citizens to convene public meetings, as a way of exercising the right to peaceful assembly. Article 3 of the law emphasises the necessity to submit a written notice to a governor or chief of police before convening a public meeting, but it does not indicate that it is necessary to obtain the permission or approval of the police or the governor. Thus, this law strengthens citizens' exercise of the right to free peaceful assembly, and it would be very dangerous to associate it with the need to obtain prior permission.

In the same context, article 4-c provides that 'Without prejudicing the right to meet, the governor or chief of police has the right to put limits on the time and location of a meeting organised under Article 3, for the purpose of traffic control.' This article does not give the chief of police the authority to allow or prohibit the convening of a public meeting; the police have only the authority to intervene to control traffic in order to preserve others' rights and freedoms.

The law defines a public meeting as 'every public meeting to which at least 50 persons are invited, taking place in a space open to the public, such as public yards and squares, stadiums, parks, etc.'. If this type of meeting is planned, its organisers must submit a written notice to the governor or chief of police. But if a meeting takes another form (for example, if there are fewer than 50 invitees), its organisers are not obliged to submit a written notice to the governor or chief of police.

Accordingly, it can be said that the Law of 1998 on Public Meetings is an achievement for the Palestinian people, serves its aspirations to be considered a democratic state, and complies with international standards of human rights, which ensure the right to peaceful assembly. It also reflects the lawmakers' awareness that the right to peaceful assembly is a foundation for democracy. It is an important qualitative step towards strengthening the freedom to convene public meetings, a civil and political activity that is important in Palestine.

This can be better understood if we take into consideration that colonial powers sought throughout history to deprive Palestinians of their right to hold public meetings, through enacting laws which sought to undermine it. Despite all of this, the period after the law came into force witnessed many restrictions aimed at preventing citizens from exercising their right to peaceful assembly, organising peaceful demonstrations and marches, or convening public meetings.

In June 1999 the PA refused to grant the Islamic National Salvation Party permission to organise summer camps throughout the Gaza Strip. On 26 July the Criminal Investigation Unit in Beit Lahia closed a summer camp organized by the al-Ehsan Charity Association in Beit Lahia. On 25 October 1999 Palestinian police prevented the Women's Affairs Technical Committee in Gaza from organising a march in protest at an explosion in a cigarette lighter factory in Hebron, which resulted in the death of several female workers.

The situation became considerably more serious when the PNA looked to take measures aimed at destroying any legal guarantee of the right of free peaceful assembly.

On 29 February 1999, after the events of Bir Zeit University on 26 February, Maj.-Gen. Ghazi El-Jabali issued a police order that prohibited the convening of public meetings without his prior permission. This contradicts Palestinian law in letter and spirit, the Law on Public Meetings in particular, and violates a basic human right to peaceful assembly. Thus it is worth discussing this matter and its effects on Palestinians' exercise of the right to peaceful assembly.

The police order issued by the chief of police to prohibit public meetings without prior permission

Palestinian local newspapers published this order on 29 February. The order stated that:

> According to the Law of 1998 on Public Meetings, and without prejudicing the right to peaceful assembly, the following has been decided:
> 1. All citizens are absolutely prohibited from carrying out marches without prior permission from the chief of police. Applications for permission must specify the date, and the route of the intended march.
> 2. Holding public meetings is completely forbidden without the prior permission of chief of police, in which the place, date, time and organizer of the meeting are specified.
> 3. According to Article 6 of the Law on Public Meetings, and without prejudicing any other penalty provided in the penal law, anyone who does not respect this order will be punished by a maximum of two months' imprisonment, or a fine not exceeding 50 JD or the equivalent in other currencies.
> 4. Chiefs of police of governates must take the necessary legal measures relevant to their authorities against violators, and must inform us of the procedures.

This order clearly violates the Law of 1998 on Public Meetings, which asserts in article 3 the right to convene public meetings without the obligation to obtain prior permission. Submission of a written notice to the governor or chief of police 48 hours before convening the meeting is legally sufficient. It is this notice that guarantees the right to peaceful assembly. To consider the permission of police to be a prerequisite for convening a public meeting restricts such a right. The law does not give the governor or chief of police the authority to permit or prevent holding a public meeting (article 4-c). It only conveys the right to put controls on the time and place of the meeting (or route of the march) provided in article 3, for traffic control purposes.

In addition article 8 suspends the Ottoman law on public meetings, which was in effect in the Gaza Strip, Jordanian law no. 60, which was in effect in the West Bank, and any other provision that might contradict the new law. So, the above police order is invalid, according to this article, as it contradicts the spirit of the Law of Public Meetings.

In light of the police order, on 29 February 2000 the PSS in the West Bank threatened to arrest some students of Abu Dies College in the West Bank for their intention to go by bus to Bir Zeit University to participate in marches in solidarity with the detained university students. The PSS considered that they did not have permission to charter the buses. Later, the driver of one of the buses was arrested. In addition, the PSS and GIS put two checkpoints at the eastern and western entrances of the university, to prevent people from reaching the university to express their solidarity with the detained students.

On 15 April the Palestinian police prevented the al-Dameer Association for Human Rights in Gaza from organising a march for the following day, from the yard of the PLC to the streets of Gaza, on the occasion of Palestinian Prisoners' Day.

On 19 April 2000 the police ordered about 100 citizens, who were participating in a march organised by the Union of the Handicapped in Ramallah, to disperse. The march, which left from the headquarters of the union near Sorda, and passed through al-Manara Square (the central square in Ramallah) and past the court of Ramallah, was in protest at the assault of a 15-year-old handicapped girl by a 55-year-old man.

The decision of the High Court of Justice

On 29 April 2000 the High Court of Justice decided to temporarily suspend the police order. This decision came after lawyers Raji

El-Sourani and Younis El-Jaro brought the issue in front of the court on 23 April, challenging the chief of police (represented by the attorney general) on behalf of political organisations and NGOs. The lawyers asked for:

1. A decision to accept the claim, at least temporarily, and to oblige the respondent to clarify his reasons for issuing the order published in *Al-Quds* on 29 February 2000, concerning public meetings.
2. The temporary suspension of the order until the court's final judgement.
3. An irrevocable decision to suspend the chief of police's order.

This took place after a consultative meeting between political organisations, NGOs and their central committee on 13 March 2000, when the decision had been taken to appoint the lawyers. The PCHR had in effect called for the pursuit of all possible means to countermand the police order. Representatives of the PFPL, the PCHR, the al-Mezan Centre for Human Rights, the Democracy and Workers' Rights Centre and the al-Dameer Association in Gaza, in addition to PLC member Kamal Shrafi, participated in the meeting. The participants concluded that the police order was illegal, and contradicted the letter of the Law of 1998 on Public Meetings. As a result, they decided to refer the matter to the judiciary, with lawyers Raji El-Sourani and Younis El-Jaro representing the political organisations and NGOs in the claim.

The court's decision was to temporarily suspend the police order. This can be considered a positive step towards strengthening the right to peaceful assembly, but it cannot be considered a fully satisfactory outcome because the order was not definitively countermanded.

It was expected that the executive order that the president of the PNA was expected to ratify in order to put the Law of 1998 into effect would contain clauses countermanding the police order and allowing the generalisation of the right to public assembly. However, the executive order, which was issued by the President of the PA on 30 April 2000, did not live up to these expectations and was disappointing, because it introduced supplementary restrictions on the right to convene public meetings, adding these to the restrictions in the order of the chief of police. It is thus necessary to review the executive order, and to discuss its effects on the exercise of the right to convene public meetings as a form of the exercise of the right to peaceful assembly.

Yasser Arafat issued the executive order in his capacity as Minister of Interior. It consists of twelve articles that define the procedures which must be followed when preparing to convene a public meeting in which 50 persons or more participate.

Article 9 of the order provides, *inter alia*, that 'organisers of a meeting or a march must comply with the provisions of the Presidential Decree (3) of 1998 on strengthening national unity and the prevention of incitement'. This article constitutes a dangerous violation of the right to convene public meetings, as Presidential Decree (3) of 1998 is controversial and vague.

Article 1 of the Decree lists several actions that are considered illegal and punishable by law, including incitement to apartheid, acts of violence or incitement to violence that endanger relations with other states, forming illegal associations, and incitement to violate agreements reached between the PLO and other states. The decree is widely controversial, in regard to its content and its ability to strengthen the right to free expression. For example, it does not define 'incitement to violate agreements reached between PLO and other states', or the boundary between a critical or opposed political position towards agreements, and incitement. Is adopting a critical or opposed position towards interim agreements considered a form of incitement? If it is so, who has the authority to decide this, the PA or Israel?

It is the same in regard to the concept of 'agreements between PLO and other states'. The decree does not define such agreements; are they the agreements the PLO has reached since its establishment, with most, if not all, of which an ordinary citizen will be unfamiliar? It is possible that people might violate them without intention, since they are not familiar with them. Or are they those agreements concerning the transitional period?

In addition, the decree itself is legally controversial concerning the validity of the agreements it mentions. It is commonly perceived that any agreement a state reaches with another state will not be valid in that state, or form part of its law, unless it is approved by its legislature. The agreements the PLO signed have not been approved by the PLC or the National Council, so it is not possible for them to become part of Palestinian local law, nor can decrees be issued in regard to them.

Consequently, the demand of article 9 of the executive order for compliance with the provisions of the decree represents an implied demand for necessary compliance with a text that it is not possible to interpret. This undoubtedly paves the way for interpreting article 9 in the way that suits for the executive, concerning the extent to which 'organisers of a public meeting comply with' the provisions of the decree.

In short, the executive claims the authority to prohibit any public meeting, if it finds this necessary according to its interpretations of the concepts. That means that prohibiting the convening of public meetings becomes the rule, and permitting them is the exception. This essentially contradicts the philosophy on which Law of 1998 on Public Meetings is based. The core of such philosophy is that permitting public meetings is the rule and preventing them is the exception.

The content of article 11 of the executive order provides that:

> the response of police to the notice mentioned in article (1) of this executive order will be a written licence, in the formula that the chief of police decides, handed to the applicant. The written licence will include the following: name of the applicant; subject of the meeting or the aim of the march; time and place of the meeting; place, route and time of the march; security conditions and controls on which the chief of police decides in order to provide protection for a meeting or a march in a way that ensures public safety, and any other conditions.

It is clear from the above article that a notice is indeed required to be submitted to the chief of police to inform him or her of the intention to convene a public meeting, but this notice is not automatically tied to an eventual permission given by the chief of police. On the contrary, this interpretation gives way to an authorisation, given by the chief of police, to hold a meeting or march. It is also clear that a licence will include, *inter alia,* 'the subject of a public meeting and the aim of a march', but it is the chief of police who defines the terms of the licence. If article 9, which provides that 'in accordance with the provisions of the Presidential Decree of 1998 on strengthening national unity and preventing incitement', is considered, it is possible that the chief of police may not permit the convening of a public meeting or organising of a march, justifying that by the non-conformity of the subject of a public meeting or the aim of a march, with the provisions of the decree. This will be according to his or her private interpretation, and based on his/her exclusive authority to decide the extent to which the subject of a public meeting or the aim of a march complies with the provisions of the decree. The chief of police in effect has exclusive authority to make this decision, and the presidential decree can be interpreted in various ways to support it.

Measures pertaining to the arrest or shooting of people on the grounds of exercising the right to peaceful assembly

On 7 and 8 August 1999 the Criminal Investigation Unit arrested 19 residents of Khan Yunis, suspected of participating in demonstrations in the city after a child was kidnapped and assaulted.

The same month witnessed the most serious case of shooting, when Palestinian security forces shot at protesters in Rafah during clashes that erupted after the State Security Court sentenced Rae'd El-Attar, aged 25, of Rafah, to death by firing squad for the murder of Captain Refa't Joudeh, aged 35, of Rafah. A member of the PSS, Mohammed Ibrahim Abu Shammaleh, was sentenced to life imprisonment, and Ussama Suleiman Abu Taha to 15 years in prison, in the same case. The firing resulted in the death of Alla' Joma'a El-Hams, aged 17, of Rafah, from a head injury, and Khamis Mahmoud Salameh, aged 17, also of Rafah, from a chest injury.

On 17 February 2000, seven children from Zo'rob Square in Rafah were arrested by the PSS and GIS, accused of throwing stones and a Molotov cocktail at Israeli patrols on the Egyptian–Israeli borders.

On 22 February 2000, in the aftermath of a strike declared by teachers of Hebron and Bethlehem in protest at the Ministry of Education's decision to decrease their salaries, pre-university students organised a sit-in before the headquarter of the North Hebron Directorate of Education in solidarity with their teachers. Police rapid intervention forces were used to disperse the students after they threw stones at the headquarters, breaking its windows. About 15 persons, most of them students, were injured and were moved to A'ali hospital in Hebron for treatment.

On 23 February 2000 Tareq Eissa, aged 17, of Nuseirat was arrested by the PSS for participating in a peaceful march organised by Hamas in solidarity with Chechnian Muslims.

On 16 April 2000 Khalil Abu Shammaleh, director of the al-Dameer Association for Human Rights, was arrested by police after the association issued a statement on a decision taken by police to prevent it from organising a march in solidarity with Palestinian prisoners for Palestinian Prisoners' Day. He was released on 17 April. (...)

15 The death penalty in Palestine[36]

Palestine Human Rights Monitoring Group

The death penalty in Palestine seems to have been reinstated with the arrival of the Palestinian Authority (PA) in 1994. The first person sentenced to death under the PA was Tha'er Mahmoud Faris, who was convicted and sentenced to be executed by firing squad in May 1995. This was done in a military court, which uses the Law of the Palestinian Revolution, approved by the PLO in 1974.

Civil law

The civil laws of Palestine include the death penalty for a variety of offences, including murder. After the Israeli occupation began in 1967, the Israeli army issued an order declaring that the death penalty would no longer be available for the civil courts to use as a punishment for crimes, including murder.

The laws regulating the death penalties in Palestine were written by the British Mandate authorities in 1936. The Jordanians added their own laws to this, as did the Egyptian military authorities in Gaza. In May 1994, President Arafat issued a decree informing Palestinians that in the areas liberated from Israeli rule, the legal systems used would be those in place before the Israeli occupation. This creates a conflict between the Israeli military decrees issued since 1967 and the earlier laws. The civil courts in general are still using Israeli military decrees as part of the official legal code, unless they have been specifically revoked. This leaves open the question of whether the death penalty is legal in the civil courts, including those under complete Palestinian civil and military control.

The Oslo Accords create a further obstacle to clarification: laws passed by the Legislative Council and approved by President

---

36 Excerpt from *Death Penalties in Palestine: 1995–1997*, March–April 1997, issue no. 2.

Arafat must be then approved by Israel, except within narrow areas fully under the control of the PA. Israel has signalled its resistance to the death penalty within the PA by stipulating that suspects extradited to the PA may not face the death penalty (Gaza and Jericho Agreement, 1994). In any case, is the decree mentioned above, depriving all military regulations of any legality, in accordance with the Oslo Accords? This question is not resolved.

Military law

None of the above discussion affects the operation of either the military courts or the State Security Courts (SSC) established in 1995. The former are legal only if used against personnel employed or connected to the various security forces. The SSCs have been heavily criticised by Amnesty International in a comprehensive report – for not following basic legal procedures, violating the rights of the accused, and refusing to allow observers at their sessions. Both of the courts have used the death penalty for convicted murderers. One of the problems with the use of the death penalty by the military courts and the SSCs is that they do not meet internationally recognised standards for legal procedure. These courts also do not have an independent judiciary.

The death penalty, 1995–7

The criminal courts have sentenced four people to death, the military courts five, and the SSCs six – all in the six months to March 1997. The trials conducted by the SSC were conducted in the middle of the night. In 1996, Rajeh Huliel Ali Abu-Sitta was sentenced to death in a trial that took 15 minutes to complete. The trial was held minutes after his arrest, at 3.00 a.m. (Two others were arrested and sentenced to death with Abu-Sitta.)

On 6 March, 1997, three more people were sentenced to death only 36 hours after being arrested for the murder of Preventative Security Service officer Ismail Hasuna. The trial was also held before dawn, and lasted only one session. The two trials mentioned represent the most severe violations of the rights of the suspects and the suspects' families. Attorneys and family visits were not allowed, and there was no time to prepare a defence or show mitigating circumstances. Abu-Sitta claims that he was beaten in the time between his arrest and the start of the trial. His family heard about the trial and the death sentence from the newspaper.

It is clear therefore that the trials conducted by the SSCs are in themselves a violation of human rights and the rule of law. There is no right of appeal. The trial of al-Sakani and al-Wadi was held in secret. The families of the accused were not informed of the court dates, and therefore could not attend or appoint a lawyer for the defendants. These violations are common in the military courts, and the PHRMG is unable to determine if in this case the violations were intentional or random.

In our opinion the operation of the Palestinian legal system is far from perfect, and that of the military courts even worse. The widespread and routine defects of the justice system (civilian and military) are an additional reason for abolishing the death penalty, which would be wrong even if the courts were above reproach.

In January, Justice Minister Freih Abu-Medein told reporters that President Arafat had commuted all death sentences by all the courts. But this statement, made to reporters as a reply to a question, did not acquire a formal status. Relatives of prisoners sentenced to death were not informed of any change, and they report that defendants were not told either. The legal states of Minister Abu-Medein's statement remains unclear.

The laxity of the rule of law, in the courts, the implementation of the death penalty, and even in the supposed commutation of all death penalties is not acceptable. The PHRMG joins Amnesty International and other international and local human rights organisations in demanding that the death penalty be abolished in Palestine. The PHRMG calls on PA President Yasser Arafat to:

1. Issue a decree forbidding courts, both military and civilian, from sentencing anyone to death, until the Legislative Council is able to pass a law abolishing the death penalty.
2. Abolish the State Security Courts. Justice Minister Freih Abu-Medein and Attorney General Khalid al-Qidrah should take immediate steps to protect the rights of defendants in the civilian and military courts, so as to ensure that justice is carried out.

Table 1 List of death penalties issued in Palestine[1]

	Name	Date	Charge	Branch	Court
1	Tha'er Mahmoud Faris	30/5/95	Murder of security forces member	Army	Military
2	Odeh Muhammed Abu-Azab	31/10/95	Rape and murder	Civilian	Criminal
3	Ala'a Abdul-Hamid Akil*	10/3/96	Murder of security forces member	Police	Military
4	Atieh Khalil Abu-Nekeineh*	10/3/96	Murder of security forces member	Police	Military
5	Matar Hanbal al-Shobaky	20/3/96	Murder, kidnapping	Civilian	Criminal
6	Wael Shaban al-Shobaky	20/3/96	Armed robbery	Civilian	Criminal
7	Salah Mata al-Shobaky	20/3/96	Armed robbery	Civilian	Criminal
8	Riad Mansur Kleib Abu-Susseen	22/10/96	Murder of civilian	Force 17	SSC
9	Rajeh Hiliel Ali Abu-Sitta	22/10/96	Murder of civilian	Force 17	SSC
10	Arafat Odeh Abu-Shbab	22/10/96	Murder of civilian	Force 17	SSC
11	Khalil Hamid Hasan al-Sakani	15/12/96	Murder of civilian & security forces member	Police	Military
12	Hatim Salameh Abu-Wadi	15/12/96	Murder of civilian & security forces member	Police	Military
13	Kheireddin al-Bheisi	6/3/97	Murder of security forces member	Police	SSC
14	Faris al-Bheisi	6/3/97	Murder of security forces member	Army	SSC
15	Mohammad al-Bheisi	6/3/97	Murder of security forces member	Civilian	SSC

Notes:
* Sentence commuted to life imprisonment by order of President Arafat.
1. Civil courts have ordered that prisoners by hanged; SSCs and military courts have ordered that prisoners be shot.

16 Press freedom violations by the Palestinian Authority[37]

Reporters Without Borders

Since the start of the second Intifada a large part of the media has been at the service of the Palestinian cause. After the 11 September 2001 attacks in the USA and consequent rejoicing by Palestinians, the Palestinian Authority (PA), afraid of seeing its image tarnished, stepped up its pressure on journalists to stop them from covering movements supporting Osama bin Laden.

The end of the year was marked by escalating violence. Palestinian President Yasser Arafat was caught in the crossfire, with pressure from radical Palestinian movements and Palestinian public opinion on the one hand, and that of the Israeli Prime Minister Ariel Sharon on the other.

The PA put pressure on Palestinian and foreign journalists to prevent them from covering these events. On 18 September, in a meeting in Ramallah with members of the Foreign Press Association (FPA), the Palestinian information minister, Yasser Abed Rabbo, declared that the PA regretted these hindrances. 'I would like to take this opportunity, in the name of the Palestinian Authority, to reaffirm that it will guarantee the security of all journalists working in the territories under its control', he said. Yet pressure has not eased and the year was marked by arrests, questioning, closure of a television channel, prohibitions on covering demonstrations and so on.

Since the start of the second Intifada both the official and private sector media have been at the service of PA propaganda. Television channels continuously broadcast programmes to the glory of martyrs, inciting hatred or murder. Certain foreign journalists, like their Palestinian colleagues, practise self-censorship for fear of threats, intimidation or violence from the security services.

37 Excerpt from *Annual Report 2002*, May 2002.

A journalist imprisoned

On 11 October 2001 in Gaza the Palestinian police arrested Alaa Saftaoui, editor-in-chief of the weekly *Al-Istiqlal*, a publication close to the radical Islamic Jihad. An article in the weekly that day had judged the PA as 'very weak' and had called for 'the dismissal of the heads of the security services'. Alaa Saftaoui was released on 17 October after six days in detention.

Seven journalists arrested

On 14 September 2001 Palestinian police arrested five journalists while they were covering a demonstration in the Nuseirat refugee camp in memory of the perpetrator of the 9 September suicide attack in Nahariya in Israel. A photographer and an editor with Reuters, a cameraman from Associated Press TV, a correspondent for the satellite television channel Abou Dhabi and an AFP photographer were released one and a half hours later, after police had confiscated their video tapes and films. During this commemoration a portrait of Osama bin Laden was brandished by youths. Four of the five journalists were Palestinians; the AFP photographer was a Norwegian. When the tapes were returned to the journalists a few days later they noticed that many of the scenes they had recorded had been deleted. During an anti-American demonstration in Gaza on 8 October a cameraman from the French channel TF1 was arrested and detained for a few hours.

On 11 October police escorted an AFP journalist out of the al-Maghazi refugee camp in central Gaza. He was detained for a few minutes, while other journalists were prevented from entering the camp.

Two journalists physically attacked

Five unidentified Palestinians beat up Sakher Abou el Oun, AFP correspondent in Gaza, on his way to the AFP agency offices on 29 July 2001. The journalist sustained serious head injuries and was hospitalised in the town. The attack followed an AFP dispatch mentioning the death of eight Palestinians, including one member of the security police, during a settling of scores between two rival clans in Gaza. The journalist blamed the attack on members of the security police.

On 21 December Saif el-Din Shahin, Gaza correspondent for the Qatar-based satellite television channel al-Jazira, was hit outside his office by three unidentified assailants. The reasons for this attack have not been determined.

Pressure and obstruction

The Ramallah offices of al-Jazira were closed on 21 March 2001 on orders of the Palestinian authorities. According to Walid al-Omary, the head of the office, on 19 March officials had asked the manager of the channel to stop broadcasting the trailer of a documentary on the war in Lebanon, which showed a demonstrator brandishing his shoe in front of a portrait of Palestinian Authority President Yasser Arafat. Since the channel refused, members of the security police occupied its offices on 21 March. According to a communiqué by the al-Jazira management, 'armed agents ordered the employees to stop their work, threatening them with arms'. The channel was reopened two days later, on orders from Yasser Arafat. In May two *Newsweek* journalists were abducted by a group of Palestinian militants claiming to be with Fatah, the armed branch of the PLO (Palestinian Liberation Organisation). They were released shortly afterwards.

Police and armed men prevented journalists in Nablus from covering Palestinians rejoicing on 11 September following the attacks in the USA. On the same day the security services summoned a freelance cameraman working for Associated Press, and warned him not to broadcast images filmed in Nablus. The secretary of the PA government, Ahmed Abdel Rahman, subsequently said that the PA 'could not guarantee the life' of the cameraman if the film was shown. The images were not broadcast.

On 18 September Palestinian police in Bethlehem announced the introduction of new regulations concerning Palestinian television and radio. These were no longer authorised to broadcast news concerning calls for general strikes, nationalist activities, demonstrations or security-related issues, without permission from the police or security services. On 20 September the PA ordered the closure of a privately-owned television channel, al-Rooat, in Bethlehem. A Palestinian senior security official, Nakhlé Kaabar, told AFP that al-Rooat would remain closed until further notice. This decision was taken after the channel broadcast a communiqué by the al-Aqsa Martyrs Brigade, a group belonging to Yasser Arafat's Fatah, which claimed responsibility for the attack that day in which a settler had been killed in the Tekoa settlement.

Palestinian police prevented journalists in Gaza from covering an anti-US demonstration on 8 October through to the end. Two Palestinians were killed during the demonstration, declared illegal by the police. The journalists were also banned from covering incidents after the funeral of one of the victims. On the same day, the PA banned filmed interviews with Palestinians about the US offensive in Afghanistan.

On 9 October foreigners, including journalists, were prohibited from entering Gaza. The PA justified this decision by explaining that it was not able to guarantee the security of foreigners.

On 12 October the PA banned journalists from covering an Islamic Jihad demonstration in the al-Maghazi refugee camp in central Gaza.

Appendix: useful addresses

Amnesty International (AI)
1 Easton Street, London WC1X ODW, United Kingdom
Tel.: + 44 207 413 55 00/Fax: + 44 207 956 11 57
E-mail: amnestyis@amnesty.org
Website: www.amnesty.org

B'Tselem (Israeli Centre for Human Rights in the Occupied Territories)
8 HaTa'asiya Street (4th Floor), Jerusalem 93420, Israel
Tel: + 972 2 673 55 99/Fax: + 972 2 674 91 11
E-mail: mail@btselem.org
Website: www.btselem.org

International Federation of Human Rights Leagues (Fédération internationale des ligues des droits de l'homme, FIDH)
17 passage de la Main d'Or, 75011 Paris, France
Tel: + 33 1 43 55 25 18/Fax: + 33 1 43 55 18 80
E-mail: fidh@fidh.org
Website: www.fidh.org

Human Rights Watch (HRW)
15 rue Van Campenhout, 1000 Brussels, Belgium
Tel: + 32 2 732 20 09/Fax: + 32 2 732 04 71
E-mail: hrwbe@hrw.org
Website: www.hrw.org

Médecins du monde (MDM)
62 rue Marcadet, 75018 Paris, France
Tel: + 33 1 44 92 15 15/Fax: + 33 1 44 92 99 99
Website: www.medecinsdumonde.org

Palestinian Centre for Human Rights (PCHR)
29 Omer El Mukhtar Street, El Remal, PO Box 1328, Gaza
Tel./Fax: + 972 8 282 4776/972 8 282 5893/972 8 282 3725
E-mail: pchr@pchrgaza.org
Website: www.pchrgaza.org

Palestinian Human Rights Monitoring Group (PHRMG)
Ragheb Nashashibi Street 5, 2nd Floor, Sheikh Jarrah, East Jerusalem
PO Box 19918 – via Israel
Tel.: + 972 2 582 3372/Fax: + 972 2 582 3385
E-mail: admin@phrmg.org
Website: www.phrmg.org

Public Committee Against Torture in Israel (PCATI)
PO Box 4634, Jerusalem 91 046, Israel
Tel.: + 972 2 563 0073/Fax: + 972 2 566 5477
E-mail: pcati@netvision.net.il
Website: www.stoptorture.org.il

Reporters Without Borders (Reporters sans frontières, RSF)
5 rue Geoffroy-Marie, 75009 Paris, France
Tel: + 33 1 44 83 84 84/Fax: + 33 1 45 23 11 51
E-mail: rsf@rsf.org
Website: www.rsf.org

Index